THE NATURAL MORAL LAW

The Natural Moral Law argues that the good can be known and that therefore the moral law, which serves as a basis for human choice, can be understood. Proceeding historically through ancient, modern, and postmodern thinkers, Owen Anderson studies beliefs about the good and how it is known, and how such beliefs shape claims about the moral law. The focal challenge is whether the skepticism of postmodern thinkers can be answered in a way that preserves knowledge claims about the good. Considering the failures of modern thinkers to correctly articulate reason and the good and how postmodern thinkers are responding to these failures, Anderson argues that there are identifiable patterns of thinking about what is good, some of which lead to false dichotomies. The book concludes with a consideration of how a moral law might look if the good is correctly identified.

Owen Anderson is an Assistant Professor of Philosophy and Religious Studies at Arizona State University. He is the author of three books: *Benjamin B. Warfield and Right Reason: The Clarity of General Revelation and Function of Apologetics* (2005); *The Clarity of God's Existence: The Ethics of Belief after the Enlightenment* (2008); and *Reason and Worldviews: Warfield, Kuyper, Van Til and Plantinga on the Clarity of General Revelation and Function of Apologetics* (2008). His articles have appeared in *Sophia*, *The Heythrop Journal*, *New Blackfriars*, and *Zygon*. He is a regular contributor to *Reviews in Religion and Theology*.

The Natural Moral Law

THE GOOD AFTER MODERNITY

Owen Anderson
Arizona State University

CAMBRIDGE
UNIVERSITY PRESS

CAMBRIDGE
UNIVERSITY PRESS

32 Avenue of the Americas, New York NY 10013-2473, USA

Cambridge University Press is part of the University of Cambridge.

It furthers the University's mission by disseminating knowledge in the pursuit of education, learning and research at the highest international levels of excellence.

www.cambridge.org
Information on this title: www.cambridge.org/9781107008427

First published 2012

A catalogue record for this publication is available from the British Library

Library of Congress Cataloguing in Publication data
Anderson, Owen, 1977–
The natural moral law : the good after modernity / Owen Anderson.
p. cm.
Includes bibliographical references and index.
ISBN 978-1-107-00842-7 (hardback)
1. Natural law. 2. Law and ethics. I. Title.
K460.A53 2012
340′.112–dc23 2012001483

ISBN 978-1-107-00842-7 Hardback
ISBN 978-1-107-66975-8 Paperback

To Jack, Lilliann, Daniel, and Andrew

Contents

Preface

As Aeneas, our great ancestor,
Did from the flames of Troy upon his shoulder
The old Anchises bear …

I chose Carle van Loo's painting *Aeneas Carrying Anchises* for the cover because it depicts an apt metaphor for this book. In the *Aeneid*, Virgil tells us that before being carried by Aeneas from the flames of Troy, Anchises prays to Jupiter for help. Aeneas then tells Anchises to gather up the sacred objects and household idols and bring them along. While Troy is burning, Aeneas escapes carrying his father and leading his son, taking with them the best of what they could save. Although this is the end of one age, as Virgil tells the story, it is the beginning of another.

Similarly, this book is about the end of one age and the beginning of another. As with the destruction of Troy, the Modern age ended in costly and devastating wars. And just as Anchises brought his idols with him, so too the new age, the Postmodern age, relies on ideas taken from Modernity, which may be responsible for the latter's ending. Anchises does not stop to think, as he prays to Jupiter, that if Jupiter could help, Troy would not be burning. But Zeus (Jupiter), as Homer tells it, was distracted on many occasions by Hera. Why save such idols? Why not rethink the presuppositions on which such a worldview is based? And what should be most troubling for Virgil, why build another empire on such presuppositions? How could such an empire hold out the hope of being the *impirium sine fine* (empire without end)?

There is a desire in the human consciousness for such an empire (city). There is a desire to build a life together that reaches the heights of human excellence. This goal cannot be achieved by a single individual; rather, it must be the product of cooperation by all. This cooperation requires a shared goal and a shared understanding about the means to the goal. That is why this is a book about law, and specifically about the natural moral law. It is a book about the good (our shared goal) and the means to the good as known by reason (the natural moral law).

However, this idea of cooperation toward a goal brings to mind another story. This is the story of when all humanity united together to pursue something that was not the good. Together they built a city, a way of life, and together they worked to build a tower that would extend to heaven. This story, in Genesis 11, immediately follows the account of the Flood in which all humans except Noah and his family had gone into violence and corruption. In such a short time after the Great Deluge, humanity was once again uniting in a purpose apart from that given by God. Rather than filling the earth and understanding what the works of God reveal about the Creator, they turned to idolatry and building the city of man based on man's law. Consequently, at the Tower of Babel, God confused languages so that unity became division and humans dispersed.

It is only in the last few centuries that humans have begun to have contact with each other at a global level. This means that once again there is the question of how humans will unite, toward what goal they will work together, and how they understand the means to that goal. What law will humans live by as they come together in the Postmodern age, and will it be a law that leads to the good or away from it?

These two stories also provide a contrast of how beliefs about God work into human life. On the one hand, although Anchises calls Jupiter the "almighty," the gods of Greek polytheism are finite and limited, with various personalities and proclivities that do not always include pursuing the good. On the other hand, in the book of Genesis, God is portrayed as the absolute creator, who imposes natural evil on the creation as a call back from moral evil. It is because God is good that the problem of evil requires an answer by theists. The event of the Tower of Babel marks a transition in the history from God dealing with humans in general to the particular account of redemption beginning with Abraham and his descendants. Although Abraham lived in a city with laws, he is said to have been looking for a city whose maker and builder is God. This contrast between the city of man and the city of God involves a contrast between two views of the good and the law that is to govern human life. As such, we will see this theme in the following study of Modernity and Postmodernity as humans respond to challenges out of the presuppositions they carried with them.

This book relies on an interdisciplinary approach. I draw from philosophy, history, jurisprudence, religious studies, and literature. Consequently, it will engage different readers in various ways. However, the underlying argument is present throughout the book and is contributed to by several supporting arguments. Every reader can engage with these arguments to examine them for soundness. Because the arguments examine assumptions about the good and what is real, active readers will be engaged in self-examination of their own beliefs about these subjects. The extent to which readers do this will be the extent to which they profit from this book.

Acknowledgments

There are many persons who need to be acknowledged as having contributed to this book. Family, friends, and students have all supported me in my thinking about, and research for, this book. I am thankful for comments and suggestions from Francis Beckwith and Stephen Grabill. Professors Michael White and Hoyt Tillman have encouraged and taught me in numerous ways and in the many subjects at which they both excel. John Berger's help as the law editor at Cambridge University Press was an indispensible support from the start. Andrew Presnell offered helpful insights and gave my manuscript a careful reading that I greatly appreciate. Finally, my thanks to my mentor, Surrendra Gangadean, who first asked me "What is the good?" and who has taught me to critically examine basic beliefs. As I wrote about subjects such as the good, and leading the examined life, I was aware of the special burden that these subjects present to an author. I have as much need as anyone else to live the examined life in pursuit of the good, and consequently any mistakes in these pages, or failures in application to life, are mine. I am thankful to acknowledge that there is a source of grace.

Introduction

The Concept of the Natural Moral Law as a Legal Theory

Law and the Good

INTRODUCTION

It takes time for belief systems to be lived out and their inadequacy revealed for all to see. The intellectual energy released in the attempt to fuse Aristotle and Christianity characterized the intellectual life for a significant portion of the Medieval Age. The incompatibility of Aristotelianism and Christianity was officially noted in 1276, but the untangling and disengaging of Christian thought from Aristotle required more time in which skeptical attacks on Aristotle's epistemology and metaphysics made known the need for a foundation on which to build anew. Out of this skeptical backdrop the Modern age emerged with thinkers like Descartes and Hobbes seeking to provide a new basis for thinking about what is certain and how the world works. Religious conflicts that retained medieval characteristics were set aside in favor of a division between private beliefs about what cannot be agreed on and public goods required by all.

Nevertheless, Modernity also lived itself out in time for all to see. Like Aristotelianism, it claimed to have provided a foundation for knowledge and a description about the world. Its denouement came in the same way, through skeptical attacks concerning the sufficiency of this foundation. Like the medieval world, the modern world drew to a close in a series of costly and deadly wars. In the aftermath, there is general agreement that the postcolonial, globalized world is a postmodern world, but little agreement about what would constitute a new foundation for rebuilding. It is the skeptical time between the death of one age and the beginning of another.

This atmosphere of skepticism influences all areas of life, not least of which is the area of law. Even the use of that term will immediately raise questions about its manifold meanings and methodological uses. Is law a description, or is it normative? Is law to be analyzed in terms of the authority from which it proceeds, or in relation to a standard of justice? What is the meaning of normative claims; how is *ought* to be understood? Are *ought* claims making cognitive statements about facts, or are they noncognitive expressions? The first question gets to the similarity or difference between science and legal theory. Scientific laws are said to be describing order in the world, regularity between cause and effect, laying bare the intelligibility and comprehensibility of the universe. Natural law has the benefit of claiming to give a similar description about human life both individual and social.

However, natural law is criticized as relying on metaphysical speculation and outmoded systems of thought about how the universe works. Furthermore, scientific laws are descriptive, whereas natural laws are prescriptive; the world of human choice is full of persons acting contrary to the natural law. In an attempt to arrive at the descriptive aspect of law, the realist traditions claimed to be merely describing law as it is. Law is separated from metaphysical speculation and is expected to follow as closely as possible the scientific method. Natural law seemed too mired in metaphysical assumptions to be of any use to a modern and scientific mind.

As Modernity progressed, scientific thinking increasingly limited all knowledge to the empirical and natural (material). Nevertheless, it rested on assumptions that could not be proven empirically. This empiricism and naturalism encouraged the embrace of nominalism. One implication was the rejection of the idea of a universal "human nature" and instead the study of only particularity and modest induction. Without the idea of a universal human nature, claims about the human good lost their meaning, and any law based on the good and human nature appeared unhelpful. The idea of the highest good was therefore challenged both by the rejection of final causes and by nominalism that denied universal natures in general and human nature more specifically.

In this book I argue that there is the highest good based on human nature and that it is readily knowable, so that the failure to know the good is a form of culpable ignorance. This involves showing how no legal theory can actually disconnect itself from the study of metaphysics (the study of what is real). The argument will be given that it is not possible to avoid resting law on metaphysics where metaphysics means a theory about what is real. Rather, the issue is to what extent given thinkers are aware of the metaphysical assumptions behind their theory of choice. Thus, the change to Modernity marks a shift not away from metaphysics, but from one set of metaphysical assumptions to another. Furthermore, because these assumptions are used to support the new tools of science, the *novum organon*, science cannot be called on to defend them without creating a circular argument as a result. The following seeks to lay bare for investigation these metaphysical assumptions and in so doing help explain the current skeptical attitude and make progress in a new foundation for the moral law.

This means that we will need to learn how to think about metaphysics in order to make progress in coming to understand law and achieving unity between legal theories. It is the absence of this that marks the age of skepticism whose function is to call into question the assumptions of a system, but which does not offer anything in replacement. Studying the natural moral law after Modernity requires exposing uncritically held assumptions that give fuel to the fire of skeptics (those who claim we cannot know), but also making progress toward a replacement that answers the challenges of the age. The natural moral law after Modernity is not simply natural law fit into Postmodernity; it is natural moral law understanding the failures of Modernity and answering the challenges of Postmodernity.

The lawyer will regard this book as an essay in critical thinking about jurisprudence for it is concerned with thinking our way backward to presuppositions that mold and shape the general framework of legal thought.[1] This is not the same as a critical-theorist approach that seeks to expose power structures on the way to the goal of addressing alienation (critical legal theory will be one of the legal theories analyzed for presuppositions). Nor is it the same as a criticism of a specific law or legal policy. I rely on a historical method to consider how presuppositions change and how they are hidden from sight through a process of intellectual neglect and avoidance. However, my main purpose is philosophical in that I will critically examine presuppositions for meaning in the hope of making progress toward a growth in meaning. These presuppositions are mainly epistemological and metaphysical; they are the presuppositions that help us understand how one legal theorist can say: "The prophecies of what the courts will do in fact, and nothing more pretentious, are what I mean by the law" and another can say: "An unjust law is no law at all."

The historical sections of this book are not meant to duplicate what can already be found in other, more detailed history books. The purpose of the historical ordering of the book is to illustrate how ideas shift through a process of challenge and response. I want to capture the interplay between the challenges of an age, how the response to these shapes epistemology and is shaped by it, and how this forms the view of the good and what is

1 Contrast this with H. L. A. Hart's purpose in *The Concept of Law*.

valuable and in turn produces a lived piety. From these relationships we can infer patterns that illustrate why the good is misidentified and therefore not known.

The concept of the good will help provide a fixed point of reference for us as we consider law. Natural law is sometimes distinguished as the legal theory concerned about the good, but I argue that the concept of the good is inescapable. The issue is not whether a given theory posits the good; the issue is what any given theory asserts to be good. A realist who says, "I'm not interested in the good, I'm interested in knowing what counts as the correct procedure for producing law so that society can have stability," is giving us a look at what he/she believes to be the good. Indeed, what any given legal theory believes to be the good is a central part of the foundation of that theory; it is a belief on which the entire theory rests. The extent to which a view of the good has been proven in contrast to its competitors will be the extent to which the foundation is solid. And so we can proceed with this question fixed before us: What is the good?

THE GOOD

This study begins with a clear assertion: Some things can be sought as ends in themselves, and some things cannot be sought as ends in themselves.[2] To say that a concept is clear is to say that it cannot be confused with its opposite. The idea of an end in itself, or the good, is one example of a clear concept. Similarly, it is clear that we make choices, that in making choices we seek to attain a goal or end, and that some goals are sought as a means to yet another goal, whereas there remains the idea of the good as an end in itself. There is a clear distinction between that which is a means, that which is an end, and that which is an effect of attaining the end. To build toward the conclusion that the good is easily knowable, I begin by highlighting views of the good in notable thinkers from the early medieval, late medieval, early modern, and late modern eras. I will use this study to make the case that beliefs about the good are relative to beliefs about human nature and the real. Legal theories are expressions of this relationship, and thus distinctions between notions such as natural law and positive law can mask rather than illuminate such beliefs.

The final goal of this study is to make the case that a global age requires a global law, and that a global law requires a clear statement of the good. There are implications that I draw from this, especially about the

[2] This is consciously different than the beginning of Aristotle's *Nicomachean Ethics*.

responsibility for individuals to know the good and the inexcusability of failing to do so. The idea of coming to unity about answers to basic questions is rarely on the agenda. People appear content with disunity, and with approaching law as a compromise between incommensurable viewpoints. I believe we should work toward a basic unity concerning what is real and what is good, and that until there is a basic unity, there will be no end to our troubles.

The contradiction of "some things are ends in themselves" is "nothing is an end in itself." If true, this makes choice empty and meaningless. If choices are made to attain an end, and this includes choices made for something that will be used as a means to another end, then choice can only be meaningful if there is an end in itself to choose.[3] Otherwise, choice is confused with not choosing because in neither case can an end in itself be attained, and one may as well not choose as choose. Therefore, choice itself, or the faculty of the will, cannot be that which is good, but instead is that which aims to achieve the good.[4] To claim that there is not end in itself and yet to make choices toward goals is a lack of integrity.

The idea of the good as an end in itself is distinct from happiness, as well as from duty, virtue, and excellence. The latter three are used as a means to an end. One is excellent to ensure one achieves a goal; a person does his/her duty to make sure society runs smoothly, or to have integrity, or some such goal; virtue is defined in relation to the goal it achieves, not the other way around. In each of these cases, the good must first be known, and then duty, virtue, and excellence are defined and understood in relation to the good.

Happiness is an effect of possessing what one believes to be good. Aristotle claimed that all men desire to be happy, but the classical world after him spent centuries debating the nature of happiness and how best to achieve it. How can all men desire it if they are not even sure what it is? Happiness has been understood as pleasure, joy/contentment, and a final blessed state, among others. Each of these is an effect of something else (rather than an end in itself) and is not sought directly as is the good. I argue that the real distinction should be between lasting and not lasting happiness. Our happiness is temporary when it is a result of our possessing something that we believe is the good but is not actually the good. This realization takes away our happiness. If we actually possess the good, we

3 Aristotle gives an argument in the *Nicomachean Ethics* to show why an infinite regress of goals is not possible.

4 This distinguishes between the will and that which the will is choosing. Therefore, the will itself cannot be the good, nor can it be the only thing that can be called good without qualification (Kant).

will be lastingly happy. The fact that happiness is an effect of understanding the good means that it is cognitive and mediate, not simply a perception and immediate (as in pleasure or the beatific vision).

Can we know the good at this stage in history? Specifically, can we know the good after the collapse of Modernity and in the age of global pluralism? I study this question by first giving a brief look at conceptions of the good in the early medieval, late medieval, and modern periods, and then looking more closely at views from the early twentieth century. This method likely will open me up to the criticism that I am only giving caricatures of these periods, but I believe this can be avoided if I have done two things: (1) accurately represented the given thinker's view of the good; and (2) showed that it is true either that the thinker shaped the period in a formative way, or that the presented view is an expression of the attitude of the period.

I want to capture the interplay between the challenges of an age, how responses to these challenges shape epistemology and are shaped by it, and how this forms the view of the good and in turn produces a lived piety. From these relationships we can infer patterns that illustrate why the good is not known. I consider a line in history that is described generally and then with greater precision in order to highlight patterns. This is a descriptive work that does not help us know which beliefs about the good are and are not justified. However, it does help us make progress is understanding what has been revealed in history as we contemplate the good.

Philosophically, I want to begin with the Socratic integration of reason and reject the bifurcation of theoretical and practical rationality made by later thinkers and assumed in much contemporary discussion. The Socratic view maintains that knowing is necessary and sufficient for choosing the good. A person does something not for the sake of doing it, but to attain some end. We do not pursue the good for the sake of that which is a means to the good, but rather we do intermediate things for that which is good. "So it's because we pursue what's good that we walk whenever we walk; we suppose that it's better to walk. And conversely, whenever we stand still, we stand still for the sake of the same thing, what's good."[5] Feeling pleasure is not the same as doing well; what is pleasant is different from what is good, because a person could be in pain yet also feel enjoyment.[6] All things are done for the sake of what is good; it is the end of all action

5 Plato, "Gorgias," in *Plato: Complete Works*, ed. John M. Cooper, trans. Donald J. Zeyl (Cambridge: Hackett, 1997), 468b.

6 Ibid., 497a.

and pursued for its own sake.[7] The lawful and the law are descriptions of states of organization and order, which lead people to the good.[8]

For Socrates, the goal of discussion and persuasion is knowledge. There are two types of persuasion: one providing conviction without knowledge, the other providing knowledge.[9] Socrates proceeds with a method of attempting to make the subject clear through discovering meaning rather than attempting to win the argument through persuasion.[10] To produce conviction with knowledge, the orator must know that about which he speaks – for instance, health, justice, or the good. In the matter of choices we are asking what can be pursued as an end, what is a means, and what, if anything, is an end in itself, which is sought for its own sake.

This also helps us understand what is meant by "law." A law describes what must be done to achieve the good. It is therefore both an "is" and an "ought." To achieve the good, a person must do this, and because the good is desired by all, a person ought to do this. The reality of false beliefs about the good helps explain why people act in competing ways (either different people or the same person at different times) – namely because of conflicting beliefs about what is good. Different societies enact different laws, and this is an expression of how they understand the good and the means to the good.

ATTEMPTS TO AVOID CONNECTING LAW AND THE GOOD

There are notable attempts to avoid connecting the law to what is good. These are also considered further in this study as we consider particular thinkers. However, it is worth thinking about some of them now in relation to the Socratic viewpoint.

Law Is the Command of an Authoritative Will

This view has been influential in a number of otherwise different legal theories. For instance, it is the definition of law used by divine command theorists like William of Ockham. It is also the theory of law used by Thomas Hobbes at the beginning of Modernity. Because of this, some scholars, like Brian Tierney, trace the origins of Modernity into the thirteenth and

7 Ibid., 500a.
8 Ibid., 504d.
9 Ibid., 454e.
10 Ibid., 457e.

fourteenth centuries. It is also the view shared by some contemporary legal positivists who seek to trace the origins of law to the correct procedure in a given society for enacting laws.

In an important way, this view of law promotes a division between the intellect and the will, which has been, and continues to be, influential in Western thought. It was not present in Socrates, as I discussed earlier, but it is seen in some aspects of Plato and in Aristotle. It is in Aquinas, and it is behind the debate about whether it is the intellect or the will that is the basis for law. The intellectualists and the voluntarists assume this division. It fueled the argument between Thomists and Ockham about the omnipotence of God, and it is related to the Euthyphro dilemma about God and the good.

Taking the Socratic approach, I argue that a law is not valid because it is commanded by the valid authority, but that a law has authority because it is an accurate description of how to attain the good. In the case of God, what is good for a being is based on the nature of that being, and so what is good for a human is based on the nature of a human. God, as creator of human nature, is the determiner of good and evil for humans. So the moral law commanded by God is given not apart from human nature as an imposition (heteronomy), but in unison with God creating human nature.

With relation to a human authority (monarch or legislator), what is willed as law is an expression of what the authority believes to be the good and how to achieve that good. Therefore, if the authority is incorrect about what is good, then its laws will describe inaccurate means to the good (although perhaps accurate means to what is falsely believed to be the good). This calls into question what it means for this lawgiver to be an authority.

If someone in authority is not ruling for the good, then this rule is either for evil or it is amoral. There are serious problems in saying that someone knowingly rules for evil. Or perhaps they rule for the evil of their citizens but for their own good. Nevertheless, evil will bring about the end of their citizens and leave them with nothing to rule and no way to rule for their own good. The claim that rule is amoral might be another form of skepticism about knowing the good, but it might also be a claim about the inapplicability of the good to most of the kinds of laws a government needs to enact. I consider this in the next session.

Law Is the Power to Change Behavior

This definition is related to the law while bearing some distinctions in focus. It moves even further from the intellect into the realm of pure force. It rests on the intuition that if there is not an ability to enforce a law, then it is not really a law; or, if a law has no consequences, then it is not really a law. There is some truth in this. However, this particular view rests on the same division of the intellect and the will. Furthermore, this division of the intellect and the will rests on skepticism about our ability to know the good and the reality of the good. Because humans cannot know what is actually good, or because there is no good, only desires, laws are expressions of individual or group preference. To make the step from preference to actual law, there must be an ability to enforce the law. This, in turn, changes behavior. Therefore, authority most simply is that which has the power to enforce laws.

This viewpoint also rests on the claim that most laws have little or nothing to do with what is good. Laws about what color of light means "stop," what side of the road to drive on, regulations on public water or electricity, kinds of zoning permits, and so forth seem like the real day-to-day business of government and also seem far removed from the discussion about what is good. This is another kind of skepticism: a skepticism about the applicability of the good to the ins and outs of life. It is indeed true that historically, much discussion about the good has promoted the viewpoint that the good cannot be known or attained until the afterlife. Thus, the challenge is about how the good applies in this life.

Initially, we can respond by pointing out that the kinds of "mundane" laws just considered collectively represent an attempt to have order and safety in society. Different societies can have different laws about what side of the road to drive on, but there must be some consensus about this, otherwise serious problems will occur. Therefore, even though these laws are not directly related to the good, they are indirectly related through the proximate goals of order and safety. Order and safety are themselves a means to humans having the ability to live their lives unmolested and unharmed in order to achieve other goals, including the good. So I do not believe we can claim there are laws that have nothing whatsoever to do with the good. However, it does remain a serious problem for the postmodern world to reject otherworldliness in relation to the good and to understand how the good can be achieved presently in this world.

Finally, this view and its skepticism about the possibility of knowledge reduce humans to appetites and actions. The phrase "brute force" describes this idea of law as the force used by brutes, not by creatures with intellects and knowledge. Because postmodern thinkers share this skepticism, their analysis of history often revolves around arbitrary power systems rooted in one group's desires and achieved through the oppression of another group whose desires go unfulfilled. What I question is the shared skepticism about our ability to know what is good, and the shared skepticism about there being a good (epistemological and metaphysical skepticism).

Positivism

These attempts to avoid relating the law with the good overlap. Positivism can be found in the previous two sections. However, it is worth considering it in more detail because of its importance. Most basically, positivism relies on empiricism. Empiricism claims that all knowledge is through sense data. This modern form of empiricism claims that a good researcher is one who describes events and seeks to find their meaning within what was experienced, not by imposing an external order from presupposed metaphysical assumptions. Because of the limits of empiricism, the adherent to this view claims that only the experienceable world (the material world, the natural world, the physical world) exists, or perhaps that only such a world can be known. Everything else is opinion and, more often than not, a hindrance to knowledge, and should therefore be jettisoned. Thus, for instance, H. L. A. Hart argues that nothing is gained by claiming that law and the natural law (or moral law) are necessarily connected, and so we should reject such an approach as unenlightening.

Once again we find that this rests on an epistemological skepticism. Has the positivist succeeded in avoiding all epistemological and metaphysical assumptions? Clearly not. Rather, what is happening is the positivist saying that only his/her assumptions can be permitted, whereas all others are dubious. Why should we accept this? An appeal to the marvels of science is not sufficient as these marvels are consistent with other presuppositions beside empiricism and naturalism (for instance, theism). Similarly, an appeal to the overextended use of superstition in the past, and all of the harms it produced, is insufficient as that only tells us to avoid superstition, not to become empiricists and reject all that is nonmaterial (supernatural). Empiricism has dogmas, and these are not provable by empirical methods.

Hart's criticism rests on the belief that there are some very general concepts, like justice, that inform law, but that natural law itself is unhelpful in giving particular laws. The idea of justice is sufficient to get us going, being a kind of intuition of sorts that is shared by all. Disagreements arise in relation to what justice looks like "on the ground," in a given circumstance.

In relation to what came before (in terms of natural law theorists), Hart has an important point. It has been difficult for natural law theorists to show

how the law is comprehensive, applying to all aspects of human life. Hart is also responding to skepticism about what we can know, and his solution is a kind of "minimal natural law" relying on ideas like justice. However, he does not really escape making assertions about the nature of things, particularly justice. Therefore, it is not at all the case that he avoids what he himself is warning against. His own analysis is a good example of the inescapable requirement to relate law back to the nature of things. Minimizing this to justice does not avoid the reality that it is really happening.

Furthermore, it is not the case that empiricism can make global claims about the nature of justice. Consistently held, empiricism leads to nominalism. This is an important part of the postmodern challenge, namely that such thinkers have, in many cases, taken empiricism to its more consistent conclusions. So, just like logical positivism, legal positivism rests on principles that cannot be proven by, and are contrary to, its definition of knowledge. That legal positivism has lingered on for so long is a testimony to there being nothing to takes its place.

Prediction

The stature of Oliver Wendell Holmes is significant enough that attention must be given to the claim that law is best understood as trying to predict the outcome of court decisions. In his "The Path of Law," he states: "[T]he object of our study, then, is prediction, the prediction of the incidence of the public force through the instrumentality of the courts."[11] The contemporary law student will find much that seems intuitively correct in this viewpoint. The feeling is that all this talk about the good and moral laws is fine for philosophers, but at the end of the day what matters is winning one's case. And it is a different kind of thinking that is needed for winning a case then is necessary for contemplation of the good.

Perhaps the common thread here is pragmatism. Oliver Wendell Holmes himself was part of the group that founded this viewpoint in America, which includes William James and C. S. Peirce. This philosophy says "truth is what works." First, we can point out that it is a philosophy, it is rejecting other philosophies, and unless it is held dogmatically, it must be shown why we should be pragmatists. It is not that the lawyer or judge is just concerned with the case, but that the lawyer as a pragmatist (or whatever else) is interpreting the case in relation to this philosophy. There are presuppositions about epistemology and metaphysics present; it is not possible

[11] http://www.gutenberg.org/files/2373/2373-h/2373-h.htm

to say "I only care about the outcome" without exposing some of those presuppositions.

Pragmatism has been a very popular and attractive view, and indeed many of the postmodern thinkers are pragmatists. We need to consider what is meant by their dictum, "truth is what works." It could be affirming the relationship between knowledge and reality, that as one comes to know the nature of things, one comes to know how they work or comes to know the means to a given goal. This is not what is meant by pragmatists. Rather, they are reducing truth to what can be measured in physical outcomes and saying "truth" simply means that which produces the desired outcome.

This is perhaps the origin of a phrase I have often heard from my students: "[T]his is what is true for me." I believe they are expressing that this is what they are comfortable with, or what satisfies them. However, statements about what satisfies are statements about the state of one's mind, not about what is mind-independent. Indeed, postmodern pragmatists have carried this viewpoint to its more consistent conclusion of non-realism.

We must hold the point that commonsense pragmatic realism is itself an epistemology and metaphysic. If it is held dogmatically, it is no different than the "superstitions" the Modern age has sought to replace. Why not go with commonsense pragmatic non-realism? Or why not say that the lawyer need not concern himself/herself with such considerations? In one sense this is true, if we reduce the lawyer to a function. But as a human, the lawyer necessarily has beliefs and is subject, like the rest of us, to the need to live the examined life and the consequences for not doing so. If Oliver Wendell Holmes is happy with his pragmatism, that is fine for him up to a point, but if he wants to argue that the rest of us should accept it, then he will need to establish the epistemological and metaphysical presuppositions on which it rests.

Noncognitivism, or Emotivism, or Anti-Intellectualism

This avoidance mechanism has been intertwined in the previous three sections but, like positivism, is worth making explicit in its own section. Like what has come before, it denies the ability for the human intellect to know what is good. Rather, it reverses the order and instead of saying that humans desire the good, it says that the good is what is desired.

This rests on an important problem, namely how there can be so many conflicting choices, laws, and societies if all humans desire the same good. Its solution is to say choices, laws, and societies are merely the expression of individual and group desire, and that is what we call "good." So once again, we are encountering skepticism. And yet this view has been formative in the Modern age, and we will encounter it again.

It is to a great extent connected to the modern world's rejection of otherworldliness and embrace of empiricism. In this life, what I know from experience is that I enjoy fulfilling my desires. I can do this in a brutish or an enlightened way, and the latter is preferred by thinkers like J. S. Mill. But really that is just a further expression of Mill's own desires and carries little weight for those who do not already share them. Stories about what will happen to me in the next life if I do not abstain from certain pleasures in this life carry no weight for a modern mind. And given that the good has been so often connected with that next world, the good becomes an irrelevant concept. Or, more accurately, the modern mind pursues pleasure in this life as the good.

I consider the last sentence to be an important observation. I am arguing that the idea of the good is inescapable where choices are being made. So it is not that the noncognitivist does not have a view of the good, but that the noncognitivist believes fulfilling desires is the good. Similarly, claims about the nature of things are unavoidable. This viewpoint, just like the positivist viewpoint, rests on numerous claims about the nature of knowledge and reality. To merely assert these is dogmatism. However, they are unprovable by empiricism. Therefore, Modernity is either as dogmatic as the medieval world it has sought to replace (a postmodern critique), or it must expand its definition of knowledge beyond empiricism.

Having considered these five attempts to define law apart from the good, I do not believe the attempt to avoid this relationship has been successful and we can proceed with the definition given by Socrates. Furthermore, we can apply ourselves to a descriptive work that brings to light beliefs about the good. As we come to understand what a given legal theorist says about the law, we will also be able to see what is presupposed about knowledge, reality, and the good in this theory. It is these presuppositions that I want to bring out and examine in the following pages.

KNOWING AND RESPONSIBILITY

Making the formal distinctions between what is a means to the good, the good itself, and the effect of possessing the good does not help us identify what actually is the good. We can quickly understand that many things commonly said to be goods, or the good, are not in fact ends in themselves: money is used as a means; developing talents and excellences within oneself is a means; the common good (referring to social stability, commodities, peace, justice, etc.) is a means of avoiding destruction and promoting individual and social development; loving relationships are both a means to the good as we work together in mutual assistance and an effect of possessing the good together (otherwise they are unloving relationships in which harm is done by not mutually pursuing the good); intuitive enjoyment of beauty is an effect of what one understands to be good and beautiful; simply being alive is not an end in itself because one can be alive but in a vegetative state in which choices cannot be made – and many more such examples can be offered. The point here is that precisely because the distinction between an end and the means to an end is a clear distinction, we can readily understand that much of what is called good is not actually the good. The implication is that either the good is hard to know and people are doing their best to understand it, or the good is readily knowable and people are not seeking to know it.

If what a person is seeking as the good is clearly not the good, then that person's choices will be made incorrectly, and the person is in a state of culpable ignorance. While each choice might be practically rational given the end that is being pursued, the wrong end is being pursued. The end can be said to be wrong in that it is not an end in itself, nor is it a means to the end in itself (or at least the individual does not understand it to be such), and it is clear that this is the case.

If what a person is seeking as the good is clearly not the good, then this person bears responsibility for this mistake. This person has a belief about their goal (this goal is good, an end in itself), which is readily knowable as false. There is no excuse for this confusion of what is and is not an end in itself. Concretely, it is inexcusable to believe that money is the good. It is inexcusable to believe that friendship, intuition, or retirement are the good. It is inexcusable to believe that the unexamined life is the good.

Combing the last two paragraphs tells us that there is a kind of guilt where one is without excuse for a choice because the choice was made with an aim at an end that is not the good. There are two parts to this inexcusability: believing something to be the good that is not the good, and a failure to know what is actually the good. One is claiming to know, asserting that something is an end in itself, which is actually a means, and it is thus clear that one does not know. Furthermore, this error about knowing directly affects how choices are made and actions are carried out.

A person reveals what they believe to be the good in making choices. So, any given person may not be able to articulate to any significant degree what he/she believes to be good, and yet their choices can be seen to aim at some end. We can call this a lack of consciousness, lack of self-awareness, or living the unexamined life. In a related way, a person may exhibit significant inconsistency in the ends at which various choices are aimed. This lack of consciousness and consistency should not surprise us, neither when we find it in others or in ourselves; nor is it limited to the working masses, but is just as regularly found among those who claim to be intellectual. It is part of not seeking to know, and thus it forms a compound with not knowing the good, which can be labeled culpable ignorance.

Claiming to know the good is to make a judgment about something as an end. In such judgments two concepts are connected to each other. A person can be questioned about their judgment, in which case supporting judgments will be given. The resulting argument can be evaluated for soundness (where soundness means the argument is valid and the premises are true). The judgments used as premises can be evaluated in terms of what each claims to be the case – for instance, by considering if something that is being sought as an end in itself is really a means to some other end.

This delineates what is meant by the term "know" and distinguishes it from common sense (culturally accepted beliefs and bits of "street smarts" about how to operate in daily life) and intuition (immediate or non-inferential beliefs, often resulting from a perception or sensory input). It may be common sense in Wall Street culture that money is the good, and a particular investor might have an intuition one morning about an investment. It may be common sense in a religious culture that God exists and direct perception of God is the good, and a particular adherent might have an intuition one morning of God's presence. These examples are different from knowing what is the good because in knowing one can actually show what is an end in itself and what is not. When questioned, the investor or religious adherent is unable to give support for their belief or their reliance on intuition; and yet competing investors and religions also use intuition to arrive at opposite conclusions. This is a kind of fideism, and is contrary to the examined life.

The implication is that failure to know the good is inexcusable, and not only is confusion about what is good and what is not an apparently commonplace error, but so too is the confusion between knowing and other kinds of support such as common sense and intuition. This is often because of a confusion between knowing as discussed in the previous two paragraphs and knowing how, such as knowing how to ride a bike. In such a case, one can know how without being able to prove how. And so it could be claimed that a person knows how to be good but cannot prove what is good.

With respect to the good as the end in itself that is chosen for its own sake, one cannot choose to be good without knowing what is good. One cannot choose the good if one does not know what is being chosen. One cannot choose the good if there is no good, or if the good is unknowable. Knowledge of the good is distinguished from belief about the good because knowing the good guarantees that one is able to choose the good, whereas in mere belief or opinion one could be calling something good that is not good.

This level of knowledge of the good can be distinguished from other levels of knowledge by identifying the relationship of more basic and less basic beliefs through presuppositions. An assertion about the best way to achieve money as the good presupposes that money is the good. An assertion about the intuitive enjoyment of beauty in a poem or sunset presupposes that the poem or sunset is being understood correctly. In the study of choice, knowing the good is more basic than knowing the means to the good. I will call this thinking presuppositionally in that we will consider how a given theory of law presupposes a belief about the good, which in turn presupposes a belief about what is real. These beliefs about what is real are the most basic of a worldview and are supported by an epistemology that must also be exposed and examined. And so thinking presuppositionally is the method of this book. It is the tool that will help us understand that law cannot avoid metaphysics or epistemology.

At this most basic level, there is a direct connection between knowing, showing, and doing that is not necessarily present at less basic levels. If one does not know the good, one cannot deliberately choose the good, and in order to knowingly choose the good, one must be able to show (to oneself at least) that something is in fact the good, an end in itself. An essential part of leading the examined life – indeed the very beginning of this process – is to know oneself. This can be understood as interrogative processes asking: Do you know the good, or do you only think you know the good?

There has been much ink spilled about *akrasia* and our apparent ability to knowingly do evil. The general consensus is that Socrates must have been wrong when he demonstrated that no one knowingly does evil. However, even Aristotle, who tried to explain how we can knowingly do evil, conceded that Socrates was technically right and that *akratic* action is like a drunk reciting Empedocles (we can hardly say he *knows* Empedocles in such a case). Aquinas also wanted to find a way to explain it and dismissed the Socratic solution. However, he concludes that Socrates was correct except that in *akratic* action, the person is failing to make a link between a universal knowledge claim (this is not good) and the particular instance (this is not good for me); this means, of course, that the person is not knowingly doing evil.

The modern solution is generally that our desires overwhelm our knowledge. We will need to consider the modern view of desire and intuition about the good. What we can note now is that the examples given are: (1) never examples of knowledge, but only belief, about the good; and (2) never get to basic examples of the good but favor examples of the nice or the practically good. It is going to be important for this study that we are careful in our use of the term "knowledge." The examples given that supposedly prove we can knowingly do evil are really, at best, examples of a confused person with multiple beliefs about what is good. For instance, I know it is bad for me to overindulge in ice cream, but I do it anyway. I know I should brush my teeth before bed, but instead I go to sleep without doing it. I know I should save my money, but I really want the newest video game, so I go out and buy it. These and a plethora of similar examples drive the point home.

However, health and financial well-being are not the good. Even if we use an extreme example, such as a heroin addict who knows using drugs is wrong but cannot stop, we still have not gotten to knowledge or the basic level of the good. The heroin addict can stop but is not willing to suffer the pains involved. And this is true in all such examples. A person who is given two or more options in some sense believes one is good but is strongly inclined to another and chooses this one. Knowledge of the good is not present in these examples. However, there is an implied belief connected with the choice: It is better to do what I most strongly desire than to do what I claim to believe is good.

Knowledge differs from opinion in that knowledge cannot be incorrect and one can give justification to show why it cannot be incorrect. The logically most basic problem in philosophy is this problem of knowledge. When an age cannot explain how it knows, and instead adopts skepticism, the next age will blossom precisely by providing a solution to this problem. In the contemporary age, justification has been understood deontologically as if one is doing one's epistemic duty. The shortcomings of this have led to externalism's claims about warrant. However, neither this form of justification nor warrant gives certainty, and so both are really just another kind of skepticism about knowledge.

One reason this occurs is because questions of what we know are kept at the less basic and practical level. For instance, Edmund Gettier became famous with his 1963 essay, "Is Justified True Belief Knowledge," in which he considers whether a character knows how many coins are in his pocket, or if he will get a raise. In one case, the knowledge claim is based on memory and experience, and in the other on the testimony of another person. Neither of these kinds of justification provides certainty (my memory of experience can be mistaken, a boss's testimony can be mistaken), and so neither is a case of knowledge.

The typical response is: So you are saying that knowledge is very rare, because we are rarely certain. Yes, of course. Neither side debates this, but one side simply changes what the word "knowledge" means by conceding there is no certainty, which is obfuscation and simple skepticism. Furthermore, perhaps most people are not actually certain about anything, and most kinds of beliefs are not such that we can have certainty. If there is to be certainty, it must be at the most basic level. It must have to do with what is clear concerning the metaphysical and moral absolutes. If we cannot have certainty here, we cannot have knowledge at any other level that assumes these basics.

Furthermore, those who claim to have knowingly done evil can be called on their bluff: Prove that you know what is good and what is evil. In my experience, this claim to knowledge quickly melts away. The person has a strongly held belief but does not have knowledge and does not know what is the good. It is no surprise that such a person is often confused and is led about by their strongest feeling or opinion at the moment. In the following, I am interested in knowledge of the good in order to avoid this kind of situation.

THE ARGUMENT

I am somewhat wary of presenting a conclusion before having studied the premises on which it rests. Nevertheless, I am going to state the conclusion toward which I will argue in order to give the reader a structured sense of where I am going and what is being said. I hope the arguments in the book will provide the missing premises.

I am making the case that the good is the knowledge of the highest reality, that the highest reality is God, that God is readily knowable, and the failure to know God is based on a few simple confusions where eternality is attributed to being that cannot be eternal; the failure to know God reveals something about the human condition in self-deception and self-justification; God is revealed to us in the works of creation and providence and not directly or intuitively in the afterlife; that the division between nature and grace, or law and grace, has been made incorrectly and instead redemptive revelation is needed to restore humans to knowing the good.

I believe I am in good company (although perhaps unpopular company) when I argue that the law begins with God and the good. It is in this way that the *Decalogue* begins, in focusing our attention on God the redeemer and that there is no higher good than knowing God. It is in this way that Christ summarizes the law in focusing our attention to love God with all of our being. Nevertheless, an important part of both Modernity and Postmodernity is the rejection of God and the claim that God either does not exist or cannot be known. The pragmatism of both eras is violently opposed to beginning with the *summum bonum*, which at first appears very impractical and irrelevant to law. Even so, we can rely on the example of Socrates from the *Apology* to be reminded that all pretensions to law or benefiting the youth rest on assumptions about what is good. Like Melitus, many in our day will resist having their assumptions about what is good challenged, and use whatever means they can to avoid talking about the good, but the human need for the good will persist.

Although I am not going to give a proof for God's existence here, I am going to argue against most of the positions that have been called on to give nontheistic accounts of what is real. I am arguing that the following is formally true: The highest good for humans is knowledge of the highest reality. As different philosophers or theologians plug in their view of the highest reality, we will begin to see how they understand the good and human nature. Furthermore, I am going to argue that attempts to avoid this formula generally represent some species of skepticism (rejecting knowledge and so locating the good in desire/appetite), and we will be considering many forms of skepticism in what follows. Thus, the goal of my argument is to clear the way for us to consider the implications of the conclusion: it must be clear what is good, the good is knowledge of the highest reality, and therefore the highest reality must be clear (readily knowable). This, coupled with widespread skepticism (or fideism) and consequent lack of knowledge about the highest reality, gives us a picture of the human condition with respect to the good.

DEWEY AND RAWLS: BASIC BELIEFS AND KNOWING THE GOOD

By way of contrast, I am introducing a thinker who made a significant contribution to the move from Modernity to Postmodernity. John Dewey was very explicit in his rejection of the good as knowledge of the highest reality.[12] Dewey recognized that at the most basic level, philosophical conflicts are epistemological. He presented his view, pragmatism, as having come of age and understood the mistakes of all past thinking – mistakes that involve making a distinction between the knower and what is known. This creates philosophical puzzles about appearance and reality, what counts as justification and the nature of being, neither of which is, in fact, either relevant or helpful.[13] Although modern thinkers like Descartes wanted to correct the errors of past philosophy, they nevertheless retained this mistake.

Dewey argues that we can put all of this behind us. This is because the biological sciences, with the foundation in evolutionary thinking, have shown us that we are simply one organism on a continuum with all other organisms. Consciously or not, Dewey is applying insights from Hume and arguing that there is no self, only experience. His solution to the problems of philosophy is to accept as a given the naturalism of evolution and the epistemology articulated by Hume, and to argue that what we have left is practical rationality toward the end of satisfying desires (especially relieving physical suffering). All truth claims can be understood as being about the utility of a given belief to bringing about the desired end.

Dewey rejects the claim that the good is knowledge of the highest reality, and that this reality is indeed God: "The theological problem of attaining knowledge of God as ultimate reality was transformed in effect into the philosophical problem of the possibility of attaining knowledge of reality. For how is one to get beyond the limits of the subject and subjective occurrences?"[14] Like other modern philosophers, he lumps all "religious" thinking into the category of "otherworldly":

> When dominating religious ideas were built up about the idea that the self is a stranger and pilgrim in this world; when morals, falling in line, found true good only in inner states of a self inaccessible to anything but its own private

[12] John Dewey (1859–1952) was an American philosopher and educator who was a leader in forming the American pragmatist school of philosophy. As a pragmatist, he believed that truth can be reduced to what works, and most of what philosophy has studied is meaningless because it cannot be applied to practical purposes. In contrast, a democracy requires citizens who are educated to solve the problems of the day.

John Rawls (1921–2002) was an American political and ethical philosopher. He offered a defense of political liberalism based on the ideas of justice and equality. He attempted to revive the idea of a social contract by arguing that a just and fair society would be one that people would agree to beforehand, without knowing where they would be placed within the society with respect to social and economic status.

[13] John Dewey, *Creative Intelligence: Essays in the Pragmatic Attitude* (New York: Octagon Books, 1970), 467.

[14] Ibid., 31.

> introspection; when political theory assumed the finality of disconnected and mutually exclusive personalities, the notion that the bearer of experience is antithetical to the world instead of being in and of it was congenial. It at least had the warrant of other beliefs and aspirations. But the doctrine of biological continuity or organic evolution has destroyed the scientific basis of the conception. Morally, men are now concerned with the amelioration of the conditions of the common lot in this world. Social sciences recognize that associated life is not a matter of physical juxtaposition, but of genuine intercourse – of community of experience in a non-metaphorical sense of community.[15]

This is a turn away from otherworldliness to mere this-worldliness. I do not believe we can simply allow this viewpoint to claim it has science on its side, or biological proof, or is riding the wave of the greatest insights in human history. It is making claims about reality that are the same in kind as those it rejects, meaning that they also must be argued for, initially, in a non-question begging. To simply argue that this viewpoint is true because it works is to beg the question (which is what his appeals to "progress" amount to, and "what works" is a relative claim).

Dewey has built on Hume, and prefigures postmodern thinkers, in deconstructing the "self." There is no self as traditionally understood. We are an organism that has experiences, and these experiences are partially thrust on us and partially shaped by us (as an organism, not a self). So Dewey can say, "knowledge is always a matter of the use that is made of experienced natural events,"[16] because he denies that there is anything else. Of course, this is a claim about what is, about being, and he must step out of his assertion about knowledge to justify that assertion. Logical Positivism was famously shown to contain this same error (defining knowledge in a way that cannot be justified by its own definition). As Alvin Plantinga has recently argued, why think our beliefs are accurate if they are the outcome of evolution or are merely neurons in our brain? For Dewey to assert as he did that science has demonstrated these things is a kind of fideism and table pounding.

Importantly, Dewey affirmed the formal relationship between the real and the good that I use throughout this book:

> The Greeks were wholly right in the feeling that questions of good and ill, as far as they fall within human control, are bound up with discrimination of

15 John Dewey, *The Essential Dewey: Pragmatism, Education, and Democracy.* ed. Larry Hickman and Thomas M. Alexander (Bloomington: Indiana University Press, 1998), 57.

16 Dewey, 1970, 47.

> the genuine from the spurious, of 'being' from what only pretends to be. … We have only to refer to the way in which medieval life wrought the philosophy of an ultimate and supreme reality into the context of practical life to realize that for centuries political and moral interests were bound up with the distinction between the absolutely real and the relatively real.[17]

The good for humans depends on what it is to be a human. Yet Dewey argues that attempts to know the real are baseless because, in some sense, everything is real. He argues that the philosophical puzzles created around searching for the real are based on the belief that this would affect one's afterlife. Modernity, he believes, has moved past this. "It is enough for our purposes to note that none of the modern philosophies of a superior reality, or *the* real object, idealistic or realistic, holds that its insight makes a difference like that between sin and holiness, eternal condemnation and eternal bliss."[18] By way of contrast, he defines pragmatism in the following manner:

> It is often said that pragmatism, unless it is content to be a contribution to mere methodology, must develop a theory of Reality. But the chief characteristic trait of the pragmatic notion of reality is precisely that no theory of Reality in general, *uberhaupt*, is possible or needed. It occupies the position of an emancipated empiricism or thoroughgoing naïve realism. It finds that "reality" is a *denotative* term, a word used to designate indifferently everything that happens. Lies, dreams, insanities, deceptions, myths, theories are all of them just the events which they specifically are. Pragmatism is content to take its stand with science; for science finds all such events to be subject-matter of description and inquiry – just like stars, fossils, mosquitoes and malaria, circulation and vision. It also takes its stand with daily life, which finds that such things really have to be reckoned with as they occur interwoven in the texture of events.[19]

Dewey affirms Bergson as identifying the ultimate with absolute flux. All is change. "[I]ntelligence means that the function of mind is to project new and more complex ends – to free experience from routine and from caprice … intelligence develops within the sphere of action for the sake of possibilities not yet given."[20] In this he explicitly rejects what he takes to be the Christian worldview. He notices that the Christian worldview is an attempt at a system, but argues it has had the wrong starting point:

17 Dewey, 1970, 57.
18 Dewey, 1998, 65.
19 Ibid., 64.
20 Ibid., 67.

> They centered about a Fall which was not an event in nature, but an aboriginal catastrophe that corrupted Nature; about a redemption made possible by supernatural means; about a life in another world – essentially, not merely spatial, Other. The supreme drama of destiny took place in a soul or spirit which, under the circumstances, could not be conceived other than as non-natural – extra-natural, if not, strictly speaking, supernatural.[21]

What both sides recognize is at stake is a system of belief, a worldview, which relies on basic beliefs about knowledge and reality to inform beliefs about morality and law. Dewey maintains that what is real is change; all is change. This is just as much a claim about the real as arguing that all is permanence, or that only God is eternal. To support his claim by appealing to natural science is to beg the question in that science has been used by all three of these basic beliefs.

I am sympathetic to Dewey's turn away from otherworldliness. I understand his description of the otherworldliness in much of Christianity to be true as a description of what people believe(d) but not true of Christianity as it becomes more conscious and consistent. In relation to knowing God as the good is the claim that God is known through the works of creation and providence, not apart from these in heaven. Furthermore, this is not merely a matter of soteriology, being saved to go to heaven, but of attaining the *summum bonum*, which is available in this life. In rejecting otherworldliness we need not join Dewey in mere this-worldliness.

And yet a feature of Modernity is to notice that, as John Rawls says:

> A modern democratic society is characterized not simply by a pluralism of comprehensive religious, philosophical, and moral doctrines but by a pluralism of incompatible yet reasonable comprehensive doctrines. No one of the doctrines is affirmed by citizens generally. Nor should one expect that in the foreseeable future one of them, or some other reasonable doctrine, will ever be affirmed by all, or nearly all, citizens. Political liberalism assumes that, for political purposes, a plurality of reasonable yet incompatible comprehensive doctrines is the normal result of the exercise of human reason within the framework of the free institutions of a constitutional democratic regime.[22]

This instantiates the solution of Modernity to the Wars of Religion: We cannot know and we must set aside those matters and learn to address practical problems alone. Rawls is also instantiating the formal relationship between what can be known, what is real, and what is good.

21 Ibid., 56.
22 John Rawls, *Political Liberalism*, Columbia University Press, New York, 2005, xvi.

I am questioning this claim that we cannot know. I agree that these systems of belief are incompatible, but I disagree that they are all reasonable. Perhaps in some minimal way they are internally consistent. However, I am going to call into question the basic beliefs on which they rest. Most basically, the two competing beliefs are the claims that "all is eternal" or "only God is eternal." The former can be expressed as "all is permanence" or "all is change"; it is also found to say "all is one" or "two beings exist (matter and spirit) both of which are eternal." Yet, all of these share in the essential claim that eternality can be attributed to something besides God, and that in this sense God the Creator does not exist. If we can make progress to show that only God is eternal – and I believe we can – then we do not need to join Rawls in his pessimism about unity of belief. I am also questioning his view of human nature, that we cannot or will not come to agreement in the foreseeable future. I believe we can, and that ultimately the earth will be filled with knowledge of the good.

Dewey and Rawls are directing their focus to an aspect of the problem of evil, the problem of pain. All humans experience physical suffering, and they believe we can unite on this as our common ground. I am arguing that the problem of evil is larger, that it most fundamentally is a problem of meaning, and that if this problem is not solved, there may not be any reason to address the problem of pain insofar as it may be meaningless to do so. We do need common ground, and I believe it is found in our ability to use reason to find meaning, and that not all basic beliefs are meaningful. We can apply this to debates in law because we should not expect those debates to be resolved as long as opposing viewpoints rest on competing basic beliefs.

CHAPTER LAYOUT

Having introduced the good, and the human responsibility to know the good, I turn in Chapter 1 to consider the postmodern challenge. To do this, I present a challenge-and-response approach to the history of thinking about the good and law. I will identify eras of time as those that worked to develop ideas about what is real and good into all areas of human life. These eras change as they are challenged in ways they cannot sufficiently answer. Modernity is one such change. These changes begin with the area of epistemology, as a worldview's source of authority is questioned. I argue that Modernity began as a new source of authority was sought after the Wars of Religion. Postmodernity is also an epistemological challenge to the modern system, including beliefs about what is good.

In Chapter 2, I make the case that all beliefs about the good presuppose beliefs about what is real and eternal. Therefore, differences about what should be lawful can be traced back to these kinds of presuppositional differences. To make this case, I consider Aristotle and Aquinas. Although close in many respects, these two thinkers are importantly different in their theories about what is real, and this influences their thinking about the highest good. I argue that Aristotle's own metaphysical viewpoint (dualism) can be shown to be contrary to reason, but also that the otherworldliness of Aquinas is not an accurate explanation of the highest good. The insight from this specific case can then be applied to the many different legal theories we study in this book.

In Chapter 3, I give an overview of thinking about the good from ancients like Cicero to the beginnings of Modernity in Hobbes. My point here is not to give an exhaustive history (for which there are already reference books), but to help interpret the history by considering representative thinkers and how they embodied beliefs about the good characteristic of their age. I will argue that, more often than not, a given thinker was concerned about a legal matter (what is just or right) but hardly noticed how this hinges on questions about what is good (and hardly worked to resolve competing visions of the good), and even less often noticed how views of the good are rooted in beliefs about what is real. My argument here is to show that Modernity began as an epistemological challenge to the previous age, and this resulted in changed beliefs about what can be known and what is real, and therefore the human good and law. I suggest there are patterns of development that we can use to understand how these kinds of changes in history unfold.

Chapter 4 picks up with the end of the Wars of Religion and the beginning of Modernity as a turn away from religious authority to what can be known by all persons, what is universal and so a source of agreement. I consider numerous European thinkers in order to make the case that Modern Natural Law begins with the physical goods of this life (physical survival). Theories of the origin of the state all start with the need for survival or working together to ensure greater physical comforts. The good is most often identified with pleasure and evil with pain. Beliefs about what is not physical are considered mere opinion with no public way of adjudicating the truth. Therefore, these are asserted to be matters in which we should have great latitude and not allow opinions to disrupt public peace. I argue that Modernity is therefore a kind of naturalized practical rationality, and that for all of its praise of reason it is really just meant as practical thinking about how this physical world works.

It should not be surprising that, given Modernity's focus on the "natural" or physical world, the philosophy of materialism or "naturalism" became the most popular theory toward the end of the modern world.

In Chapter 5, I consider how naturalism became prominent, particularly in the study of law (in the scientific and legal sense, given that I believe these are related). The scientific naturalism of the nineteenth century became the foundation for ethical naturalism that flourished then and throughout the twentieth century. As was the case in earlier parts of Modernity, Naturalism has argued that survival and physical goods are the basis for human society. However, this belief has taken it a step further in arguing that only the material world exists, and all knowledge is therefore limited to facts about the material world. This is the philosophical basis for positivism. I end by arguing that we can know that only God is eternal, and that God as the creator is the determiner of good and evil for humanity.

Given the background assumptions of Naturalism, the twentieth-century legal and ethical philosophers sought objectivity in some natural feature of the world. In Chapter 6, I consider the development of this thinking, noting that it is largely noncognitive because knowledge is limited to facts about the physical world and moral statements are not facts of this kind. Furthermore, objectivity was generally sought for in the idealized self, which is a kind of concession to the need for God as the metaphysical absolute.

In Chapter 7, I consider some examples of contemporary Natural Law thinking. Such thinkers present themselves as staying away from metaphysical considerations and instead offering a kind of practical rationality about human flourishing. Although I believe this kind of approach is superior to alternatives such as positivism, relativism, deontology, and consequentialism, I argue that we must know the *summum bonum* to make real progress in natural law thinking. In general, these thinkers either stay away from defining the highest good or concede that perhaps we achieve it in the next life. By way of contrast, I suggest that the knowledge of God as the highest good is made available through the works of creation and providence and should be our starting point in thinking about the natural moral law.

The challenge from Postmodernity undermines this kind of practical rationality and exposes the assumptions to all pretentions of neutrality or objectivity. Chapter 8 considers postmodern thinkers and their various challenges to the modern world as well as the implications for continuing any kind of Modernist vision in natural law (limiting natural law to practical rationality about human flourishing). I argue that Postmoderns are helpful in reminding us about the role of presuppositions, and that no theory of the good, law, or the state is without presuppositions about what is real. However, I also argue that Postmodernity takes a turn toward a kind of mysticism that is antirational and in doing so undermines any possibility for this form of Postmodernity to make a meaningful contribution to knowing what is eternal and what is good. Those postmodern thinkers who wish to limit themselves to pragmatism keep one foot in the modern world of practical rationality and one foot in the postmodern world of deconstructing hidden presuppositions.

In Chapter 9, I present my own view of the natural law as the moral law. I argue that the good is knowledge of the highest reality, and that this means that the good is knowing God the Creator. All attempts to deny God are based on confusions of what is eternal and what is temporal (for instance, attributing eternality to the material world, or the individual self). Rather than beginning natural law with physical survival, I argue that humans do not live by bread alone and that finding the meaning in the world is more important to human survival (in two senses) than mere physical bread. Although this moral law is consistent with the approach of the *Decalogue* (beginning with God) and how Christ summarizes the law (love God with all your heart, mind, soul, and strength), I argue that it is knowable from general revelation and that the failure to know is inexcusable and is the basis for needing redemptive revelation in scripture.

I conclude the book with a study of how "hot button" legal debates of our day are based on presuppositions about the good and what is real. Such debates get all of the attention, and the suggestions that we should shift the discussion to the good will not register in many spheres. Nevertheless, I argue that these debates will not be resolved until the good is known and kept in the center of our thought.

CONCLUSION

Modernity began by searching for a certain foundation in contrast to the turmoil and chaos in which the medieval world ended (the Wars of Religion). Neither the *cogito* nor Locke's empiricism were able to give this certainty. Descartes's clear and distinct ideas were guaranteed by God, and he says we know God because we have a clear and distinct idea of him (a circular argument). Hume drew out the logical implications of Locke and these led to skepticism. Reid and Kant worked to reinvigorate the Enlightenment, but the following centuries have shown that these as well led to fideism (mere assertion about common sense, which is actually culturally relative) and skepticism (Postmodernism).

We will be asking the following questions: Is it clear what is good? Can we know the good, or are there only opinions about the good? What happens when a person or culture settles for an opinion about the good and does not know what is good? We will look at the unfolding of Modernity in order to answer this last question, and use this to energize our own pursuit of knowledge of the good.

1

The Postmodern Challenge

From Modernity to Postmodernity

> Mephistopheles. *To you no goal is set, nor measure.*
> *If you should like to nibble everything,*
> *To snatch up something on the wing,*
> *May all agree with you that gives you pleasure! …*
>
> Faust. *I feel that I have made each treasure*
> *Of human mind my own in vain,*
> *And when at last I sit me down at leisure,*
> *No new-born power wells up within my brain.*
> *I'm not a hair's-breadth more in height*
> *Nor nearer to the Infinite …*
>
> Mephistopheles. *Humanity's most lofty power,*
> *Reason and knowledge, pray despise!*[1]

In this selection from Goethe's *Faust*, Mephistopheles tempts Faust with pleasure and encourages him to despair of reason and knowledge. This is a particularly successful temptation because Faust already believes that he has achieved all there is of value from reason and knowledge, and this had not gotten him any closer to the infinite and was therefore insufficient for the good life. As in the Garden of Eden, the temptation here is to determine what is good and evil for oneself, to do what gives pleasure to the self. Similarly, as in the Garden, the tempter serves as a test that reveals how well the good and God are understood. Faust presumes that he has already exhausted knowledge, that he already knows enough or that what he did know was insufficient because it did not bring him closer to infinity. Had Faust really made each treasure of the human mind his own,

1 Johann Wolfgang von Goethe, *Faust*, trans. George Madison Priest (Chicago: Encyclopaedia Britannica, 1980).

or had he come short in knowing what is actually good? The temptation by Mephistopheles indicates that Faust did not know.

This relates to our current chapter, because the change from Modernity to Postmodernity involves a turn from reason and knowledge. The ills of Modernity have sometimes been blamed on reason and the presumptions of "Enlightenment thinking." Rather than taking this route, I explore the extent to which Modernity actually used reason as opposed to coming significantly short in the use of reason. This coming short is particularly in identifying presuppositions and critically examining them for meaning. In doing this, important patterns about law and the good are exposed for consideration.

AFTER MODERNITY

In the following chapters, I trace changes in thinking about the law and the good over a large period of time. Many of these ideas and thinkers will be considered from multiple perspectives in more than one chapter in order to more robustly wrestle with their legal theories. Of necessity, this examination will require that we go beyond strict limitations of legal theory and consider broader moral/ethical theories and the epistemological and metaphysical assumptions on which they rest. Before doing this, I turn to articulating some of the historical and philosophical patterns that have come to the surface in more detail.

LAW AND JUSTICE

The good provides a means to unify the many disparate definitions of the concept law. Whether law is a command or categorical imperative (do the good), an obligation (I should be good to others), a right (humans have a right to the good), a hypothetical imperative (if you want to achieve the good, you should do the following), or some such example, in each case one must know what is good to make sense of the concept of law. Indeed, in the following it is argued that law is an outcome of a formal relationship between the ideas of the good, human nature, and what is real or eternal. Specific laws presuppose a belief about what is good; beliefs about what is good presuppose beliefs about human nature; beliefs about human nature presuppose beliefs about what is real or eternal. Laws are designed to explain the means to the good.

A person's belief about the good is relative to that person's beliefs about human nature. What it means to be a human is presupposed in knowing what it is to be a good human, or to achieve the human good. When faced with a problem about what should be done, the relationship between beliefs about what is good and choice becomes more concrete. This relationship applies to how "law" is understood, because the moral law is concerned with identifying the good and describing the means to the good.

The formal relationship between choice and the good discussed in the previous chapter has as an implication the claim that distinctions between natural law and positive law are superficial. The rejection of "natural law" is, upon examination, the rejection of "that natural law." Upon inspection, all who reject natural law replace it with a framework that contains the conceptual relationship between law, view of the good, view of human nature, and beliefs about what is real. Therefore, the problem is not whether to employ natural law or not, but rather which presuppositions about nature one holds as accurate. To avoid ambiguity, I refer to this law as the moral law, noting that there are reasons why some prefer what they call positive law and others natural law. Uncovering the presuppositions of a given legal philosophy about what is good, about human nature, and about metaphysics can take work. Uncovering one's own presuppositions can take work.

Indeed, it is this process of uncovering presuppositions that will be the focus of the historical elements in this book. Modernity began with presuppositions. These are expressed in every area of human life. Insofar as these presuppositions were incorrect, they led to decay and collapse. Postmodernity is struggling to make sense of this collapse. Postmodernity has presuppositions. These are being applied in every area of human life, which has reached a new global age. This work gives a historical conceptual map that provides the necessary orientation for thinking about contemporary challenges and responses.

Critically examining the presuppositions of an era and their implications for law is the focus of the philosophical elements in this book. Critical examination asks what judgments mean. Modernity was called the victory of nominalism. Postmodernity shares this nominalism. What does it mean to say that there are no universals, only particulars? What is the implication of this for human nature and the good? For law? Critical examination is a search for contradictions. Can it be the case both that there is an end in itself and that there are no universals? Can it be the case that the good is knowable and that all knowledge is from sense experience? Critical examination begins by searching to uncover what is most basic and inquire into the meaning of a system's most basic assertions.

Rather than thinking of the interplay between challenge and response in terms of a Hegelian dialectic, what can be understood is that the tension of challenges and the eventual response brings to light how presuppositions have shaped the age that is challenged and where its presuppositions were insufficient. The kinds of challenges that result in age-shifting responses are those that most clearly bring to light that the presuppositions were not actual instances of knowledge. This is a kind of reverse-dialectic in that it uncovers what is presupposed rather than simply moving to a synthesis. It is a critical dialectic that calls into question critical theory and assumptions about alienation; the presuppositions of these views must also be critically examined.

Challenges are challenges because they require work toward greater consciousness and consistency. The initial challenge of the Reformation required greater consciousness of shortcomings in soteriology and greater consistency about the nature of God's justice and mercy. When a unifying response could not be found and what some believed to be the good and the means to the good were threatened, it is not surprising that devastating war was the result. Attempts to reduce these wars to merely political or economic struggles are attempts to reduce human beliefs to behavior, but the reality and role of beliefs persist.

THE TWILIGHT OF IDOLATRY

Presuppositions that hinder knowledge and responses that do not resolve disputes are identified by a particular term by two thinkers at the opposite ends of Modernity. That term is idols. In his *Novum Organum*, Francis Bacon identified four idols that he believed were a hindrance to knowledge. These were specious reasoning or distractions that kept people from knowing. On the other side of this age, Friedrich Nietzsche also identified four idols in his *Twilight of the Idols*. These were errors in causal thinking, especially as it relates to morality, religion, and the good life. Based on false beliefs about reality, these idols encouraged false causal reasoning and a deceived life. We can use this terminology to say that false presuppositions are idols in that they are misrepresentations about reality. Challenges to these idols reveal that people do not know but only think they know. Cultural collapse (internal struggles such as the Wars of Religion, World War I, and World War II) is the inherent consequence of this disunity and as such should serve as a call back to serious thinking about presuppositions. What kinds of idols characterized Modernity?

A legal system can be based on an idol. It can be based on false thinking about what is good and false assumptions about what is real. Appealing to justice, or the current legislative means for enacting laws, does not avoid this problem, because one can have an idol of justice (calling something just that is not just), and the current legislative process can be based on false thinking about reality. In this sense, challenges arise to expose idols and call humans to think about how their lives have been based on these idols.

In the Scriptures, it was Baal and Ashtoreth that were the idols to which Israel often turned. The offspring of these two was the golden calf. Baal, as the representative of power, and Ashtoreth, as the representative of sexual enjoyment, are still popular idols that many people pursue in the belief that sex and power will bring lasting happiness. While "gross" idolatry of statue worship is less common today, the same kind of attitude prevails as the good of knowing God is neglected in favor of these pursuits.

PATTERNS WITHIN MODERNITY

To make progress toward my conclusion about the good and Postmodernity, I need to flesh out Modernity and its patterns. There are formal patterns that can be identified about the good and epistemology, which serve to illuminate how the failure to know what is clear about the good has implications in human life and history. We have already discussed the pattern of challenge and response and how this brings presuppositions into the light. This can be further elucidated by noting that it is a pattern of idols, the inherent consequences of these idols, and the response these consequences generate that are being revealed.

Where the response is a reaction to inherent consequences without actually calling into question the presuppositions of the age, it can be identified as part of a cycle of the life span of the age. For instance, Modernity can be divided into the Enlightenment, Romantic, and Pragmatic eras. These are differentiated as emphasizing thinking, feeling/intuition, and will/action. There are reasons for speculation about why this pattern falls out in this way. What we can note here is that as the Enlightenment drew out the implications of its presuppositions to their conclusion of skepticism (notable in David Hume), the Romantics sought for an alternative knowledge window into reality (notable in the German Idealists), and as this response began to blur all distinctions and again lead to the implication of skepticism, another route was advocated by Pragmatists (notable in Russell's rejection of Bradley).

This is the pattern revealed in thinking one knows when one does not know. A response is pursued (British empiricism), but it does not actually provide knowledge and is shown to end in skepticism (Hume). A response to this is given (intuition), and once again this was a case of thinking one knows when one does not know. A response is given to this skepticism (what works is what is true), and this too ends in skepticism (because what works depends on what is real). Out of exasperation with this process, some in Postmodernity disclaim truth and knowledge, although we will study if this can in fact be done. One of the thinkers we will study, Christian Thomasius, said of the esoterics and mystics that they make too much of the will and belittle the light of reason: "[N]o one can understand the mystics because they strive to write in an incomprehensible way and want to eradicate reason completely."[2] It may be that the postmoderns are the mystics of our day.

Within these eras that together compose Modernity there can be smaller generational patterns.[3] The idols of one generation form the basis for the next generation's thinking. This new generation rejects these idols, although they do so from within the framework in which they were taught to think (meaning the idol is still present in presuppositional form). This process can go on to the third and fourth generation, during which time pressure builds and challenges, both internal and external, require attention. The cycle of such generational responses has been studied in detail by Strauss and Howe in *The Fourth Turning* and need not be duplicated here. What is of central importance to this study is the formal similarity between these generational and era responses to previous idols: In each case, what has gone before is shown to have claimed to know when in fact knowledge was not present. The challenges themselves show that there was not knowledge, but rather assertion.

This gives us another pattern, the pattern of fideism and skepticism. Fideism is the assertion that one should believe without proof because proof is not necessary. When the fideist is challenged as to why his/her form of fideism should be accepted over another form, no reply can be given (without the contradiction of giving proof). On the other side, the skeptic agrees that proof is not available but argues that in its absence, one must withhold belief. The conflict between these two camps often absorbs most of the energy of a generation or era, and ignores the shared presuppositions that give rise to the false dilemma. In the case of Modernity, both sides share the presupposition that proof is empirical, and both agree that there is no empirical proof for many religious and moral beliefs, but then the argument ensues about whether one should continue to accept such

2 Christian Thomasius, *Essays on Church, State, and Politics*, eds. Ian Hunter, Ian Ahnert and Frank Grunert (Indianapolis: Liberty Fund, 2007).

3 William Strass and Neil Howe, *Generations: The History of America's Future, 1584–2069* (New York: Morrow, 1991), 538.

beliefs without empirical proof. If this presupposition were questioned, the debate would be irrelevant.

Indeed, it is precisely this futility that an age-shifting challenge brings to light. An inadequate epistemology leads to challenges – those in authority claim to know but, upon examination, are shown to not know. I will call this a flawed foundation. The foundation of an age is the set of beliefs about epistemology, metaphysics, and ethics, or about authority, reality, and the good life. The implications of these most basic beliefs are drawn out into the less basic areas of human life. It is most often the case that the less basic areas of human life are the areas that get all the attention, and this is precisely why challenges require working to uncover the presuppositions behind human actions.

There are noticeable patterns in this area of human action. Earlier I stated the dual problem involved in not knowing the good: failure to know what is clear and putting in the place of the actual good something that is not an end in itself. Now, if we combine this dual problem with one more element, a pattern will emerge. This additional element is inherent to the very act of claiming to know what is good – the need for meaning. As persons seek to understand, seek to find the meaning that is in the world, they are making knowledge claims about reality and the good. When they fail to know what is clear, as in the case of calling something the good, which is not an end in itself, they will fail to find the meaning that is in the world. They will act to achieve their perceived, falsely named "good," the idol, but this idol will not bring about the desired effect. Idols bring about a temporary effect since they are not actually ends in themselves. The good brings about a lasting effect. I use the term "happiness" to denote this effect, although I do not want this confused with pleasure but instead understood as related to joy and contentment.

Indeed, in the absence of happiness, persons pursue pleasure. We can say that the good brings lasting happiness,[4] and idols bring temporary happiness; as the latter fail to bring about lasting happiness, persons must do more and more to get the temporary happiness. The pattern is that idols require excessive behavior in areas that provide pleasure. This pattern takes time to unfold in human history, so that what counts as excessive grows over time and context. There is a limit to excess, however. It is in excessive behavior that a civilization commits suicide, allowing external challenges to gain victory.

4 No evil can befall a good man; Socrates, *Apology*.

We can borrow a phrase from Confucius – "the rectification of names" – and his insights about what happens when names are distorted.

> If language is not correct, then what is said is not what is meant; if what is said is not what is meant, then what must be done remains undone; if this remains undone, morals and art will deteriorate; if justice goes astray, the people will stand about in helpless confusion. Hence there must be no arbitrariness in what is said. This matters above everything.[5]

Confucius suggested one solution: returning to ancient usages by the sage kings. I do not believe tradition or "original usage" resolves the problem. Rather, I am arguing that whatever word we use, we have the concept of "the end in itself." This has been called "the good." However, "the good" has also been equated with virtue, duty, excellence, or happiness. To rectify the name of "the good," we must carefully make the distinction between the end in itself, the means to this end, and the effect of possessing the end.

To call something the good that is not an end in itself is to distort the term. To work toward a goal that is not an end in itself is a similar mistake. To have failed to think through one's choices and goals is a distortion of one's humanity as a thinking and choosing being. If we do not properly name the good, we cannot choose the good or accurately speak about what is good or what is lawful to achieve the good. The result is, as Confucius described in his day, cultural collapse and widespread ignorance.

Two opposing camps developed their ethical theories from this framework in the Modern age. One said that because happiness is the effect of possessing what one desires as good, the health and success of a society can be measured by the happiness of its members. What is of utility in achieving happiness, or what results in the consequence of happiness, is what should be sought. The other responded by arguing that there is not a relationship, in this life, between doing what is good and being happy. Therefore, a person should consider one's duty to the social contract. From these two theories can be derived many other related schools of thought, such as those that appeal to tradition, intuition, ethical egoism, existentialism and absurdism, humanism, and stoicism.

Transcending these particular schools is talk about rights. Generally speaking, a right is something obligated to a person necessary to achieve the good. Thus, Modernity spoke about rights conferred by nature and

5 *The Analects*, 13.3, http://www.analects-ink.com/mission/Confucius_Rectification.html.

nature's God (pre–social contract) and rights that were part of the social contract. How these rights are understood depends on a given thinker's ethical theory. They began with the right to the achievement of one's desire resulting from work: property. They can be expanded to include what is necessary for work and property. They can also be understood in the duty framework as one having a right only to that which can be universalized.

In general, Modernity is characterized by the view that humans are equal and therefore have the same rights. Specific conflicts within modern history are often about expanding this belief to be more consistently applied. This is consistent with the starting concern of finding what is common to all in the face of partisan division. It also makes the important point that there is one shared humanity, so that what is good for any individual human is also good for other humans in their shared nature.

So here are the patterns we have identified:

1. Presuppositional pattern: Beliefs about the law presuppose beliefs about what is good, which in turn presuppose beliefs about human nature and what is real. A given person will justify their beliefs on the basis of their presupposed epistemology. Because all legal theories presuppose beliefs about human nature and what is real, all share this formal pattern of being "natural laws."
2. Pattern of change: Persons and groups hold to worldviews more or less consciously and consistently. Challenges about the meaning of a worldview force change through growth in consciousness and consistency.
3. Pattern of decay: Where a worldview has misidentified what is real, there will also be misunderstanding of human nature, the good, and law. Misidentification of the good leads to meaninglessness, and meaningless (where not corrected through knowing the good) leads to excess in seeking to fill the void of meaning. Historically, excess has been identified in lust, greed, gluttony, and envy.
4. Pattern of epistemology: The highest source of authority is the basis of support for knowledge claims about our most basic beliefs. When this source is misidentified (as the senses, intuition, common sense, tradition) the result will be thinking one knows when one does not know. This will lead to either the abandonment of knowledge claims (skepticism) or to bald assertion (fideism/dogmatism).
5. Pattern of responsibility: Persons or groups will hold others responsible for what is believed to be clear. What is clear is the basis for common ground. Therefore, when what is clear has not been accurately

identified, challenges will bring this to light and common ground between people will break down.

6. Pattern between duty and happiness: When the good is not kept at the center of ethical discussion as distinct from both duty and happiness, these will be elevated improperly and become the basis for ethical theories. The pattern of this neglect of the good is a stalemate between those theories that emphasize duty/virtue/obligation and those that emphasize happiness.
7. Pattern of the unexamined life: The unexamined life begins with a casual attitude wherein a person thinks he/she knows when he/she does not know; when challenged, this progresses into self-deception about one's condition and self-justification through rationalization. When challenges persist, there will be an attempt to destroy that which challenges while preserving the self-deception and self-justification. Historically, these have been identified as attitudes of sloth, pride, and anger.

NATURAL LAW AND ALTERNATIVES

The idea that the good is relative to human nature has been called natural law and distinguished from other theories about what constitutes a law. Moral theorists attempt to articulate moral laws, which are broader than civil laws but share some of the same thinking about their status. This concept of human nature is basic to the study of natural law. Natural law is the theory of law that derives the good from human nature. That is, what is good for a being depends on the nature of the being; what is good for a horse depends on the nature of a horse, and the like. So what is good for a human, what a human can seek as an end in itself, depends on the nature of a human. Indeed, the very ability of humans to choose and seek sets them apart from animals, vegetables, and minerals and offers a clue into the unity of human nature.

Natural law as a legal philosophy is said to be distinguished from other legal philosophies because it derives law from the nature of a being. By way of contrast, legal positivism maintains that laws are given force by the authority that makes them, and legal realism is a descriptive theory claiming that law is the practice seen in the judicial system. These do not need to be incompatible; indeed, I argue here that they are either, upon inspection, doing essentially the same thing, or the latter two are kinds of skepticism about the good.

Positivism refers to the laws made by humans. This does not need to conflict with natural law because the natural law must be applied in a given historical context. However, when the term means "worldview positivism,"[6] it means a philosophy that claims that there are no universals, no human nature on which to base a law, and therefore laws proceed from the will (voluntarism) rather than the intellect. This can be understood as an epistemological claim or as a metaphysical claim. Both, if consistently held, end in skepticism. As an epistemological claim, the positivist is saying that human nature and the good cannot be known and therefore cannot be the basis for law. As a metaphysical claim, the positivist is saying that only particulars exist; drawn out to its conclusions, this undermines the ability to think or communicate, because no thoughts or claims are ever the same. As noted earlier, positivism is either an application of natural law theory or a kind of skepticism about the good.

Legal realism can be likened to epistemological externalism. It describes external actions that result in valid law. Law is a real state of affairs in the world that is the result of a particular process or is being carried out in a particular situation. There is nothing inconsistent with natural law and legal realism at this point. Just like an externalist might say that a description of what people are doing when they "know" is compatible with an internalist account of knowing, so too a legal realist's description can be compatible with the idea of a natural law where a legislator knows the good and the historical setting and makes a positive law on this basis. However, like externalists, legal realism can make a further claim that this kind of description is all that there is. This can only be the case if the good cannot be known, and therefore assumes skepticism. If I can know the good and give an account of this knowing, then an external description is not "all there is."

I have presented research at a conference, which may embody another kind of legal philosophy: critical legal theory. This is a theory that seeks to expose power structures behind legal codes. It is a reductionist theory that reduces human beliefs to power relations in the world of politics and economics. As such, it forms part of the response of Postmodernism to the collapse of Modernity and will be considered in kind at a future point in this book. The question most commonly asked at this conference was: Who gets to decide what counts as "reason"? For now, it is sufficient to note that it is another kind of skepticism about human beliefs concerning the good: Such beliefs are simply covers for ethical egoism and the pursuit of power to attain happiness.

6 Heinrich Albert Rommen and Thomas R. Hanley, *The Natural Law, a Study in Legal and Social History and Philosophy* (St. Louis: B. Herder Book Co., 1947), 290.

SKEPTICISM ABOUT KNOWING THE GOOD AND THE NATURE OF THINGS

Where these theories are not expressions of skepticism they are not essentially different. This is true even when they make strong statements against natural law, such as in the case of thinkers who say that an ought cannot be derived from an is.[7] In each case, the thinker or theory presents a view of what is real, of how human nature fits into this, and subsequently what is good for human nature. Thus, a theory that claims only the material world exists and that humans are on a continuum with animals will not surprisingly say that the good is the satisfaction of desires. The difficulty is not that this framework is not shared in a formal sense, but that one must do the work to uncover and "flesh out" the given thinker's views on reality and human nature. Not all thinkers are systematic or comprehensive, and instead give a small flicker here and a slight glimpse there of an overall view. Just as I endeavor to understand the presuppositions of Modernity, so too I endeavor to understand the presuppositions of the thinkers we study. What we find is that they follow the formal pattern that can be stated as follows: Beliefs about what is real produce beliefs about human nature, which produce beliefs about what is good and of value.

This means that natural law is a philosophically ambiguous concept. It must be contextualized within the framework of beliefs about the good, human nature, and what is real. Talk about natural law that does not do this will be speaking about different conceptions of law. This accounts for why natural law can be evoked from opposing political philosophies, and can be – and has been – used to support both sides of competing issues. It is not possible to simply defend natural law as a viable legal philosophy for the contemporary world. Rather, one must defend a specific natural law nested within specific beliefs.

This requires taking stock of the failure of Modernity to provide a lasting foundation for the natural law that constituted shared life. For all of its claims, it failed to get to what all humans share in common, and without this it is impossible to communicate (consider the discussion in Plato's *Gorgias*). Identifying the inadequate foundation of Modernity will be the work of another chapter. Here we can note that the failure to identify a lasting foundation has inherent consequences. The idea of inherent consequences will also be a part of the natural law – the result of not keeping the moral law involves inherent consequences rather than imposed

7 Hume, G. E. Moore (naturalistic fallacy).

consequences (such as being thrown into hell at a future time). Thus, not keeping the law has inherent consequences beginning with not providing a foundation for the law and the resulting collapse.

If a purpose of law is to describe consistent connections, then the moral law describes the consistent actions required to achieve the good. This involves practical rationality but is more than that because it also requires knowing what is actually the good and what only appears to be the good. It is a law of choice founded/grounded on the good for human nature. Making a choice requires having the correct information about the goal of the choice. Incorrect information either about the means to the correct goal or in not knowing the correct goal leads to the devastating consequence of failing to achieve the good. Although the formal language masks the seriousness of this consequence, it is, by definition, the worst that can happen.

The concept of teleology fell out of favor in Modernity because of its connection with Aristotelian metaphysics and the medieval mindset. Here the term is used in a way that is different than found in Aristotle where it indicated being drawn toward a goal. This led to a natural law defined by the Medieval as imposed on human nature externally. By way of contrast, what I mean is simply "goal oriented." This distinguishes teleology from consequentialism and deontology because the former focuses on the affect of the goal and the latter focuses on the means to the goal. In this sense, Modernity is not an improvement over the Medieval; it exchanges heteronomy for a lack of focus on the good.

An important criticism of natural law theory is detailed by Alasdair MacIntyre[8] in his chapter "Intractable Moral Disagreements" for the book *Intractable Disputes about the Natural Law*. If the natural law is universal, why is there so much disagreement about it? Furthermore, if it is known through reason, and humans are supposedly rational animals, how can such disagreement be explained? Why can't all persons be convinced by the rational arguments for natural law? MacIntyre contextualized the question by suggesting that those holding to utilitarianism and deontology have different standards for reasoning. According to MacIntyre, there are no neutral and thus universal principles of reason that can be appealed to in order to adjudicate this difference. Rather, the superior theory is known

8 Alasdair MacIntyre (b. 1929) is a Scottish-born American philosopher best known for arguing that Aristotelian ethics can be reintroduced as relevant to solve contemporary disputes. He has also argued for the incommensurability of philosophical traditions such as Aristotelianism and Confucianism.

in its ability to explain the failings of other theories and indeed to predict them.

To understand moral deliberation, MacIntyre accepts the Aristotelian division of reasoning into theoretical and practical reasoning. For Aquinas, the good is that which comes under the apprehension of practical reason. As an empiricist, Aquinas believed that the good is known immediately through experience, although the highest good as a vision of God is not know through an experience in the body. Essentially, the good is heaven and the beatific vision, with this-worldly goods being concerned with stability in society and life as one pursues the *summum bonum*. Aquinas contrasted this view of the good with eleven alternatives, such as pride, wealth, and glory, in each case showing that such worldly enjoyments and goals are not sufficient to be the end in itself. Moral disagreements are about mistakes in practical reasoning rather than about what is the apprehended end of practical rationality.

Of course, Modernity rejected this view of the good, with Hobbes getting things started by asserting that there is no *summum bonum*. MacIntyre is partially correct in his identification of this shift as being a result of the search for moral standards that do not require theological grounding. However, he does not make the connection that I intend to make as the center of this study: If we cannot know the metaphysical absolute, we cannot know the moral absolute, and if we cannot know the moral absolute, we cannot be held responsible for failing to be good. Modernity did not simply claim that we cannot know God; as it progressed, it encountered many competing views of the metaphysical absolute. Indeed, some of these had always been present in Western civilization but had been allowed to remain ambiguous under the word "God." Are some views of God in fact misrepresentations (idols), and if so, which?

This can be called philosophical ambiguity. The moral intractability that MacIntyre discusses is really a result of this kind of ambiguity. Persons can all claim to agree that God exists and yet have disagreements about the moral law. However, as we trace the disagreement backward into presuppositions, we find that there is most likely disagreement about the nature of God. Because Modernity encountered many non-theistic views, I will use the term "metaphysical absolute" rather than "God." Nevertheless, this ambiguity continues sometimes to be encouraged by theists who claim that "deep down, everyone believes in God," where the term is permitted to refer to non-theistic concepts of the metaphysical absolute.

In his chapter mentioned earlier, as well as in his famous book, *After Virtue*, MacIntyre makes the case that there has been a loss of moral foundations, and that ultimately moral foundations must be grounded in theological foundations. In his chapter he calls for a theological understanding of reason. I am also using this term "foundation," although in a slightly different way than MacIntyre. His use is ultimately fideistic. Oliver Wendell Holmes rejected natural law as a mere return to tradition. He believed that his specific moral tradition, with its brand of theistic assumptions (allowing that there could be other forms of theism that do not lead to the beatific vision as the good), is the correct view because it can explain the errors of other views. He uses an analogy from Galileo and Ptolemy to make this case. There are a few obvious problems with this view. One is that this standard is itself a principle of rationality that MacIntyre is assuming to be neutral. Second, he only compares this to a limited number of Western moral philosophies, and not to some of the non-Western philosophies that claim to be able to explain the errors of theism. Third, whether or not someone is convinced is not proof of the soundness of an argument; indeed, it seems that most people are convinced by unsound arguments (consider popular marketing campaigns). His fideism enters through the claim that the beatific vision is the good without having given rational justification for his underlying metaphysical absolute (instead he asserts that it is better than the other alternatives of Modernity).

MacIntyre claims that there are no neutral principles of rationality that will convince everyone of a given viewpoint. I agree that reason is not neutral precisely because it supports some conclusions and not others, but I do not believe that its failure to convince everyone is proof against its being universal in all thinkers. This assumes that persons are actually using reason rather than only having the potential to use reason. Or more precisely, it assumes that persons are using reason fully rather than only using it partially seeking. This failure to use reason fully is one that must be addressed in this study. How does the natural law explain this problem, and what is to be done about it?

REASON AND KNOWING WHAT IS REAL

The first step to answering these questions is to consider the implications of an answer. If it is the case that persons could use reason fully and yet not know the metaphysical absolute and the corresponding moral absolute, then there can be no responsibility for being good rather than evil. I might be accidently good, or I might be good in a way that is consistent with my view of the metaphysical absolute, but in neither case can I know if I am actually good.

The need to know the law in order to do the law is an important principle. Aquinas states it as the need to promulgate the law. If this does not happen, persons cannot know the law and cannot be held responsible. Challenges to this principle sometimes confuse it with Kant's is/ought principle that involves his beliefs about freedom. However, whether one is a compatibilist or a libertarian does not change the need to know the good in order to choose the good.

The more important challenge to this principle has been from voluntarism, which claims that the will precedes the intellect. Voluntarism is a theory that attempts to explain why we appear to know the good but not do it, and also tries to preserve the omnipotence of God by protecting him from a situation where he must obey the commands of reason. For this view, violation of the law is a result of the will and not ignorance. Indeed, it seems to be a consistent view within the framework of dividing theoretical and practical reason. Can we question that division?

Socrates provides an example where there is no such division. Specifically, Socrates argued that if one knows the good, one will choose the good. Failure to be good is a result of ignorance, culpable or otherwise. People always act for what they believe to be good; no one purposely does what is believed to be evil. This has sometimes led to the Socratic position being classified as saying that knowledge is virtue. However, it could also be understood as claiming that there is a kind of knowledge of the good that is an end in itself. Upon examination through dialogue, those who claim to know the good but not do it are shown to not really know but only think they know.

If we must be able to know the good, we must be able to know human nature and the real. Consider an example from one-time dean of Harvard Law School, Roscoe Pound. In his *An Introduction to the Philosophy of Law*, he considered twelve conceptions of what law is, and in each case we can see that there is a reliance on a belief about what is real. For instance:

1. Divinely ordained set of rules or actions
2. A tradition given to humans about how to live and enforced by vengeful forces of nature
3. Custom of men of old who learned safe conduct in the relation to divine spirits
4. A set of rules based on the nature of things as understood by Roman philosophers
5. An idea of law where humans organize a society and appoint a legislature as the best means of securing obligations and peace in this life

6. Law is the reflection of divine reason governing the universe
7. The body of command given by a sovereign as the only basis for authority in human life.

Pound provides more conceptions, but they illustrate the same point. In each case the law is shaped by the beliefs about what is real of a given society. Should we think this is somehow different now? Or does leading the examined life require us to identify what presuppositions about human nature and reality underlie our own conception of the good and law? In the chapters that follow, I lay a foundation for how we can make progress in knowing what is real, in a way that is relevant to knowing the good and the law.

To accomplish this, we will now turn to the natural law theories of Aristotle and Aquinas. Although similar, these two thinkers nevertheless give very different views of the highest good, and this can be traced to how they understand the metaphysical absolute. I argue that this can help us understand how progress about the good must first be preceded by progress in knowing what is eternal.

2

Traditional Natural Law

Differences in Aristotle and Aquinas

> *The good Master said to me: "Thou does not ask what spirits are these that thou seest. Now I would have thee know, before thou goest farther, that these did not sin; and though they have merits it suffices not, because they did not have baptism, which is part of the faith that thou believest; and if they were before Christianity, they did not duly worship God: and of such as these am I myself. For such defects, and not for other guilt, are we lost, and only so far harmed that without hope we live in desire." Great woe seized me at my heart when I heard him, because I knew that people of much worth were suspended in that limbo. ... He drew out hence the shade of the first parent, of Abel his son, and that of Noah, of Moses the law-giver and obedient Abraham the patriarch, and David the King, Israel with his father and with his offspring, and with Rachel ... I saw Electra ... I recognized Hector and Aeneas, Caesar in armor ... and alone, apart, I saw the Saladin. ... Here I saw Socrates and Plato ... Democritus, who ascribes the world to change; Diogenes, Anaxagoras, and Thales, Empedocles, Heraclitus, and Zeno ... Euclid the geometer, and Ptolemy, Hippocrates, Avicenna, and Galen, and Averroes.*[1]

In this passage from Dante we are told that there are some who did not sin, and yet did not achieve a blessed afterlife, and therefore did not achieve the good, because they did not have sufficient special revelation. Although these persons excelled in their lives and did not sin, they are condemned to a hopeless condition. This suggests that the natural law is not sufficient to identify and achieve the good. If true, it follows that most of the humans that have lived could not have known the good or the means to the good. It means that the most excellent humans who live apart from special revelation are not able to know the *summum bonum*. This is not because of the need

1 Dante Alighieri, *The Divine Comedy*, Canto IV, trans. Charles Eliot Norton (Chicago: Encyclopaedia Britannica, 1980).

for regeneration, but because it is beyond human capabilities. Furthermore, this failure carries with it a punishment of hopelessness. This relates to the following chapter, in which we explore the relationship between Aristotle and Aquinas with the goal of arguing that the problem is not lack of special revelation, but that although it is clear what is good, humans have not known what should be known because they have not been seeking.[2]

BENEFITS AND SHORTFALLS OF NATURAL LAW

Classically, natural law has made the case that there is a universal law that can be known through reason by all persons. This is an attractive notion following the twentieth century that has seen tremendous moral terror often based on the denial of universal human nature. Because Modernity came to a close with such a bloody and morally egregious century, the hope is for a law that could provide a foundation to safeguard against future occurrences of these events. Such a law would provide universal human rights and values that in turn would provide the foundation for interaction between cultures. It would also provide a standard for determining if a given positive law is just. If there is no natural law, it has been argued that the only remaining option will be the rule of the powerful, or the majority, or some similarly arbitrary system. The following is a more specific study of why natural law is often dismissed as too ambiguous and easily appropriated by competing legal and moral viewpoints. To accomplish this, we will utilize the relationship between the good, human nature, and the real in order to understand how even thinkers as closely allied as Aristotle and Aquinas can differ significantly about the good when there are differences about what is ultimate and real. This will provide us with an initial step toward the conclusion that greater and more attention to epistemology and metaphysics is necessary to avoid the deficiencies of the Modern age. Agreement on a global law would first require agreement on the good.

One major critique of natural law theory is that it, in fact, does not provide universal standards but instead can be (and has been) used to prove any position. In the history of thought, there have been multiple thinkers who have based their ethical theories on what they believed to be natural law, and these theories are logically contradictory. Opposing political parties have made reference to natural law in order to support opposing legislation. What any given thinker has called natural or natural law has more often than not turned out to be a rationalization of cultural standards.

[2] Parts of this chapter are based on my research which appeared in *New Blackfriars*, Vol 87, Is 1012.

Thus, even though in theory natural law has many benefits, the critic can rightly point to a very disappointing history.

The purpose of this chapter is to examine this critique and to consider whether it is realistic to believe that natural law theory can achieve the ideal of universality. To do this, we examine two thinkers who are central to natural law thinking, and who would be expected to have very similar conceptions of natural law: Aristotle and Aquinas. What will be seen is that these thinkers have important differences in their ethical theories, which at first glance lends support to the previously mentioned critique. However, upon examination, it will be discovered that these differences in ethical theories arise from differences between these thinkers' perceptions of human nature. These particular differences, in turn, can be further traced to a difference in view of the two thinkers on the origin of human nature. Here I argue that even though the critic of natural law is accurate in pointing out a disappointing history, this does not indicate a necessary failing in natural law theory. It certainly does not indicate a need to avoid metaphysics because such avoidance only masks the origins of ambiguity in natural law. Rather, it highlights the need for more careful work in epistemology and metaphysics.

If the good is derived from one's view of human nature, which in turn is derived from one's view of the real, then natural law theory can only achieve universality through first coming to a consensus on human nature and, before that, coming to a consensus on the origin of human nature and what is real (the eternal).[3] It is precisely because this has not been done that there are differences with respect to the content of natural law. These differences are only an indication of logically more basic differences with respect to views of human nature and the eternal. Thus the critique of natural law theory should provide an impetus to reexamine the relationship between theories of human nature and theories of what is real and eternal, and to achieve consensus about these matters.

TELEOLOGY IN ARISTOTLE AND AQUINAS

In studying natural law, one inevitably encounters Aristotle and Aquinas.[4] These thinkers made important contributions to natural law thinking, and

3 This chapter uses the term "eternal" to refer to that which is self-existent, as opposed to dependent on another for existence. The eternal therefore has no beginning.

4 Aristotle (384 B.C.–322 B.C.), Greek philosopher, student of Plato, and tutor to Alexander the Great. He broke with Plato over the nature of change and forms and began his own school called the Lyceum in 335 B.C. His emphasis on a more empirical and this-worldly

given that Aquinas builds on Aristotle, one can find an overlap in their theory. Consequently, one would expect that if natural law can provide a universal system, such a system would be found in Aristotle and Aquinas. Their common starting point is the affirmation that all actions aim at some end. This is how Aristotle begins his *Nicomachean Ethics*, and it is why both thinkers are called teleological. Frederick Copleston says of Aristotle's ethical theory that it is "frankly teleological. He is concerned with action, not as being right in itself irrespective of every other consideration, but with action as conducive to man's good. What conduces to the attainment of his good or end will be a 'right' action on man's part: the action that is opposed to the attainment of his true good will be a 'wrong' action."[5] Or, as Ralph McInerny summarizes, "human action is ordered to an end; we act for the sake of an end insofar as we have a reason for action."[6]

Of course, it is this teleology that has made Aristotle unpalatable for many modern thinkers. Aristotle is not usually thought of as a natural law thinker in a strict sense. Yet, as Copleston points out, Aristotelian ethics is goal oriented, and that goal is the human good based on human nature. Further, Aristotle is commonly considered to have made a seminal contribution to natural law thinking. For the purposes of this study, he is classified as a natural law thinker because he bases his ethical theory on what he believes to be human nature. The fact that Aristotle bases his ethical theory on human nature, and Aquinas does the same, and yet they come out with different theories, appears to give credit to the previously mentioned critique of natural law. To have consensus about the natural law, there must be consensus about the metaphysical absolute. It is not the case that Aristotle and Aquinas can be lumped together on one side, with atheists on the other; Aristotle is a dualist and Aquinas is a theist, and the differences between dualism and theism are logically similar to the differences between theism and atheism (both cannot be true).

These two thinkers differ in important ways: They have different views of the eternal, and therefore different views of the human good. This

approach to change has been contrasted with Plato's more rationalist and otherworldly approach.

Thomas Aquinas (1225–1274), an Italian Dominican theologian. Known as the great systematizer of scholastic philosophy and theology, he is the author of the *Summa Theologiae* and *Summa Contra Gentiles*. In both he relied on Aristotle as the best representative of what natural man can achieve through reason.

5 Frederick Charles Copleston, *A History of Philosophy, Vol. 1: Greece and Rome* (Petaluma: Search Press, 1994), 323.

6 Ralph McInerny, "Ethics," in *Cambridge Companion to Acquinas*, eds. Norman Kretzmann and Eleonore Stump (Cambridge: Cambridge University Press, 1993), 198.

becomes important for natural law because the specifics of the law, the precepts for daily life applicable to concrete situations, are based on the human good. Thus, differences of opinion about the human good, even where they are small, can lead to exponentially larger differences about the natural law. This chapter argues the following: (1) natural law is based on the human good; (2) the human good is based on human nature; (3) human nature is based on what is real/eternal; (4) differences in belief about what is eternal will lead necessarily to differences in belief about human nature, the human good, and natural law; (5) natural law presupposes that the eternal is knowable; and (6) holding a person responsible for knowing and doing the natural law requires first holding the person accountable for knowing what is eternal.

One's view of the natural law is based on one's view of human nature. Human nature is what all humans have in common at all times. The natural law must be universal because human nature is universal. If there is a natural law, it applies to all humans just because they are humans. The critique on which this study is centered is best regarded as an epistemological critique: We cannot know human nature, and this is evidenced by the long history of disputing; thus we are left with only positive law. A less powerful reading of the critique is the metaphysical claim that there is no human nature. For a variety of reasons, I set aside this metaphysical critique for a later time. This chapter is therefore concerned with the epistemological reading of the critique: Natural law requires that human nature is knowable.

ARISTOTLE

> Now we call that which is in itself worthy of pursuit more final than that which is worthy of pursuit for the sake of something else, and that which is never desirable for the sake of something else more final than the things that are desirable both in themselves and for the sake of that other thing, and therefore we call final without qualification that which is always desirable in itself and never for the sake of something else.
>
> Now such a thing happiness, above all else, is held to be; for this we choose always for self and never for the sake of something else, but honour, pleasure, reason, and every virtue we choose indeed for themselves (for if nothing resulted from them we should still choose each of them), but we choose them also for the sake of happiness, judging that by means of them we shall be happy.[7]

7 Aristotle, *Nicomachean Ethics*, 1.7, translated by W. D. Ross.

Aristotle began the *Metaphysics* by asserting "all men by nature desire to know." This claim unites a fact about humans with human desire and implies something about what humans ought to do (they ought to know). Furthermore, it is a good example of how a natural law is proven to be the case in that arguing against it is self-refuting – the alternative cannot be the case.

According to Aristotle, the goal of metaphysics is to come to know what is eternal (without beginning or end), as opposed to that which is transitory or potential.[8] For the rest of this book, I will refer to this idea as the eternal (the metaphysical absolute, the real). Aristotle analyzed change in terms of actuality and potentiality. Matter without form is pure potentiality. Matter is given form but not existence (it has always existed – it is eternal). This becomes relevant for morality and natural law when we ask: What ought I to do? The assumption behind this question is that the answer might be different from what I in fact do. A contrast thus arises between how things are in terms of my actions and what my actions ought to be. This change involves changing from potentially being excellent to achieving excellence in actuality. "There must be, in the individual person, an intellective *psuche* that manifests an acquired *hexis* (or *habitus*, in the later scholastic tradition), which is the developed potentiality for knowing. Within the context of Aristotelian metaphysics, this premise seems to be relatively straightforward: in order for an agent to know or to understand, that agent must have a potentiality or *dunamis* for knowing/understanding."[9] Indeed, Aristotle's solution to earlier Greek philosophical problems about being and becoming is to suggest that everything can be conceived of in terms of the concepts "actuality" and "potentiality." Change is the process of what is potential striving to become actual according to the given form of a given. Humans are in the process of going from differing levels of potentiality to actuality in living according to the human form; this is one of the most important purposes of law.

Aristotle believed that the purpose of the law and the state is to make men good:

8 "With what category of being, then, is metaphysics especially concerned? With that of substance, which is primary, since all things are either substances or affections of substances. But there are or may be different kinds of substances, and with which kind does first philosophy or metaphysics deal? Aristotle answers that, if there is an unchangeable substance, then metaphysics studies unchangeable substance, since it is concerned with being *qua* being, and the true nature of being is shown in that which is unchangeable and self-existent, rather than in that which is subject to change." Copleston, *A History of Philosophy, Vol. 1: Greece and Rome*, 291.

9 Michael White, "The Problem of Aristotle's Nous Poietikos," *The Review of Metaphysics* 57 (2004).

> The man who is to be good must be well trained and habituated, and go on to spend his time in worthy occupations and neither willingly nor unwillingly do bad actions, and if this can be brought about if men live in accordance with a sort of reason and right order, provided this has force – if this be so, the paternal command indeed has not the required force or compulsive power (nor in general has the command of one man, unless he be a king or something similar), but the law has compulsive power, while it is at the same time a rule proceeding from a sort of practical wisdom and reason.[10]

For Aristotle, the question therefore becomes what is the actuality of human nature toward which those with potential human nature are moving:

> Just as for a flute-player, a sculptor, or an artist, and in general, for all things that have a function or activity, the good and the "well" is thought to reside in the function, so would it seem to be for man, if he has a function.... What then can this be? Life seems to be common even to plants, but we are seeking what is peculiar to man. Let us exclude, therefore, the life of nutrition and growth. Next there would be a life of perception, but it also seems to be common even to the horse, the ox, and every animal. There remains, then, an active life of the element that has a rational principle ... human good turn outs to be activity of soul in accordance with virtue, and if there are more than one virtue, in accordance with the best and most complete.[11]

This illustrates that Aristotle's approach to ethics is based on his view of human nature and on the general truth that human nature is that which is peculiar to humans. The life according to reason is the happiest life because it is the life of a human. Second to this is the life of virtue where we observe our duties and obligations to one another.[12] This highest life, however, is the life where one most closely resembles God: "Therefore, the activity of God, which surpass all others in blessedness, must be contemplative; and of human activities, therefore, that which is most akin to this must be most of the nature of happiness."[13] This is the pattern I attempt to illustrate in this chapter: One's view of the metaphysical absolute will determine one's view of human nature and the good. Precisely because Aristotle and Aquinas differ about the nature of God, they differ about human nature and the good.

From these considerations Aristotle concluded that there is an eternal prime mover: "Obviously, therefore, the substance or form is actuality.

10 Aristotle, "Nicomachean Ethics," in *Aristotle II*, trans. W. D. Ross, Vol. 21 (New York: Encyclopedia Britannica, 1952), 339.
11 Ibid. (i.6.1098b)
12 Ibid. (x.7.1178).
13 Ibid. (x.8.1178.20).

According to this argument, then, it is obvious that actuality is prior in substantial being to potency; and as we have said, one actuality always precedes another in time right back to the actuality of the eternal prime mover."[14] This eternal prime mover, the Unmoved Mover, is thus pure actuality without any potentiality; it is the source of change in other beings from potentiality to actuality. In some readings of Aristotle, there are multiple unmoved movers, at least one for each celestial sphere. The unmoved mover of the outer sphere is still given preeminence, because the movements of the lower sphere can be regarded as accidentally (albeit not essentially) moved in imitation of the perfection of the outmost sphere.

For Aristotle, the Unmoved Mover is pure actuality and is the origin of change from potentiality to actuality. The Unmoved Mover is not itself made of matter, and seems to be intelligence. Sometimes the Unmoved Mover is thought of as starting motion, the same way the first domino in a series begins the motion of the rest of the dominoes. This is not an accurate picture. The Unmoved Mover initiates motion through its actuality and perfection. All other beings have some potentiality remaining in them, striving toward actuality. The actuality of the form of human nature is eternal and causes change in those with potential human nature. Aristotle thus gives us his view of the eternal:

> It is clear then from what has been said that there is a substance that is eternal and unmovable and separate from sensible things. It has been shown also that this substance cannot have any magnitude, but is without parts and indivisible (for it produces movement through infinite time, but nothing finite has infinite power; and, while every magnitude is either infinite or finite, it cannot, for the above reason, have finite magnitude, and it cannot have infinite magnitude because there is no infinite magnitude at all). But it has been shown that it is impassive and unalterable.[15]

Aristotle's metaphysical view has been called dependent dualism, because change is explained in terms of the potential striving to become like the actually perfect. He applies this same framework to human nature. Humans are potentially excellent, and ethics studies how humans can become actually excellent. For Aristotle, excellence involves possessing certain virtues with the aim of being happy. The good life is where a person actually has the excellences of the human form that are potentially present. These excellences are found in the virtues of which Aristotle speaks throughout

[14] Aristotle, "Metaphysics," in *Aristotle: 1*, trans. W. D. Ross, Vol. 86 (New York: Encyclopedia Britannica, 1952), 576.

[15] Ibid., 603.

the bulk of the *Nicomachean Ethics*, and also in the contemplative life he mentions in the last book of that work. These virtues revolve around the social life and what is necessary for flourishing as a social being. Therefore, a natural law based on the Aristotelian view would aim at giving prescriptions on how to live the virtuous life as understood by Aristotle. Aristotle's view can be summarized as follows: All is eternal (in that there is no creation *ex nihilo*) and yet only the Unmoved Mover is pure actuality; the rest of the cosmos strives to reach pure actuality from the state of potentiality; the good life for a human is to achieve excellence that is potentially present in human nature; achieving these excellences (or virtues) will lead to happiness.

AQUINAS

Aquinas relied on the Aristotelian framework while making some important adjustments. He generally accepted the Aristotelian view of man as a social being, and the virtues as outlined by Aristotle. However, he had a very different view of God than did Aristotle. It is even questionable as to whether the term "God" should be applied to Aristotle's view of the eternal. This study continues to use the term "eternal" and to distinguish Aristotle's view of the Unmoved Mover as the eternal (and the cosmos itself, given that for Aristotle, there is no creation *ex nihilo*) from Aquinas's view of God as the eternal creator.

Aquinas introduces a distinction, not present in Aristotle's metaphysics, between "nature" and "grace." For instance, there are natural goods and spiritual goods. "Can a person have a plurality of ultimate ends? If health counts as an ultimate end, our answer of course will be in the affirmative."[16] Aquinas seeks to reconcile or, more pessimistically, to accommodate Christian theology with Aristotle's philosophy:

> It is on this basis that Aquinas distinguishes between an imperfect and a perfect realization of ultimate end. The philosophical ideal does not conflict with the Christian as if both were doctrines of what perfectly realizes the ideal of human happiness. The pagan philosopher's realization that our conceptual reach exceeds our practical grasp provides the basis for Aquinas to speak of the complementarity, rather than the opposition, of the philosophical and theological.[17]

[16] McInerny, *Ethics*, 199.
[17] Ibid., 214

Aristotelian moral philosophy is presupposed in the *Summa* and is thought to be equivalent to "philosophy" and "reason/rationality." This means that while Aquinas believed that Aristotle "got it right" on the level of nature, there is a higher level of grace of which Aristotle was ignorant. Aquinas suggests that Aristotle was only speaking of imperfect happiness as available in this life, and that lasting happiness is achieved in the beatific vision. However, Aristotle does not make this distinction and only speaks of one kind of happiness.

It should not be thought, however, that Aquinas believed that Aristotle made a mistake, or that there are two kinds of truth that are about the same object and yet contradictory. Copleston does note some tension between Aquinas's Christianity and Aristotelianism, but the general framework is that the natural man can go only so far with reason (and Aristotle went about as far as possible); one can get the whole picture only when grace is supplied. Aristotle's picture is therefore not wrong but only incomplete:

> St. Thomas's Christian faith frequently impinges on or has some effect on his philosophy. For instance, convinced that man has a supernatural final end, and a supernatural final end alone, he was bound to envisage the term of man's intellectual ascent as the knowledge of God as He is in Himself, not as the knowledge of the metaphysician and astronomer; he was bound to place the final goal of man in the next life, not in this, thus transmuting the Aristotelian conception of beatitude; he was bound to recognize the insufficiency of the State for fulfilling the needs of the whole man; he was bound to acknowledge the subordination of State to Church in point of value and dignity; he was bound, not only to allow for divine sanctions in the moral life of man, but also to link up ethics with natural theology, and indeed to admit the insufficiency of the natural moral life in regard to the attainment of beatitude, since the latter is supernatural in character and cannot be attained by purely human means. Instances of this impinging of theology on philosophy could no doubt be multiplied; but what I want to draw attention to now is the latent tension on some points between St. Thomas's Christianity and his Aristotelianism.[18]

Aquinas believed that the natural man could fulfill all the commands of the natural law, but fallen man cannot fulfill all the divine commandments without healing grace.[19]

[18] Frederick Charles Copleston, *A History of Philosophy, Vol. 2: Augustine to Scotus*. Petaluma: Search Press, 1994), 428.

[19] Thomas Aquinas, *Summa Theologica*, ed. Mortimer J. Adler, Vol. 19 (Chicago: Encyclopaedia Britannica, 1955), 826. Part 1 of the Second Part Q 109. A. 4.

Because the law is grounded on reason, limits placed on reason will limit the natural man's ability to know and do the law. Hence it is significant that Aquinas believed the natural man cannot know, from reason, that matter is not eternal. Aquinas did not believe that reason can prove that the world was created (the implication is that Aristotle did the best he could). It is in special revelation that one discovers the doctrine of creation.

Although God created the world freely, Aquinas did not think this means God created the world in time. God could have created the world from eternity – it requires special revelation to know if this is or is not the case. That this had been shown to be an impossible supposition St. Thomas refused to allow. Aquinas did not believe that it could be philosophically proven that there was a first moment, and he did not believe it could be philosophically proven that the world did not have a first moment (against the Averroists). This means that Aquinas did not believe theism can be proven philosophically, and that dependent dualism remains a viable option only precluded by special revelation.

Thus, the Thomistic natural law will necessarily involve aspects that Aristotelian ethics do not, giving rise to the differences that the critic points out. There are also important differences between Aquinas's view of God and the Unmoved Mover: God is the creator and God is personally concerned with the creation. Aristotle's Unmoved Mover is intelligence, and therefore in a sense personal, but there is no way for a human to have a relationship with the Unmoved Mover as can be had with God. Furthermore, grace is needed as a source of healing. For Aristotle, happiness can be achieved in this life; for Aquinas, only imperfect happiness can be achieved in this life. For Aristotle, law and the state can make a person good so that they achieve happiness in this life; for Aquinas, law and the state can only help persons achieve imperfect happiness and must be infused with the work of the church in dispensing sacraments to prepare people for perfect happiness in the next life.

UNDERLYING DIFFERENCES IN METAPHYSICS

Aristotle as a dependent dualist and Aquinas as a theist begin their systems with differing and competing views of the metaphysical absolute and law. This has gone unnoticed in the sense that Aristotle's dependent dualism as a rejection of theism is not viewed in the way Hobbesian materialism as a rejection of theism is viewed. And yet it should be obvious that Aristotle's dualism and Aquinas's theism are vastly different. Aristotle took for granted the eternality of the material world. While the Unmoved Mover is said to be the first mover, this first is not to be understood as acting temporally, because Aristotle says that motion is necessarily eternal. Further, the Unmoved Mover is not the creator of matter, which, according to Aristotle, has existed from eternity (as has the cosmos as a whole).

With the addition of grace and scripture comes the ultimate end of the beatific vision. Recall the passage quoted earlier in which Aristotle speaks about the end of human nature. Human nature does not – nor could it, in his worldview – include this supernatural end. Yet also recall that Aristotle's ethics is based on human nature and the end of human nature. This means that Aristotle's ethics will be different from that given by Aquinas. Aquinas adds grace and special revelation: It is through special revelation that truths about the immortality of the soul, and the higher goal of knowing God, are revealed. According to Aquinas, a full understanding of natural law requires a knowledge of this higher goal of knowing God. Some of the precepts of natural law will be aimed at this end and therefore will differ from precepts based purely on Aristotle's metaphysics.

Aquinas's position can be summarized as follows: Only God is eternal (everything else was created by God *ex nihilo*); humans can know that God is creator and personal, but they cannot know that God created matter *ex nihilo* apart from special revelation; there is a lower level of the good life available to all through general revelation (natural philosophy); the best life is available only through special revelation. Consider this general statement by Aquinas:

> It is therefore evident that as regards the common principles, whether of speculative or of practical reason, truth or rectitude is the same for all, and is equally known by all. As to the proper conclusions of the speculative reason, the truth is the same for all, but is not equally known to all; thus it is true for all that the three angles of a triangle are together equal to two right angles, although it is not known to all. But as to the proper conclusions of the practical reason, neither is the truth or rectitude the same for all, nor, where it is the same, is it equally known by all. Thus it is right and true for all to act according to reason.[20]

However, what end can reason attain? It cannot attain theism apart from special revelation. We can only know God as the one who forms and governs the world, but this is consistent with Platonic and Aristotelian dualism. In this passage we also see the bifurcation of practical and speculative reason, which needs to be further analyzed.

[20] Ibid., part 1 of Second Part Q. 94. A. 4.

RESULTING INFLUENCE ON THE FORMULATION OF LAW

The division between speculative or theoretical reason and practical rationality is an Aristotelian introduction not found in the earlier Socratic approach. Theoretical reason can be used to know some truths, but does not necessarily alter the affections. Consequently, practical rationality is the process of reasoning about how to achieve what one wants. This leads to the divide between what one knows (from theoretical reason) and what one wants. In terms of the ability for speculative/theoretical rationality to know the metaphysical absolute, these thinkers must arrive at different conclusions. For Aquinas, speculative reason requires that we believe in God the Creator, and for Aristotle, speculative reason requires that we believe there is no Creator. For a more concrete example, consider the following:

> As Augustine says (De Lib. Arb. I,5), 'that which is not just seems to be no law at all'; therefore the force of a law depends on the extent of its justice. Now in human affairs a thing is said to be just from being right according to the rule of reason. But the first rule of reason is the law of nature, as is clear from what has been stated above (Q. XCI, A. 2, Reply 2). Consequently every human law has just so much of the character of law as it is derived from the law of nature. But if in any point it differs from the law of nature, it is no longer a law but a corruption of law.[21]

Human laws should be framed in a general rather than a particular way:

> Whatever is for an end should be proportionate to that end. Now the end of law is the common good; because, as Isidore says (Etym. V, 21) 'law should be framed not for any private benefit, but for the common good of all the citizens.' Hence human laws should be proportionate to the common good. Now the common good comprises many things, as to persons, as to matters, and as to times. Because the community of the state is composed of many persons, and its good is procured by many actions; nor is it established to endure for only a short time, but to last for all time by the citizens succeeding one another, as Augustine says.[22]

Law and legislation must take into account man's ultimate end, and yet just what this is differs in Aristotle and Aquinas. Hence any particular law must be based on natural law, which is based on human nature and the eternal. Aquinas denies that a person can lead the good life without knowing God

[21] Ibid., Q. 95. A. 2.
[22] Ibid., Q. 96. A. 1.

and receiving the grace of God, although the natural man can have some good proportionate to his nature:

> Human nature needs the help of God as First Mover, to do or will any good whatsoever, as stated above (A. I). But in the state of integrity of nature, as regards the sufficiency of the operative power, man by his natural endowments could will and do the good proportionate to his nature, such as the good of acquired virtue, but not surpassing good, as the good of infused virtue.[23]

Both Aristotle and Aquinas would agree that we should act in order to achieve the good and that the good is based on human nature, and yet they arrive at very different views of how we should act. The natural man can achieve the goods of virtue, but not "infused virtue" from healing grace or the beatific vision. The problem for natural law theory is that these two systems will end up producing natural laws with different content. Even though these two thinkers are very similar, their differences with respect to the nature of the eternal are enough to make for very different views of the human good. The reason that natural law can be criticized as able to support any position is that this criticism does not notice philosophical context: natural law #1 presupposes metaphysical absolute #1, whereas natural law #2 presupposes metaphysical absolute #2, and so on. Failure to notice these differences results in philosophically ambiguous claims about the natural law.

Differences at the level of natural law are indications of differences at the more basic levels. Aristotle believed that the cosmos is eternal whereas Aquinas believed that God created the cosmos. If a person achieves excellence in philosophy, which one are they to believe? Further, in Aquinas's worldview, God is personal. For Aquinas, the good life includes having a personal relationship with God, and yet there is nothing like this for Aristotle. The differences between these thinkers about the nature of the cosmos and what is eternal result in important differences in their theory of natural law. It therefore seems to be theoretically possible to arrive at a universal natural law only by coming to consensus on the nature of the eternal. Philosophical ambiguity about the metaphysical absolute must be cleared up if there is progress to be hoped for in law.

[23] Ibid., Q. 109. A. 2. Aquinas also asserts that without grace, man cannot fulfill the law (Part 1 of Second Part Q. 109. A 4).

KNOWING WHAT IS ETERNAL

Aquinas gave four standards that must be met for a law to be just, and one of these was that the law must be promulgated or made known. This is an expression of the general principle that one cannot be held responsible for what one cannot know. Adding this to the pattern that the good presupposes human nature and the metaphysical absolute, we can conclude that: If the eternal is not knowable, then neither is human nature, the human good, or natural law. Or reversing this, natural law theory presupposes that the metaphysical foundation of the natural law is knowable. The eternal must be knowable if there is to be a natural law. It is thus necessary first to establish what is eternal and then to move on to determine the natural law based on the eternal. This can be called a "presuppositional approach": The more basic truths must be established before the less basic issues are dealt with.

A central difference between Aristotle and Aquinas about the eternal is whether matter is created or not. Aquinas appeals to special revelation in order to settle this question, which is epistemologically unhelpful in coming to consensus because (1) Aristotle did not have access to this special revelation, and (2) not everyone agrees as to whether there is special revelation and as to just what counts as special revelation. Therefore, staying within the realm of reason, which is accessible to all, I suggest a way of achieving consensus on this issue through presuppositional thinking: Aristotle believed that matter is eternal (although dependent), and Aquinas believed that this could not be disproved through reason: "The First Mover is not a Creator-God: the world existed from all eternity without having been created from all eternity. God forms the world, but did not create it, and He forms the world, is the source of motion, by drawing it, i.e. by acting as final cause."[24]

Aristotle, on the other hand, believed that matter is eternal because "neither the matter nor the form comes to be-and I mean the last matter and form. For everything that changes is something and is changed by something and into something. ... Note, next, that each substance comes into being out of something that shares its name."[25] For Aristotle, creation *ex nihilo* is not possible. He correctly asserts that "nothing" cannot cause something to exist, although he does not seem to consider the possibility of God causing matter to exist from or of nothing (this is not an uncaused

[24] Copleston, *A History of Philosophy, Vol. 1: Greece and Rome*, 315.
[25] Aristotle, *Metaphysics*, 599.

event because God is the cause). But this raises a dilemma for Aristotle: Either matter has some actuality without the Unmoved Mover and is then not dependent, or matter has no actuality without the Unmoved Mover and then is brought into being by the Unmoved Mover. Aristotle cannot accept the first option because he himself argues that matter cannot be independent of the Unmoved Mover. Matter without form is, according to Aristotle, pure potentiality; but if matter has some actuality apart from the Unmoved Mover, then it is not pure potentiality anymore. Matter without form is pure potentiality until it is given form, and therefore actuality, by God the Creator. However, the second option implies that while matter exists eternally in the mind of the Unmoved Mover, it only actually exists through a creative act. If reason apart from revelation can demonstrate this, then Aquinas gave up too soon on the ability of reason.

Aquinas himself argues for the existence of God by asserting that there is no composition of the existence and essence of God, that for God, these are the same. If they were not, "if there were composition of essence and existence, for instance, God would owe His existence to another being, which is impossible, since God is the first Cause."[26] This implies that only God is eternal and self-maintaining, and all else owes its existence to God. Further, this is shown through reason.

That reason can demonstrate that matter is not eternal can be further seen in Aquinas's consideration of time. The problem that Aquinas said cannot be solved by reason is the following: Did God create the world from eternity or in time? The solution given by reason (as opposed to special revelation) is that God created the world and time itself. Aquinas affirmed that time is the measurement of change, or motion, in terms of before and after. Thus, if there were no object that is in motion, there would be no time. Further, Aquinas affirmed that for God, who is eternal, there is no time. Consequently, matter is dependent on God for its existence, and the act of creation is the act that brings time into existence through bringing changing beings into existence. Time is not eternal, but rather had a beginning. Consequently, it can be shown by reason that matter is not eternal.

This argument is valid if one first assumes that there is a substantial difference between God and the created order. Aristotle did not make this assumption but instead believed that all is eternal and explained difference and change by the process of potentiality and actuality. Aristotle maintained that theism is impossible. What is the status of this belief? Is Aristotle culpably ignorant on this point? What are the implications for his

[26] Copleston, *A History of Philosophy, Vol. 2: Augustine to Scotus*, 349.

error on his legal theory? These questions need to be considered in relation to how natural law will be implemented and in terms of the ethics of belief about the metaphysical absolute.

This argument at least indicates the possibility of knowing God the Creator through general revelation and therefore undermines the idea that Aristotle exemplifies the natural philosopher. This consideration of the creation of matter is meant to illustrate that it is possible to discern through reason the nature of the eternal. Consensus can be achieved about the eternal, and this implies that consensus can also be achieved about human nature, the human good, and the natural law. One need not appeal to special revelation to argue that the world was created and is not eternal. Indeed, the scriptures assume this but do not prove it. There can certainly be more questions raised about this issue, but the intention has been to show that Aristotle and Aquinas did not exhaust the possibilities of reason; instead, it seems that they did not use reason enough and missed the alternative that matter is dependent and created, as is time itself.

KNOWLEDGE AND RESPONSIBILITY

Having first established that it is necessary to know the eternal in order to establish a universal moral law, it can then be asked whether all or only some need to be able to know the eternal. Responsibility is relative to how much a person can know: If persons cannot know the law, they cannot be held responsible for obeying or disobeying the law. Given that knowing the natural law requires first knowing what is eternal, holding persons accountable for knowing the natural law requires also holding them accountable for knowing the eternal. If the eternal is not knowable by all, a universal natural law is not achievable. Knowing the eternal is therefore a necessary condition for knowing the human good and natural law, although it may not be sufficient (more is needed).

To say that humans must be able to know is a statement about human nature, not about a specific human or about a given historical condition. For instance, some might argue that post-lapsarian humans cannot know God and therefore the ought/can principle does not apply to them. However, the reason these humans are post-lapsarian is because they did not do what they were able to do. They fell from the state of innocence because of not keeping a commandment that they could have kept (and the commandment included knowing the difference between God and humans, that they cannot be like God in the sense in which they were tempted – the determiner of good and evil). Furthermore, even in a post-lapsarian state, humans are able to know God in the sense that they are the kinds of beings that can understand premises and draw conclusions. However, they are said to be not seeking and therefore not understanding or knowing. The failure to seek does not change the reality that they can know (if they sought).

If humans are responsible because they have the ability to know the natural law, then humans must have the ability to know what is eternal. Appealing to intuitional agreement about less basic examples of law (do not murder) only ends in philosophical ambiguity as the meaning of such laws is traced to their more basic presuppositions. Knowing the eternal is a necessary condition for knowing the good, so that if we hold people responsible for knowing what is good, we must also hold them accountable for knowing the eternal. Thus, the first level of responsibility for a human is knowing what is eternal. The differences in worldviews and the various systems of law that these produce are a result of differences in views about what is eternal, and humans can be held responsible for dealing with these differences through the use of reason.

The criticism this chapter has addressed is: Natural law theorizing is not helpful because natural law has been used to support contrary positions on just about every issue. This criticism has a basis in historical truth. However, the question is whether this is a necessary quality of natural law theory or if it can be overcome. Here it has been argued that it indeed can be overcome. The differences in systems of natural law have been traced to differences in views about human nature and the eternal. If two thinkers as close as Aristotle and Aquinas have differences that affect their theories of law, how much more will thinkers with more consciousness about their metaphysical differences disagree about the law? Therefore, if a universal natural law is to be presented, one that is unified and can offer helpful insights and solutions to the issues facing humanity today, then there must be a consensus on what is eternal. As long as there are differences of view about the eternal, there is no hope of a universal natural law. An implication of this solution is that humans are responsible to know what is eternal. All responsibility with respect to the natural law presupposes that humans are responsible for knowing what is eternal. It is therefore not only theoretically possible to have a consensus on what is eternal, but humans have a responsibility to acquire this knowledge.

Natural law theory asserts that the law is based on human nature, and there is only one human nature. Therefore, there is only one natural law. The emphasis in natural law theorizing must be on obtaining a correct view of human nature on which a natural law can be based. Because one's view of human nature depends on one's view of the origin of human nature, a correct view of human nature will first require having a correct view of the eternal. The critique of natural law considered in this chapter hopefully encouraged a rethinking of the differences currently widespread about what is eternal, and also encouraged natural law thinkers to work toward a consensus about what is eternal, human nature, and the human good, in order to lay the foundation for a natural law.

CONCLUSION

Long-standing disagreement about the purpose and content of law reveal that there is also disagreement about the presuppositions of the law. Unfortunately, Modernity increasingly moved away from attempting to settle these kinds of differences and instead proposed that the solution to disagreements could be attained in a secular state that set metaphysics aside. The result was that although the secular state does indeed have metaphysical presuppositions (often naturalism), these have been given a free pass as either nonexistent or neutral. Furthermore, viewpoints that were more aware of their metaphysical assumptions were identified as divisive, and persons were required to set aside these viewpoints when entering into the public sphere where law is debated. In the next few chapters, we trace some of this history and consider attempts to provide a natural law that is free from metaphysics.

3

Patterns in Historical Development

Ulyss. The heavens themselves, the planets, and this centre
Observe degree, priority, and place,
Insisture, course, proportion, season, form,
Office, and custom, in all line of order;
And therefore is the glorious planet Sol
In noble eminence enthroned and sphere
Amidst the other; whose medicinable eye
Corrects the ill aspects of planets evil,
And posts, like the commandment of a king,
Sans check, to good and bad. But when the planets
In evil mixture to disorder wander,
What plagues and what portents! What mutiny!
What raging of the sea! Frights, changes, horrors,
Divert and crack, rend and deracinate
The unity and married calm of states
Quite from their fixture! O, when degree is shaked,
Which is the ladder to all high designs,
The enterprise is sick![1]

In this passage from *Troilus and Cressida*, Shakespeare portrays Ulysses as stating a very common Ancient and Medieval belief about how "nature" works. There is a kind of order and symmetry to nature, and any departure from this brings great problems. This helps us understand how the term "nature" is philosophically ambiguous, and how appeals to "natural law" must take into account their worldview context to know what "nature" and "natural" mean. What is agreed upon is that the good for a being is according to the nature of that being. Ambiguity arises because there is disagreement about the nature of things; there is disagreement about what

1 William Shakespeare, *Troilus and Cressida*, Act 1, Scene III.

is real. A consideration of noted philosophers who have contributed to natural law thinking from the Ancients to the Post-Moderns will help illustrate this and make our path smooth in clarifying the natural moral law.

ANCIENT, EARLY MEDIEVAL, HIGH MEDIEVAL, MODERN, AND POSTMODERN

Why speak about Modernity in the past tense? Doing so seems to assume something contentious, that there are such things as historical eras, and that the one called "Modernity" has come to an end. To speak of historical eras raises a whole set of questions. Are there actually such things or are they merely helpful heuristic devises? Either way, how can they be identified? If real, how do we know what demarcates an era, and if simply a teaching tool, how do we avoid arbitrariness rooted in the teacher's preferences?

Because this is not a book on philosophy of history, some nuances of these questions must go unanswered. However, it is necessary to ask if what we call Modernity is simply a continuation of themes found in the Medieval age or if something new began in the seventeenth century. Or perhaps it will be conceded that something new began but the date must be pushed back to the thirteenth century. On the other end, some might say that Modernity has not ended but has shifted into a new phase, perhaps called liquid Modernity. In my approach to this question, I hope to capture the flow of history (as opposed to sharp demarcations between "eras," and the reliance of the present on past choices), that there are patterns of challenges and response that can be identified, studied, and understood, and that these patterns can be clustered together to form eras within the larger flow of history.

Identifying the patterns is the key to an accurate assessment of when an era begins and ends. When the focal point becomes religious, political, economic, or legal institutions, the temptation is to mark eras with the beginning or end of such institutions. For instance, it might be claimed that modern law can trace its origin to Gratian in the twelfth century (Francis Oakley) or modern political bureaucracy to the development of the French government in the thirteenth and fourteenth centuries (Brian Tierney). An alternative is to consider the kinds of questions being asked in an age, how these are rooted in historically unique challenges, and how answers to these questions set the context for further challenges. Physical continuity of institutions does not guarantee intellectual continuity.

I will especially rest my case on the idea that eras are best demarcated in relation to epistemology; changes in epistemology result in changes in how challenges (even if they are similar challenges as seen in the past) are answered.

I believe it is safe to assert that an Augustinian/Platonic epistemology dominated the early medieval period, that it was replaced by a Thomistic/Aristotelian epistemology in the High Middle Ages, and that another shift in epistemology best identified with Descartes ushered in the Modern age. Similarly, the end of Modernity came with the failure of this epistemology and the rise of skepticism as the belief that knowledge is not possible.

Thus, I maneuver in difficult waters and affirm that there is such a thing as Western civilization that has a continuity back to the Greeks, but also that there are eras within this history that present unique sets or patterns of challenges. Furthermore, these challenges press persons and groups to become more conscious of what I will call their foundation, and to develop this foundation more consistently. The foundation is the set of beliefs that are assumed by the rest of a worldview and that answer basic questions about knowledge, reality, and value. Challenges to a foundation can be either internal, by others sharing a worldview, or external from a competing worldview.

Because of these considerations, I date the beginning of Modernity to the mid-seventeenth century. It begins in the collapse of the medieval manner of dealing with internal challenges, broadly construed as the use of force to compel others toward religious consent. The Reformation called into question the authority structure of the medieval world. Earlier reform movements had appealed to this authority structure for change, or had been stamped out through violence (Augustine: compel them to enter). One era closes and another begins with the failure of this practice culminating in the Peace of Westphalia (1648). In this general time, there is the end of the Wars of Religion, the writing of the Westminster Confession, the English Civil War and the recalling of Charles II by the English, the work of Descartes in pursuit of what can be known with certainty, and the work of Hobbes to explain the life of man in the temporal order.

The Reformers shared the medieval focus on soteriology, although they called for greater consistency with the Scriptures as the foundational document. Because the competing appeals to authority were not resolved, and the Wars of Religion left Europe exhausted, a new focus on the temporal order emerged and gave us the term "secular." Religion continues to be about what happens after death, but that is left to individual choice. Shared life must be about what can be known and agreed on, and this life is the only candidate remaining. The focus on this individuality (in religious belief and conscience, in consent to be governed, in knowing what is certain) is the unfolding story of Modernity. It is a story of attempting to find freedom and autonomy apart from identifying the good.

THE ANCIENTS

> Indeed, it is a strange-disposed time: But men may construe things after their fashion, Clean from the purpose of the things themselves.[2]

To set the context of the movement from Modernity to Postmodernity, it is beneficial to understand patterns of thought that have been influential from the ancient world through the medieval and into the modern and contemporary (Postmodern) periods. This is not intended as an exhaustive history but rather as a chance to identify patterns that developed in thinking about the good and the natural law. For the ancient period I introduce some insights from Plato, and then use Cicero as a lens through which to understand these patterns.

PLATO

> When a person starts on the discovery of the absolute by the light of reason only, and without any assistance of sense, and perseveres until by pure intelligence he arrives at the perception of the absolute good, he at last finds himself at the end of the intellectual world, as in the case of sight at the end of the visible.[3]

Plato does not necessarily factor into the history of natural law.[4] Yet, given his stature and influence on Western thought, he must be considered to some extent. This is especially the case in reference to his thinking about the good and what is real.

Historically, Plato sets the tone for discussing the good in *The Republic*. Although the discussion is initially about justice, it turns quickly to defining justice in terms of doing good to one's friends. The distinction is made between something appearing to be good and actually being good, and the implication that it may be believed that one is doing good to a friend when in fact harm is being done. "Many a man who is ignorant of human nature has friends who are bad friends, and in that case he ought to do harm to

2 Cicero, in Shakespeare's *Julius Caesar*, Act I Scene III.

3 Plato, *The Republic*, trans. Benjamin Jowett. (Chicago: Encyclopedia Britannica, 1980), p. 397.

4 Plato (428/427 B.C.–348/347 B.C.) was a Greek philosopher. The student of Socrates and teacher of Aristotle, Plato started the Academy that is considered the foundation for the Western university. Plato taught a kind of dualism in which there are eternal forms to which the material world (without beginning, although changing) only roughly conforms. The human soul is also without beginning, and knowledge is a kind of memory of past perception of the forms. The Socratic form of questioning and inquiry became the standard at the Academy, which later became known for its academic skepticism.

them; and he has good enemies whom he ought to benefit."[5] Knowing what is good for a being requires knowing the nature of that being. "He is a friend who is, as well as seems, good; and that he who seems only, and is not good, only seems to be and is not a friend."[6]

Socrates is challenged by Thrasymachus, who says that justice is the benefit of the strong. Again, this initiates a conversation about what is benefit, or what is good. In this branch of the conversation, Socrates introduces the idea of natures and ends. He asks: "Would you not say that a horse has some end?"[7] This sounds foreign to modern ears, in a time when discussion of ends is not common. However, it is not entirely abandoned even today. The modern naturalist would say that the end of a horse is survival and offspring. Socrates makes the point clearer by noting the end of our various sense organs; in the case of the ear and the eye, it is, respectively, to hear and see. Furthermore, "now I think you will have no difficulty in understanding my meaning when I asked the question whether the end of anything would be that which could not be accomplished, or not so well accomplished, by any other thing."[8] So, the end of human nature must be something that humans can accomplish, and which is not accomplished by other things (or else it raises the question as to what extent the two natures are different).

Socrates maintains that the end of the soul is "to superintend and command and deliberate and the like."[9] Therefore, a good soul is a good superintendent, and an evil soul is an evil superintendent. One of the ends that Socrates names for the soul is life, and the result of being a good soul is to live well. I do not take his use of the term "life" to refer only to physical life, but to the life of the soul, which is especially related to knowing the highest reality (Book VII of *The Republic* gives Plato's view of the highest good). To live well as an excellent soul is to know this reality. A soul that is ignorant of the most important things is not wise, or excellent, nor can it be said to live well. The effect of living well is happiness (as opposed to saying happiness is itself the good).[10]

In Book VII of *The Republic*, Plato gives us the allegory of the cave. In this story, he describes how the direct vision of the forms is the highest good. This preserves the formal claim that knowledge of the highest

5 1.334
6 1.335
7 1.352
8 1.353
9 1.353
10 1.354

reality is the good. However, knowledge by inference has replaced knowledge by direct vision – a kind of intuition. Many Christian philosophers have replaced the forms with God and argued that the highest good is the vision of God. One problem with this view is that if God is a spirit whom no human has seen or can see, then there is no direct vision of God (of the essence of God). Another problem is that intuition (a direct perceiving or immediate awareness) is not the same as knowledge. Intuitions are often mistaken, and perceptions must be interpreted. In both cases there must be some other standard that can be appealed to in order to guarantee knowledge rather than mere opinion.

Plato says "As being is to becoming, so is pure intellect to opinion. And as intellect is to opinion, so is science to belief, and understanding to the perception of shadows."[11] Plato gives us the formal relationship between good and being, saying that the highest good for humans is knowledge of the highest being. The highest being is that which is unchanging and eternal. Because Plato has accepted dualism in which matter and ideas are both eternal, he elevates the ideas above matter because ideas are unchanging whereas matter is always in a state of change. The manner in which the good is grasped is through direct perception, following the analogy to sight and the eye: "The time has now arrived at which they must raise the eye of the soul to the universal light which lightens all things, and behold the absolute good."[12] He also calls this a "beatific vision."[13] Later we will see how this is translated into Christianity by maintaining the formal relationship between the good and being, but substituting direct vision of God for direct vision of the ideas or forms.

In Book X of *The Republic*, Plato describes the soul's journey after death. He describes passing through a judgment and then entering into another body of animals or humans. He claims that this has been going on from eternity. That is, the human soul is eternal and therefore uncreated. This is an assumption of his that he never critically examines. It is essential to his view of knowledge, where knowledge of the forms is a kind of memory from past perception of the forms. It makes any attempt to fuse Plato and Christianity impossible in that Plato attributes the eternal nature of God to the human soul.

In *The Republic*, Plato gives a number of important conceptual tools that aid us in this study, specifically that the good for a thing is based on

11 Plato, *The Republic*, book VII, 398.
12 Ibid., 401.
13 Ibid., 389

the nature of a thing, and that the nature of a thing involves accomplishing its end. Some might say that Modernity, as the triumph of nominalism, rejected these insights. I do not think so. Rather, I believe that formally, these insights remain, but they were given new content. That is, human nature has been reduced to the needs of the body, and the end of human nature is simply to satisfy these needs. Hobbes and Locke disagreed about how to best satisfy these needs, but not that this was the goal of the state. Likewise, postmodern thinkers say nothing that could undermine this assertion, but rather claim that each individual is its own nature (there is no universal human nature), and that the satisfaction of individual desire is the end of individual action. As we proceed, we consider in more depth the many attempts to deny the relationship between the good, human nature, and the end of knowing the highest reality.

In *The Republic*, Socrates concludes that the purpose of the law is to guide the citizens in cultivating their higher element until they have set up a ruler in their own hearts so that they go their own way not needing the law.[14] In his *Laws*, Plato considers more worldly concerns about how the law is to be formed. Specifically, "Now we ought always to cooperate with the lead of the best, which is law. For inasmuch as reason is beautiful and gentle, and not violent, her rule must needs have ministers in order to help the golden principle in vanquishing the other principles. … While the city, receiving the same from some god or from one who has knowledge of these things, should embody it in a law, to be her guide in her dealings with herself and with other states. In this way virtue and vice will be more clearly distinguished by us. And when they have become clearer, education and other institutions will in like manner become clearer."[15] The actual laws that Plato articulates reflect his understanding of human nature and what is eternal. Nevertheless, he has given us a formal relationship that holds between how a civilization understands the good, how it determines law, and the boundaries of institutions within that civilization such as education. Modernity has not shown this formal relationship to be false, but it has replaced Plato's belief about what is eternal with its own, transitioning from Theism to Naturalism.

I rely on considering how various thinkers understand what is eternal in order to think about their view of the good. Some thinkers might claim that nothing is eternal, others that the material world or the self is eternal. In Modernity, the existence of God has been questioned and the

[14] Plato, *The Republic*, book IX.
[15] Plato, *The Laws*, 650.

weaknesses of the traditional proofs exposed. However, we must not take this to mean that some other view of what is eternal has been proven. Rather, we find a kind of common-sense realism that assumes the material world (in some form or another) has always existed, or we find skepticism about this point. I argue that attributing eternality to anything besides God ends in contradiction. This helps us make our way to understanding the good as knowing God, and not a direct vision of God, but rather knowing God through what has been made.

CICERO

Cicero's works abound with references to the natural law, and he brings his own understanding to this Stoic notion in a way that influenced later ages.[16] He was influential in Augustine's appreciation of philosophy, in Aquinas's view of the natural law, he appears in Limbo in Dante's *Inferno*, and he had a pronounced affect on the Enlightenment. He is a helpful example of the attempt to approach ethical and political issues apart from, or with little critical work in, metaphysics or epistemology. He also gives us a look at the ancient schools of thought concerning the good, and this demonstrates certain patterns that arise when the good is misidentified, which continue to be relevant for us today.

In Cicero's books, *On Moral Ends* and *On Moral Duties*, we are given a look at the competing schools of thought concerning the good life and at Cicero's own method of adjudicating between them. Because little writing remains from the Stoic tradition, Cicero is our main source of understanding this tradition. However, Cicero himself takes the approach of an Academic Skeptic. The Academic Skeptics believed that certainty was not possible, and instead what one must do is understand as best as possible each viewpoint and then select the one that seems most plausible. Of course, the problem is precisely how to identify what counts as plausible. Beside searching out and rejecting contradictions at one level, the emphasis for Cicero is often on certain common-sense notions and appeals to traditional ideas. Often, what counts as common sense is informed by his metaphysical outlook, which is taken for granted rather than critically examined (this is what I mean by finding contradictions only at one level, not at more basic levels).

16 Marcus Tullius Cicero (106 B.C.–43 B.C.) was a Roman statement, lawyer, and philosopher.

The ethical discussions of Cicero's contemporaries assume that our ethical aims are limited to the fulfillment of our human nature as then understood; they are all naturalistic, in a common understanding of that term. Plato does not appear as a participant in these debates because his most striking claim is that the virtuous person should "become like God," transcending human nature as much as one can. This idea does not fit into Hellenistic ethical debate at all, although it was to have a great future in later antiquity.[17]

Cicero provides an account of the differences between Epicureans and Stoics. The common assumption of this debate was that happiness is the good. The differences were about what exactly happiness is and how best to achieve it. The Epicureans identified happiness with the maximizing of certain kinds of pleasure. Epicurus denied that there is a God (or at least that the gods cared about humans) or a soul. For these beliefs, Dante assigned him a place among the heresiarchs in graves outside the city of Dis, whereas Cicero is found in Limbo, the place for those who did the best they could without knowledge of Christ.

In contrast to the Epicureans, the Stoics believed that the best way to achieve happiness was to live a life of virtue. Zeno, the founder of the Stoic tradition, is understood to have thought that "the goal of human striving was life according to nature. This was the same as the virtuous life. The reason was that any individual nature is a part of the nature of the whole cosmos, and so life according to nature means life according to right reason; and living according to right reason is living virtuously. In such virtue does eudaimonia or human happiness consist."[18] Or, as we see from the character Laelius in Cicero's *De Republica*:

> True law is right reason in agreement with nature; it is of universal application, unchanging and everlasting; it summons to duty by its commands, and averts from wrongdoing by its prohibitions. ... It is a sin to try to alter this law, nor is it allowable to attempt to repeal any part of it, and it is impossible to abolish it entirely. ... And there will not be different laws at Rome and at Athens, or different laws now and in the future, but one eternal and unchangeable law will be valid for all nations and all times, and there will be

17 Cicero, *On Moral Ends*, trans. Raphael Woolf, ed. Julia Annas (Cambridge: Cambridge University Press, 2001).

18 Christopher Wolfe, *Natural Law Liberalism* (Cambridge; New York: Cambridge University Press, 2006), 269, http://www.loc.gov/catdir/toc/ ecip061/2005027578.html and http://www.loc.gov/catdir/ enhancements/fy0633/2005027578-d.html

> one master and ruler, that is God, over us all, for he is the author of this law, its promulgator, and its enforcing judge.[19]

This shows a formal pattern that, I argue, will always be present, although any given thinker will be more or less aware of this fact. This pattern is the relationship between the source or origin of human nature, human nature, the good, and the law. Here there is reference to God, although we need to define this term for the Stoics, and God has given a universal law that applies to all humans and leads to the good life. Cicero represents many others in that he wants to directly approach questions about the good life and the law, but he assumes a great deal about human nature and God. These terms are philosophically ambiguous and create serious disagreements in legal and ethical matters. If these earlier steps are incorrect, that will infect the conclusions drawn about human nature, the good, and the law. It is my assertion that one positive contribution Postmodernity makes is the attempt to expose some of these assumptions, although I also argue that it does not go far enough in doing so.

Cicero represents the Epicureans as saying "Now since the highest or greatest or ultimate good – what the Greeks call the *telos* – is that which is a means to no other end, but rather is itself the end of all things, then it must be admitted that the highest good is to live pleasantly."[20] Cicero attributes this to a kind of empiricism and has his Stoic character present arguments about the limits of the senses and that pleasure is not what makes life enjoyable.[21]

By way of contrast to the Epicureans, the character Cato says that "the final aim, then, is to live consistently and harmoniously with nature. This being so, all who are wise necessarily live happy, perfect and blessed lives, with no impediment or obstacle, lacking nothing. The controlling idea behind not only the philosophical system I am discussing but our lives and destinies too is the belief that what is moral is the only good."[22] So again, happiness is the goal, and it is only the moral life that achieves lasting happiness. Pleasures come and go, and a person who seeks pleasures is subject to the changes of fortune. But the Stoics believed they could insure themselves against such threats by reducing their desires and behaving morally in any situation, thus guaranteeing they were not disappointed by unfulfilled desire.

19 Quoted in: Ibid., 157.
20 Cicero, *On Moral Ends*, 17.
21 Ibid., 39.
22 Ibid., 73.

In this context, virtue is understood as a kind of practical rationality. "The Stoics (following up indications in Plato) call virtue the skill or expertise of living; it is the disposition to make the right practical decisions, so that the virtuous person acts well in the way the expert produces good results."[23] Cicero himself indicated the circularity of this definition through one of his characters in *On Moral Ends*:

> You show, at least to your own satisfaction, that what is moral is the only good. You then claim, however, that there are starting-points laid before us which are adapted and suited to our nature, and that it is in selecting from among these that virtue may arise. It was wrong of you to have located virtue in an act of selection, since it means that the ultimate good will itself be in pursuit of some further thing.[24]

If virtue, or morality, is excellence in practical rationality, then it is really a means to the good, not the good. This is indeed how Socrates defined it. So here is the second kind of pattern that we can find in studying these ethical debates from antiquity. This pattern is a false dichotomy between virtue and happiness without reference to what is actually an end in itself. So, we will often find either virtue or happiness (duty or pleasure) emphasized by a given school of thought, and contended with by another school that emphasizes the other. It is seen here, and it is seen more than 2,000 years later in Alasdair MacIntyre's *Whose Justice Which Rationality*. It is my goal with respect to this pattern to continually bring our attention back to the good as an end in itself, and remind us that virtue is a means to this goal, and happiness is an effect of attaining this goal, but neither is the goal nor can the good be reduced to either.

We can also see here the division between practical and theoretical rationality. In Socrates, these were united in the simple affirmation that no one can do evil knowingly; knowing what is good is necessary and sufficient to do what is good. However, as a larger and larger wedge is driven between these, theoretical reason takes on a more otherworldly or ascetic and withdrawn countenance, whereas practical rationality seems more applicable to the problems of this life. Furthermore, the subjects of theoretical reason are considered obscure and difficult, whereas practical rationality can be mastered more readily. Book IV of *On Moral Ends* begins with the characters discussing how obscure and difficult it is to understand the metaphysical foundations of the Stoic worldview, and agreeing that this difficulty is

23 Julia Annas (ed.) in Cicero, *On Moral Ends*, xix.
24 Ibid., 105.

part of the nature of the topic and not a result of affectation.[25] This division continues into the present time, and I believe reuniting reason is part of the solution for understanding law and the good.

Returning to Cato, we can see the relationship between human nature and the good when he extends his explanation in saying, "What remains is that the supreme good is to live applying one's knowledge of the natural order, selecting what accords with nature, and rejecting what is contrary. This is what it is to live consistently and harmoniously with nature."[26] For us, this is another example of the pattern mentioned earlier. The question is: What is nature? The Stoics believed in the eternal recurrence of all things. Nothing transcended the cosmos; this is all that exists. Thus, any references to God must not be understood in a theistic sense. Whatever else God is for the Stoics, God is not the creator (*ex nihilo*), but is immanent to the creation.

By way of contrast, the Epicureans were atomists who believed that only material objects exist. Plato was a dualist and affirmed the reality of both the material and spiritual world, giving emphasis to the spiritual world where the greatest good can be achieved in direct perception of the forms. Aristotle was also a dualist, although he differed from Plato in his understanding of spirit and instead seems to have thought of matter and spirit in terms of potentiality and actuality. Nevertheless, he too thought of the highest good, as represented in Book 10 of the *Nicomachean Ethics*, as a direct contemplation of God, who is in eternal contemplation of himself.

> It is worth noting that this second assumption tacitly rules out theories which aspire to unworldly ends that transcend human nature, such as Plato's idea that virtue is "becoming like God" and Aristotle's position in the work that we read as book 10 of the Nicomachean Ethics, that our final end is to contemplate abstract truths. In the period we are concerned with, such theories were not part of the mainstream discussion of ethics.[27]

For all of the emphasis by Socrates on the examined life, critical analysis of these metaphysical assumptions seemed to play little role in the academy. Plato and Aristotle were understood to have a disagreement about whether virtue was sufficient for the happy life.[28] Aristotle thought that examples such as king Priam of Troy who was virtuous but given a terrible

25 Ibid., 90.
26 Ibid., 75.
27 Ibid., xxv.
28 Ibid., xx.

fate were sufficient to show that virtue plus the common goods of life were needed for happiness. Cicero presented arguments for this position, against Stoicism, but his goals seems to be consistent with Academic Skepticism in presenting all views and allowing his readers to decide which seems most plausible.

In *On Moral Duties*, Cicero does begin to give an account of the natural law, and he grounds this in the idea of justice. Justice requires that we harm no other unless provoked by injury, and that we treat common things as common and private things as belonging to the one who owns them. Furthermore, the basis of justice is in keeping faith, or following through on promises and agreements. This beginning point will be attractive to thinkers in Modernity because it seems to provide a natural law that does not start with metaphysical speculation. Whatever our religious or philosophical background, we can all agree about justice. The problem arises for both Cicero and Modernity in answering the question from the individual "Why should I care about any of this?" in a way that does not get into metaphysical discussion.

Cicero's response is to assert that we should care because this is what is in accordance with nature. Indeed, individual pursuit of wisdom and knowledge should be put in second place to the pursuit of the common good and the duties of social justice. However, to the individual asking the question this will be mere dogmatic assertion. Indeed, the individual can find real problems in the Stoic view of nature. For instance, the eternal recurrence asserts that all things have existed from eternity and go through exact cycles of repetition. Yet, if all things tend toward sameness unless acted on by an outside source, and nothing is transcendent (no outside sources), then if the cosmos had existed from eternity, it should already have ended in sameness (e.g., hot and cold becoming warm). Furthermore, if it is true that everything I do has already been done and will be done again without deviation, then no choice I make has any meaning. These logical and existential problems are enough to raise concerns about Cicero's view of nature and all the implications for virtue and the good life. Perhaps other philosophies that also believe in eternal cycles, such as Hinduism, have more consistently worked out this existential problem and at least see the need to escape the cycle of death and rebirth in order to achieve the highest good. But if nothing is transcendent, and there is only this cycle, then escape is impossible.

Plutarch gives an account of the death of Cicero. He fled the forces of Marc Antony but was eventually caught. As the soldiers approached the litter in which he sat, a tired and weary-looking Cicero leaned his head out and bent his neck for execution. He was found because he had been betrayed by a servant. His head and hands were cut off and displayed as a warning to others. Had Marc Antony been defeated sooner, Octavius would most likely have allowed Cicero to live. But this was the twist and turn of fate. Plutarch compares the deaths of Cicero and Demosthenes and concludes that the death of Cicero evokes our pity, whereas in Demosthenes we find something admirable.

EARLY MEDIEVAL ATTITUDES

As noted earlier, Cicero has been influential down through the centuries. I want to give a brief look at his influence on Augustine, and Augustine's influence on the Early Middle Ages. Augustine particularly mentions this influence in *The Confessions*, Book 3.[29] Here he recounts his days as a student, and having read Cicero's *Hortensius* (now lost), which kindled his love for philosophy. He recounts that "it was this book which quite definitely changed my whole attitude and turned my prayers toward thee, O Lord, and gave me a new hope and new desires. Suddenly every vain hope became worthless to me, and with an incredible warmth of heart I yearned for an immortality of wisdom and began now to arise that I might return to thee." Among other things, he was attracted to Cicero's method of academic skepticism in that the many schools of philosophy were put forth and their problems displayed.

However, in this same Book 3, Augustine also gives us a good look at the path of his intellectual growth. He became disturbed by problems raised by the Manichaeans about the nature of God, and the reality of evil:

> In my ignorance I was much disturbed over these things and, though I was retreating from the truth, I appeared to myself to be going toward it, because I did not yet know that evil was nothing but a privation of good (that, indeed, it has no being); and how should I have seen this when the sight of my eyes went no further than physical objects, and the sight of my mind reached no farther than to fantasms? And I did not know that God is a spirit who has no parts extended in length and breadth, who being has no mass – for every mass is less in part than in the whole – and if it be an infinite mass it must be less in such parts as are limited by a certain space than it is infinity. It cannot therefore be wholly everywhere as Spirit is, as

29 Saint Augustine of Hippo (354–430), last of the early Church fathers. His conversion, engagement with church struggles such as the conflict with Donatism, and his analysis of the fall of Rome and contrast with the City of God have all greatly impacted later ages.

> God is. And I was entirely ignorant as to what is that principle within us by which we are like God, and which is said in Scripture to be made "after God's image."[30]

In this passage we see once again the pattern of how epistemology informs metaphysics, and how together these give rise to beliefs about human nature and the good. We find Augustine affirming theism over Greek dualism. God is the creator of the material world and of the human spirit. Nevertheless, we also find a kind of otherworldliness that had, and still has, substantial impact.

To illustrate how metaphysics forms and limits beliefs about the good, and to give an example of the characteristic patterns of an age, I will begin with the Platonic influence on Augustine. "Augustine shares with the ancient philosopher the conception of ethics as an inquiry into the supreme good: that which we seek for its own sake never for the sake of some further end, and which makes us happy."[31] Given that all persons want to be happy – which is an objective state, not merely the temporary satisfaction of whatever desires one has at the moment – all persons want the good. According to Augustine, this is only possible in the afterlife with God. The best we can have in this life is the promise of the good in the next life. Augustine believed that the good is a direct apprehension of God after death. This illustrates a pattern between what is lasting and ultimate and the good. Platonic dualism asserts that the material world is an impermanent shadow in relationship to the unchanging ideal realm. Augustine attempted to fit Christianity into this framework, and so the good is equated with perceiving God in the next life, whereas this world is one of preparation, but ultimately transient.

Thus we can see that Augustine responded to the challenge of the changes in the world of his day by looking to the good in the next life. Augustine says, "As for this mortal life, which ends after a few days' course, what does it matter under whose rule a man lives, being so soon to die, provided that the rulers do not force him to impious and wicked acts."[32] The civil government is necessary to restrain wickedness and injustice; it is necessary because of the Fall. It is not necessary, however, to attain the good that is finally realized only in the next life.

30 Augustine, "Confessions," in *Augustine*, trans. Edward Bouverie Pusey, ed. Mortimer Adler. Vol. 18 (Chicago: Encyclopedia Britannica, 1952), 3.12.

31 Bonnie Kent, "The Moral Life," ed. A. S. McGrade (Cambridge: Cambridge University Press, 2003), 232.

32 St. Augustine, *City of God*, trans. Henry Bettenson (London: Penguin Books, 2003), v.17.

Consider Augustine's conversion in the garden and the passage that he read from Romans 13:13–14. Although in some sense his intellectual conversion preceded this point, he had continued to struggle with immorality that grieved his conscience. It is at this point that he decided to act on the Romans passage and make a life change. Struggle with immorality and the grief of conscious that accompanies this are not unique to Augustine. His solution, however, is an illustration of his Platonism and belief about the good. Rather than marrying the woman he had been with for years, he sent her away and after some struggles remained celibate for the remainder of his life. This withdrawal from married life is indicative of the belief that celibacy is a higher spiritual state because it avoids the physical desires that are hindrances to the higher spiritual goals. The idea that he had an intellectual conversion and only later a moral conversion is a Platonic interpretation of what was going on; immorality is a result of the corrupting influence of the body, but the mind knows what is good and strives to be freed from the bodily influence.

This view dominated the early medieval period, sometimes known as the Dark Ages. It can be seen in a de-emphasis on this world and a preoccupation with the next life, in intellectual life being carried out in the seclusion of monasteries, of the use of force to compel others to enter the church, and the increasing power of the papacy as the holder of the keys to what is of highest value: the beatific vision.

HIGH MIDDLE AGES

The shift to the High Middle Ages can be illustrated in Aristotle's influence on Aquinas who is considered the great systematizer of medieval thought. Aristotle sought to remedy problems in Plato by emphasizing knowledge of the world through the senses. Aquinas accepted that all knowledge is from sense experience, and so speaks of the highest good as a kind of apprehension of God in the next life: the beatific vision. There is not a particularly strong division between this life and the next life, and indeed Aquinas spends time talking about how God is experienced out of the body, because all knowledge is from experience. This life involves a preparation for that experience, with grace being issued in the form of the seven sacraments. There is a particular theme worth considering here. This theme is the skepticism about the power of the intellect to know God and an emphasis instead on direct apprehension.

This attempt to fuse a religious tradition with Aristotle is not new. Indeed, the Christians were the last of the three theistic traditions to attempt it. It is worth comparing Al-Ghazali and Aquinas.[33] Both initially tried to fuse their religion with Aristotle. Both believed that Aristotle represented the best and highest use of the human mind to know. And yet both ended up abandoning this pursuit for mysticism. Aristotle's empiricism provides a kind of negative theology, not the kind of knowledge of God needed for a full love of God. If Aristotle is the best and therefore only option with respect to the intellect, then access to God must be achieved in some other way, namely through mystical awareness.

For Islam, Al-Ghazali's work brought about the end of philosophy. However, Aquinas did not write anything after his change to mysticism. This influence is felt indirectly in that Aquinas is held up by many as the best and highest expression of theology. If this is the farthest we can go, but much more is needed, then the implication is that we must turn away from the intellect. Those in the West who reject Christianity will use this to argue that the human mind cannot know such things, and therefore they are not relevant for public life.

So while the High Middle Ages were a rebirth, a renaissance, they also carried a seed that would bear the fruit of the Inquisition and the Wars of Religion. The argument about when to date the origins of Modernity can be nuanced by noting that Modernity is responding to insufficiencies in the medieval world, but also relying on some tools it had been given by that time period. Examples of these are the attempts to canonize law and to reform Church government.

GRATIAN AND CANONIZATION

Some scholars argue that the beginnings of Modernity can be found in the work of Gratian and his *Decretum Gratiani*, which became the first part of a larger set of six books called the *Corpus Juris Canonici*.[34] Gratian

33 Al-Ghazali (1058–1111) was a Muslim theologian and mystic. His book, *The Incoherence of the Philosophers*, showed how philosophers (such as Averroës) who had embraced Aristotle had consequently rejected belief in God in favor of belief in the eternality of the world. Because Aristotle was equated with reason, Al-Ghazali argued in favor of mysticism.

34 Gratian (b. eleventh century, d. 1159) was an Italian Benedictine monk whose *Concordia Discordantium Canonum* (generally known as the *Decretum Gratiani*) collected almost 4,000 texts and sought to harmonize contradictions in these. This became a standard book for teaching law.

produced this work in the twelfth century, and together these legal texts were authoritative in the Roman Catholic Church until 1918. I believe we can find here work that continued into Modernity, albeit with a distinctively medieval stamp. Specifically, the legal profession was an important part of the development of the European university system beginning at Bologna and continuing at Paris, Oxford, and elsewhere. Nevertheless, studies retained the medieval bifurcation of the world into this one and the next one, and those who wanted to study one went into theology, whereas those with a concern for this world studied law. Law was given a subordinate place to theology – a trend completely reversed in Modernity.

The idea behind Gratian's work was to offer a systematized and coherent account of law that took under consideration divergent but influential traditions. He worked to make a coherent picture of Roman law, the Bible, and Church Fathers. By placing apparently competing texts next to each other, Gratian could then offer his own interpretation of how to find unity in the legal theories. This same dialectic method was used by others in theology, such as in Peter Lombard's *Sentences*, but also to show that there was not agreement in tradition, such as Abelard's *Sic et Non*. Martin Luther later referenced the contradictions in Church Fathers, councils, and papal decrees to make the point that they cannot be our highest authority.

Brian Tierney notes that the medieval canonists did generally argue that the church was superior to the kings,[35] but he also notes that Gratian and others articulated offenses for which the pope could be removed. In an important sense, this gave law a high authority, which is consistent with the Counciliarist movement that began during the Great Schism of the fourteenth century. Nevertheless, Tierney says:

> [T]he growth of the Corpus Iuris Canonici from the appearance of Gratian's Decretum to the outbreak of the Great Schism is, in effect, to record the process by which the Church became a body politic, subject to one head and manifesting an external unity of organization. If the ancient doctrine of papal primacy was the corner-stone of ecclesiastical unity in the Middle Ages, the canon law was the cement, which, it was hoped, would bind together the whole vast fabric of prelates and peoples and princes.[36]

35 Brian Tierney, *Foundations of the Conciliar Theory: The Contributions of the Medieval Canonists from Gratian to the Great Schism* (Oxford: Oxford University Press, 2008), 12.

36 Ibid., 14.

This role of canon law is precisely why I see its influence as part of the Medieval Age. Its use was to affirm the outward organization of the Roman Catholic Church and to bind together the diverse peoples and nations of Europe in which that church had influence. Even if it in some ways prefigures the doctrine of *lex rex*, it was, more essentially, part of the medieval framework that gave rise to the Wars of Religion.

The concern for external and organizational unity trumped questions of doctrine in the premodern world. Beside specific heresies, which were treated with violence and compulsion, humanists and reformers were expected to work within the confines of this organization. Erasmus encouraged this attitude in contrast to Luther. Politically, Charles V argued for unity as the only solution against the "Turkish threat," and argued that questions of doctrine should be put aside.

The Reformation called into question this organizational unity and its authority, including the cement of canon law. Canon law lost its adhesive value when questions were raised about what exactly the doctrines are that make up the building needing cement. Once canon law was called into question, at least by implication, it opened up new ways of thinking about legal theories. Hobbes, Grotius, and others sought to fill this lacuna.

The wars that erupted throughout Europe were about competing conceptions of the good life and therefore competing conceptions of law and its origin. Appeals to tradition, Greek, Roman, or Christian, were insufficient to settle these differences. Although sharing a broadly Christian framework and the specific concern about soteriology, important differences about what this meant led to divisions. What began as division matured into the wars that brought about the violent end of the medieval world. It is true that law works as a kind of cement, and this decay required a new law, the one that set aside theological divisions because no solutions to them had been found.

THE COUNCILIARIST MOVEMENT: AFTER MUCH DISCUSSION

Francis Oakley notes three intense challenges that arose during the thirteenth and fourteenth centuries and called into question authority structures at the foundation of that time period.[37] These were challenges about the relationship between temporal and spiritual authorities, the dispute over the Franciscan doctrine of apostolic poverty, and the papal schism

[37] Ibid., 63.

beginning in 1378. Oakley studies the Counciliarist Movement as the form of church government affirmed by the Council of Constance (1414–1418) and not changed until the First Vatican Council. In it he sees the mixed form of government proposed by Aristotle and relied on by modern constitutionalism.

I consider this from a different perspective. The role of church councils reaches back to the beginnings of Christian history, indeed into Acts 15 and the Council of Jerusalem. Following that model, the councils form to address a challenge through the process of much discussion (Acts 15:7). In Jerusalem, the discussion was about the relationship between circumcision and being a Christian: Must one be circumcised to be saved, or are sacraments such as circumcision necessary for salvation? Succeeding counsels considered challenges of their day. Notably, Nicea considered the question of the Trinity. Oakley notes the four marks of the church designated in the Nicean Creed:[38] one, holy, Catholic, apostolic. Given their cumulative nature and their reference back to the apostolic council, successive councils cannot contradict earlier councils; the church is one.

Now, consider the Council of Constance. Oakley is correct about one of its goals: ending the Papal Schism. However, another important goal was to denounce the work of John Hus and John Wycliffe. These reformers are denounced for, among other things, teaching that salvation does not come through the sacraments. Notice that in this teaching they are not introducing a new doctrine but referring back to the decision of the first church council at Jerusalem recorded in Acts 15. Salvation does not come through the sacraments, circumcision, or baptism. They were a precursor, a "morning star," to the Reformation teaching that justification is through Christ alone, and sacraments are a sign not the reality..

The importance of church councils is therefore not in the division of powers (a teaching found in Aristotle and thus not modern or medieval); rather, it is a reflection of how challenges are addressed. They are answered not by a lone and purportedly brilliant scholar, not by a person at the head of an institution, but rather represent the outcome of the congregation of elders going through a process of much discussion in pursuit of consistency with earlier conclusions applied to new challenges in relation to the scriptures. Oakley is correct to affirm the councils as an important part of historic Christianity. Indeed, the model of this first council in Jerusalem, adopted by the Presbyterians in their ecclesiology, arguably has been the basis for the American representative government (consider the number

[38] Ibid., 65.

of Presbyterian signatories, and the English calling the Revolution the Presbyterian Revolt). So obviously the question will be to what extent the councils to which Oakley refers were consistent with previous councils (such as the decision as Jerusalem) as opposed to alternative councils/confessions like the Westminster Confession, which summarized the Reformation position against sacramentalism and Roman Catholic soteriology.

THE REFORMATION

I am including the Reformation as part of the medieval world because it shares more with that view of authority and social structure than it does with Modernity. Although the Reformation challenge to the Roman Catholic Church focused on soteriology, it was most basically an epistemological challenge. Consider Martin Luther's famous assertion at the Diet of Worms:

> Unless I am convinced by the testimony of the Scriptures or by clear reason (for I do not trust either in the pope or in councils alone, since it is well known that they have often erred and contradicted themselves), I am bound by the Scriptures I have quoted and my conscience is captive to the Word of God. I cannot and will not recant anything, since it is neither safe nor right to go against conscience. May God help me. Amen

Appealing to Papal decrees that justify the sale of indulgences, or councils that support this doctrine, would not be sufficient to answer the challenge because the challenge is about how these persons know in the first place. Furthermore, force or coercion cannot change Luther's beliefs; rather, he required an argument with reference to a legitimate authority. To say that the Holy Spirit guides the popes or councils is to say that the Holy Spirit has contradicted Himself, or to beg the question of which belief is guided by the Holy Spirit. Luther therefore provided the example of Scripture and reason (non-contradiction) as such an authority that can be applied to popes and councils.

The Reformation quickly divided into factions about soteriology and the nature of God, which had an enormous effect on law and political theory. These can be broadly construed as the Lutheran, Reformed (Calvnist), and Anabaptist branches. The Lutherans were influenced by nominalism and so tended toward divine command theory and a rejection of natural law.[39] This also supported the Lutheran view of law and grace, where law

39 Philip Melanchthon is an exception worth studying. Consider his *Orations on Philosophy and Education*.

only leads to death (as opposed to being the description of how to achieve the good), and grace is needed to rescue us from the consequences of law. This also resulted in a "Two Kingdoms" theory of church and state relations where these are two incommensurable areas of life, and while the Christian can be a good citizen, the Church should not impose morality on law. This is also an amillennail view of history where the Church and the world continue side by side until the end of history, and the Church is not triumphant in discipling the nations.

The Augsburg Confession, written to explain the Lutheran position to Charles V, emphasizes a very simple view of church unity based on the teaching of the Gospel and administration of the sacraments. I believe this is influential on the rest of Modernity in that religion is preferably very simple, and great latitude is given to whatever people might disagree about. Simple and universally knowable are confused in this view. Unity and maturity in belief are opposed in this view. It can be true that a Christian is one who accepts the Gospel, but not true that staying at such a level of immaturity in belief is the goal of the Christian church. This view of the unity of the Church is consistent with the Lutheran view of amillennialism and the Two Kingdom theory. It is also very important to thinking about the role of religion in the modern world.

The Reformed Churches were generally more ready to accept natural-law thinking.[40] Theologians like Calvin and Turrentin made reference to the natural law. Indeed, Calvin began his exposition of the Moral Law with the affirmation that the *Decalogue* is this law, committed to writing in order to better teach humans the knowledge of God and of themselves.[41] However, he also stated that this law is only "meagerly and obscurely" given in the natural law. This is a pattern in some Reformed thinking, to say that the natural world gives a bare and minimal revelation of God and the good, and special revelation is needed to more fully explain these. Furthermore, after the Fall, even this bare knowledge has been effaced.

I said this is what some Reformed thinkers taught because it is not how this tradition is best exemplified in the Westminster Confession of Faith. This Confession begins by affirming that the goodness, wisdom, and power of God are clearly known from the works of creation and providence so that ignorance of these is inexcusable. It also maintains in chapter 19 *Of*

[40] For a helpful work on this, see Stephen Grabil's *Rediscovering the Natural Law in Reformed Theological Ethics*.

[41] John Calvin, *The Institutes of Christian Religion*, abridged ed. (Grand Rapids: Baker Academic, 1987), 272.

the Law of God that God gave to man a moral law, summarized in the *Decalogue*, and which is the means to knowing the will of God. In contrast to the Lutheran division of law and grace, the Confession affirms that these uses of the law "sweetly comply" with the Gospel. The goal of the law, indeed the chief end of man, is to glorify God in all that by which he makes himself known, in all His works of creation and providence (Shorter Catechism Questions 1, 46, and 101).

Reformed soteriology affirmed that all humans are in total depravity, meaning that they are not able to do their duty before God. For some, this has been taken to mean that while the law requires humans to know God, after the Fall, humans are not able to know God. I do not believe this entails a rejection of the "ought/can" principle. Even in the post-lapsarian condition, humans are the kinds of beings that can know God (as opposed to minerals, vegetables, and animals). Their inability stems from their not seeking God, although if they did seek, they would know God and in this sense they can know God. Their post-lapsarian condition is defined by this culpable ignorance, not contrary to it.

Even so, in some Reformed thinkers we see a move to anti-intellectualism stemming from piously affirming the need for special revelation and grace. One example is Pierre Bayle, whose attacks on reason were intended to show the folly of the human mind and the need for God's grace, but were taken by "free thinkers" in the generations after him to argue the general folly of religious belief. An example of how he used apparent contradictions to undermine ethical thinking is that while we are commanded to prevent evil, God could easily prevent evil in the world and does not.[42] Bayle did not believe that evil disproves God's existence, so he was making the case that these are simply contradictory and we cannot know. This "problem of evil" remains unsolved at the heart of Modernity, and is responsible for the turn toward Postmodernity, so we should not conclude our study without having addressed it.

Whereas Lutheranism was amillennial, Reformed thinkers tended to be postmillennial, affirming that the glory of God fills the earth and that through the work of the Church the knowledge of the glory of God will fill the earth. By way of contrast, the Augsburg Confession rejected this as "certain Jewish opinions, that before the resurrection of the dead the godly shall take possession of the kingdom of the world, the ungodly being everywhere suppressed." This demonstrates the continued division within

[42] Richard H. Popkin, *The History of Scepticism: From Savonarola to Bayle*, rev. ed. (Oxford; New York: Oxford University Press, 2003), 415.

Christianity about the goal of the Church in relation to the unbelieving world.

The third branch of the Reformation – the Anabaptists – is generally understood to be antinomian and anti-state. This is not merely a result of their having been persecuted. Rather, the Anabaptists believed that the New Testament is the only relevant special revelation for Christians and gave it a literal reading that did not permit drawing inferences such as "households were baptized, households include infants, therefore early Christians baptized infants." This literal reading was applied to law and grace, and flesh and spirit, in a way that promoted individual piety and otherworldliness. Those within this tradition also tend to understand "sola scriptura" to mean "*solo* scriptura" and are therefore against creeds and confessions. All of this has been very impactful on Modernity: a strong separation of church and state; assigning religion the role of individual piety but no corporate function; religion is about how to be pious to get to heaven.

The Reformation set the stage for the beginning of Modernity because it called into question the authority structures on which knowledge claims rested. The divisions it created did not acknowledge a shared authority and therefore quickly became violent. These Wars of Religion caused terrible destruction. The fear of their return forced modern thinkers to find a common source of authority to which all persons could appeal. Physical survival in the natural world presented itself as a solution.

MODERNITY: THE TRIUMPH OF NOMINALISM AND IMPLICATIONS FOR NATURAL LAW AND THE GOOD

I am beginning my study of the Modern age at the end of the Wars of Religion (1648). This also corresponds with the high point of the English Reformation (the Westminster Confession of Faith) and roughly with the work of Hobbes and Descartes. We are especially interested in Hobbes because of his influence on political and legal thought.

In general, I am making the case that historical ages end with wars that exhaust and decimate. These wars make prominent that the given peoples do not have the means to solve problems and settle disputes. In this case, the disputes were "religious." They were particularly focused on soteriology, and behind that they were about epistemology (what authority can we appeal to in order to say we know).

The Modern age was shaped by a repulsion at the waste of these wars. This extended into the subject of debate: soteriology. The focus on what must be done to secure a blessed afterlife took attention away from this world. And so Modernity can be said to be a turn away from otherworldliness to increasing this-worldliness; its this-worldliness is noted in its emphasis on observation of how this world works through experience and repeated testing; an emphasis on the common goods of this life by which is meant those things necessary for survival and enjoyment; an increased distancing of religion and the state; an increased distancing of religion and whatever is public; and the search for naturalistic explanations in all areas of life, including law.

Modern thinkers blamed the Wars of Religion on insoluble disputes concerning the next life, complex interpretive difficulties connected to ancient texts, and personal opinion camouflaged as special insight about the will of God. In the place of these, modern thinkers viewed themselves as setting aside the passions, the superstitious, the personal and biased, in favor of cool and calculating rationality that sought for conclusions unmoved by personal considerations or feelings.

For the purposes of this study, we can isolate the focus of the Modern age as a turn away from law rooted in religious justifications and a search for a natural explanation that could respond to the skeptic. Descartes is acknowledged as the example of this for epistemology. Rather than appealing to Aristotle, who in turn relied on common sense and empiricism and accepted uncritically beliefs like the eternality of the world, Descartes sought for what can be known with certainty. In a similar way, early modern legal theorists sought to find a basis for law that could resist skeptical attacks by beginning with what was considered to be self-evident or indubitable. Whether or not they succeeded, this method is a mark of the modern approach to knowledge in all areas. It is the attempt to know from general revelation what is certain and so cannot be doubted without abandoning rationality.

Thomas Hobbes is a good representative of this kind of work. I consider him in more detail later. Here it is helpful to note that he began his considerations of the law of nature with the fear of death and desire to survive. He illustrates the shift in Modernity from calling the good the desirable, and instead defining the good as the fulfillment of individual desire. Following from this, but also related to the change in metaphysics from Aristotle, Hobbes rejected the idea of teleology and final causes. This is true about his materialism, which only recognizes efficient causation, and it is true for his psychology, which understands humans to be moved by desire but not guided to some final end. Indeed, he explicitly claims that there is no *summum bonum*. His understanding of the *summum bonum* is somewhat stilted, however, in that he rejects it on the grounds that once attained, there is no future good. Hobbes is correct that whatever is the highest good must be something that can be both attained in the present and grown further into the future.

CONCLUSION

Although Modernity borrowed ideas from previous ages, going all the way back to the Greeks as well as the Scriptures, a change occurred after the Wars of Religion that I identify as mainly epistemological and secondarily metaphysical and legal. Authority structures that medieval thinkers could appeal to in order to justify knowledge claims were no longer accepted as authoritative by all Europeans. A shift occurred in the search for authority to the individual's senses and desires. This had profound impact on legal thinking as well as beliefs about the good. Examples of this impact will be seen in the next chapter as we study notable contributors to modern legal theory.

4

The Challenge of Modernity

Religious Wars and the Need for Universal Law

Glou. But I, that am not shaped for sportive tricks,
Nor made to court an amorous looking-glass;
I, that am rudely stamp'd, and want love's majesty
To strut before a wanton ambling nymph;
I, that am curtail'd of this fair proportion,
Cheated of feature by dissembling nature,
Deform'd, unfinish'd, sent before my time
Into this breathing world, scarce half made up,
And that so lamely and unfashionable
That dogs bark at me as I halt by them;
Why, I, in this weak piping time of peace,
Have no delight to pass away the time,
Unless to spy my shadow in the sun
And descant on mine own deformity:
And therefore, since I cannot prove a lover,
To entertain these fair well-spoken days,
I am determined to prove a villain
And hate the idle pleasures of these days.
Plots have I laid, inductions dangerous
By drunken prophecies, libels, and dreams,
To set my brother Clarence and the King
In deadly hate the one against the other.[1]

In this passage, Shakespeare portrays Richard, Duke of Gloucester and future Richard III, as an example of a shift from medieval to modern thinking. The deformed, "unfinished" Richard would have been understood to be out of the natural order by the medieval world. However, his cunning and Machiavellian attitude makes him a quintessential modern politician.

1 William Shakespeare, *Richard III*, Act I Scene I.

His deformities do nothing to hinder his ability to lay traps and conspire his way to the throne.

MODERNITY AND SKEPTICISM

To understand natural law after Modernity, I take some time to discuss the development of Modernity out of the Religious Wars in Europe and the impact these had on religious law. The Modern age emerged from the Wars of Religion, which ended in 1648 with the Peace of Westphalia. This had an important impact on legal theory, because the Canon Law of the Roman Catholic Church could no longer be applied to all regions, as some were ruled by Protestant leaders. This would especially become a problem for international law where a legal code was needed that could be applied between countries with contrary religious laws. Thus, the idea of a natural law had important implication on international legal theory.

In the place of specific religious traditions, philosophers and legal theorists sought what could be universally agreed on. Ultimately this was reduced to the secular realm (because beliefs about the supernatural are not universal), where the idea was that laws should govern "goods" rather than direct one to "the good." There is a noticeable shift to discussion about private property and the rights of a human with regard to property. However, this does not disprove the formula I suggested in the previous chapter (beliefs about the metaphysical absolute determine beliefs about human nature and the good), but rather adds an important dimension: the role of epistemology.

Although Modernity is typically characterized as beginning with the Enlightenment, or before that with the Renaissance and its high view of human reason, I argue that a kind of skepticism about what is not observable became the norm. This view says that laws can only be made about what is knowable, and what is knowable is the material world (as opposed to the supernatural). The problem of Modernity is, therefore, a positing of the reality of the material world over other worldviews, and this will be criticized in Postmodernity as a construct used to legitimate certain power centers.

The Wars of Religion were the final challenge that ended more than a century of struggle about how to understand human life and the good. Aquinas articulated the view of the good held more or less consciously by persons in the medieval world. The good life involved direct apprehension of God in the next life. The authority of the church was called on to justify the belief in sacramentalism. The value of this life relates to the beatific vision in the next life. Debates about land ownership and property between monastic groups or between Franciscans and the Papacy assumed this background worldview. When this authority was called into question by the Reformation, knowledge claims were shown to be opinions and a new source of authority was sought.

As we have learned earlier, the shock of the Wars of Religion forced early modern thinkers to reconsider their assumptions about the world and the good. There was a refocusing on this life and skepticism about the next life and the exact means of attaining blessing there. This is a shift from the *summon bonum*, identified as the beatific vision, to the common goods of human life. This illustrates all of the patterns identified earlier. The institutions of Modernity are built to protect what is common to all from what is partisan. Those who persist in believing in heaven or the beatific vision can do so in private. A conception of general revelation has prevailed, which represents common ground (in contrast to special revelation) but which gives only a bare natural theology of a first cause and designer, and the world is given to humans for use and enjoyment.

Although there are important differences among the views of the thinkers I consider here, there are also important similarities that set the tone for Modernity's thinking about natural law. Without fail, each thinker begins with some notion of self-preservation in the sense of staying physically alive and improving the comfort of one's life. This is made into more than survival, and therefore a moral law, by blending it with some form of the golden rule or second greatest commandment. But again, this is restricted to consideration of this world and what is needed for physical life and comfort. Goods, or public goods, refer to items and objects that are desired for the improvement of one's physical condition. Law is restricted to rules that order society so that individuals can pursue such goods with minimal interference, and society can grow in these goods as a whole. It is easy to see how there is a temptation to reduce these laws to measurements of economics or pleasure, to consider them as entirely socially relative and positivistic, and to completely divorce them from morality that seems to be concerned with one's condition in the next life.

Modern legal theorists work to respond to the ethical egoist by explaining why these laws should be observed. This takes a limited number of forms based on the dichotomy between deontology and utilitarianism. Some respond by arguing that in human life, certain obligations arise and we must observe these, and where we do not, other humans are justified in various degrees and levels of coercion. Others respond by enticing the ethical egoist through the promise that this is indeed the path to greatest happiness.

Here I will study thinkers, from Hobbes to Kant, who set the boundaries for the Modern age and offered solutions to the problems that were being wrestled with. It will become evident that many contemporary attitudes and modes of thinking are still informed by, and limited by, these solutions. This includes a template for law that restricts it to the ordering of goods for this life and draws a distinct line between law and morality. This view of law is grounded on the restriction of reason, beginning after the Wars of Religion, which increasingly limited reason to practical calculations about the material world and was skeptical about the ability for reason to know anything else. Since laws can only be made about what can be known, this restriction on reason was also a restriction on law.

Rather than beginning with the Revolutionary era that overturned the old order, I begin with the end of the Wars of Religion and the solution found in the Peace of Westphalia. I am labeling this kind of peace "skepticism." Rather than beginning with an earlier point when reforms were sought or initial peace treaties given (Peace of Augsburg, 1555), I begin in 1648 because these earlier times still sought to have church influence as a source of knowledge. I do not begin with a time when theological solutions were still considered helpful. I begin with a time when there was a turn to general revelation. There is a turn to what all people can know from reason, and a turn to how people know and understand. There is a turn to explanations of the origin of knowledge and of society that are discoverable by reason (where reason is defined in a limited way, usually referring to naturalism or practical rationality).

I speak about skepticism as the denial that knowledge is possible. I distinguish knowledge from opinion where the latter is possibly in error. I distinguish both as beliefs from sensations, images, and intuitions, which are immediate and are not assertions. I distinguish knowledge that I am studying from knowledge by acquaintance, and from knowing how (to do something). So, I am studying how the modern world – and now the postmodern world – stands in relation to knowledge, how the modern world failed to provide for knowledge, and that the postmodern world is the outcome and end stage of that process. Skepticism includes direct and explicit rejections of knowledge, but it also includes the more common and subtle rejections of knowledge where true belief that is rationally justified is set aside as insufficient or unnecessary for knowledge. I distinguish rational justification and reason from appeals to personal experience, testimony, common sense, warrant, and tradition, which do not guarantee the truth of belief. I distinguish reason from attempts to grasp reality directly (immediately) through intuition, and from pragmatism that reduces truth to what works/satisfies. I distinguish less basic knowledge from knowledge that is about what is more basic and most basic. What is less basic assumes what is more basic, and the most basic is assumed by all else. In a most basic sense, reason is that by which we identify concepts, form beliefs, and grow in consistency.

In keeping this focus, I will be studying many different twists and turns given in attempting to avoid knowledge or justify not having it. The lack of knowledge and the justification for its absence will be the underlying theme studied in both Modernity (and, by implication, Premodernity) and Postmodernity. This study follows claims about knowledge, where what is most basic is not known, and how this becomes exposed in contrast to claims about what is known. I must confront claims that knowledge is best understood as external description, claims that imply knowledge is not possible from the first-person perspective. In many cases, such claims rely on Gettier-type examples that are purported to have shown conclusively why knowledge cannot be defined as "true, justified belief." An alternative is to take such examples as an opportunity to question our assumptions about strong and weak justification.[2] I argue strong justification avoids these problems.

Strong justification aims at establishing the certainty of a belief by showing that its opposite is impossible. Weak justification is more akin to the common sense of daily life. Much contemporary epistemology takes for granted that common sense is knowledge. However, philosophy has always asked for stronger justification to support ordinary, or commonsense, claims made about reality and the good. I distinguish knowing if a judgment is true from knowing what a judgment means. The critical use of reason is to test for meaning by applying the laws of thought; where these laws are violated, there is no meaning, and where there is meaning, these laws are being used. Most basically, skepticism rejects the laws of thought and rejects meaning, and for this reason skepticism is inexorably linked to nihilism.

Early modern thinkers began searching for "natural" laws in the common life of humans. Setting aside theological considerations based on special revelation, these laws were understood to govern the "natural" life

[2] Edmund Gettier's 1963 short article, "Is Justified True Belief Knowledge," caused a storm among epistemologists. In this article, Gettier gives examples where "justification" is equated to sense data, memory, and testimony of others, and sets up problems that show how these come short. This is a serious problem for those who equate knowledge with ordinary or commonsense belief, but not for traditional epistemology that distinguished knowledge from opinion owing to the former having certainty and ruling out all alternatives.

of humans in the sense of life in the world. This naturalism projected the current conditions of human life into the past to explain the origins of human society in a state of nature. To study these trends, I begin with Hugo Grotius, although we can note his reliance on earlier thinkers like Francisco Suarez. Grotius used the insight from Suarez that law is based on a God-given, and therefore "natural," propensity of humans toward society, which in turn produces customs and international law.

HUGO GROTIUS

Grotius is called the father of natural law, and this can be taken to mean the father of secular natural law.[3] His legal theory is secular in that it is anti-metaphysical and anti-essentialist. He sought common ground that could unite people and did so using universal precepts from which a law could be derived. To achieve this universality, he imagines back to a time of the state of nature (or projects such a state in the present using war as an example). This is supposedly a state in which religious divisions are not yet present and out of which humans form a society. The thinking is that by using this method we can isolate the universal and natural principles on which to base a universal legal and political theory. Although God is sometimes spoken of as the Creator, reference to God is minimal, and God plays a minimal role in human life (Creator, Designer, and perhaps future Judge). There is also a focus on this life, what all persons can share in common and agree on, and on the public goods of this life. Religion and the afterlife are left to the areas of personal conviction.

This approach does not require actually resolving religious disputes, but allows for them to continue and for wars to be governed by the natural law. Living during the Wars of Religion, Grotius demonstrated a concern for unity among Christians and saw this as achievable in the kind of universal law he articulated. This is in contrast to the use of force to compel others in religious matters, and also to believing that agreement can be reached in religious divisions after much discussion. The perhaps unintended consequence of his approach was to minimize religious divisions as unresolvable for the reason of being unknowable. That is, there must be a certain amount of latitude in what is acceptable to society in religious divisions, because we as humans cannot know which is actually correct.

3 Hugo Grotius (1583–1645) was a Dutch statesman and jurist, and is best known for his work on international law. His 1625 book, *On the Law of War and Peace*, is the basis for modern thinking about international law.

It has been pointed out by competent scholars that Grotius does not mark a sharp break from previous legal thinkers, and that he relies on concepts discussed by philosophers like William of Ockham. It would be impossible to find any thinker that is not influenced by those preceding, and so this is undoubtedly true. However, I am suggesting that he does mark a difference and that he can be put at the beginning of a new age called Modernity because of his epistemological approach. No longer can religious law based on metaphysical principles be relied on, the divisions between religions are too great. Canon law can serve only within the Roman Church. Earlier thinkers would not have taken this view. Like Descartes, Grotius sought to reject previous religious assumptions in the search for certainty on which to build a system. This is not merely the "two swords" approach, or the "two kingdoms" approach; this is a claim about knowledge. Humans can know, have certainty, about some matters in this life, but religious beliefs do not rise to this level. This bequeaths an important framework to Modernity.

To determine universal principles, Grotius abstracts "human nature" and comes up with two principles that he believes can serve as the basis for natural law. These principles are self-preservation and the need for society. This is the beginning of almost all modern thinking about natural law. Grotius seems to believe that the unifying element in human life can be found in physical needs. The natural concerns of human nature are shared across human civilizations and by religious sects that otherwise hate each other. This, by consequence, places a restriction on what humans can know and what can bring humans together. The universality of physical needs is taken as the appropriate starting point for a universal law. What is particular to various religious sects must be the result of uniqueness in their history and environment and cannot be resolved through the use of reason.

Grotius often wrote about reason in relation to the law. Natural law is based on right reason in conformity with these principles of self-preservation and the need for society. Although somewhat lengthy, the following selection helps illustrate his general approach and many of the points made about him thus far:

> But it must be owned that a Man grown up, being capable of acting in the same manner with respect to things that are alike, has, besides an exquisite desire of society, for the satisfaction of which he alone of all animals has received from nature a peculiar instrument, viz., the use of speech; I say, that he has, besides that, a faculty of knowing and acting, according to some general principles; so that what relates to this faculty is not common to all

> animals, but properly and peculiarly agrees to Mankind. VIII. This sociability, which we have now described in general, or this care of maintaining society in a manner conformable to the Light of human understanding, is the foundation of Right, properly so called; to which belongs the abstaining from that which is another's, the restitution of what we have of another's, or the profit we have made by it, the obligation of fulfilling promises, the reparation of a damage done through our own default, and the merit of punishment among men. IX. From this signification of Right arose another of larger extent. For by reason that man above all other creatures is endued not only with this social faculty of which we have spoken, but likewise with judgment to discern things, pleasant or hurtful, and those not only present but future, and such as may prove to be so in their consequences; it may therefore be agreeable to human nature, that according to the measure of our understanding we should in these things follow the dictates of a right and sound judgment, and not be corrupted either by fear or the allurements of present pleasure, nor carried away violently by blind passion. And whatsoever is contrary to such a judgment is likewise understood to be contrary to natural right, that is, the laws of our nature.[4]

His limitation of human needs to the physical also serves to limit the role and function of reason. This is really a description of practical rationality, as we will see in so many of the thinkers considered here.

The turn to physical goods in this life, and preserving society in conflict with other societies, is a turn away from religious disputes and promotes a kind of skepticism about the ability to find unity in religious matters. This did not make disagreement go away, and we can see how these religious beliefs continued to be important to people's lives in their search for meaning. Consider some of the notable disagreements that continue even in the present as political philosophers attempted to give a merely this-worldly explanation of political and legal origins.

THOMAS HOBBES

In *The Leviathan*, we can identify a formula that sets the pattern for Modernity's thinking in many areas.[5] Hobbes argues that knowledge is attained through the senses, that there is no natural knowledge of what

4 Hugo Grotius, *The Rights of War and Peace* (Ithaca: Cornell University Library, 2009), xvi.

5 Thomas Hobbes (1588–1679) was an English philosopher and tutor to young Charles II. His book *Leviathan* (1651) argued for a basis of law in the will of the king or ruling authority. He is considered a materialist, and gave arguments against the possibility of spirit.

occurs after death, nor is there anything that is not material, and that religion is the result of fideism responding to fear. Like Descartes, Hobbes sought to establish an alternative to the influence of Aristotle and Scholasticism. Unlike the rationalists, however, the empiricism that Hobbes embodies came to dominate the modern world. Even where modern thinkers wrestle with problems shared by the Medieval and the Ancient, they approach solutions differently.

It is said that Hobbes's life began with fear, his mother giving birth prematurely upon hearing about the approach of the Spanish Armada. Fear is what characterizes life in the state of nature, and it is this state into which England had deteriorated during the English Civil War. *The Leviathan* proposes a solution to this condition and a foundation for unity and peace; to do so, Hobbes must give us a theory of knowledge and an explanation of what is real. Hobbes is a materialist in the sense that he limits knowledge to the material world (we know through the use of our senses; ideas are memories of what has been sensed or imaginations where senses are combined in different ways; memories are just fading senses) and rejects as real anything that is not material. He affirmed that the individual is the unit of responsibility and all voluntary acts are aimed at what the individual believes to be good. Good and evil are the objects of the passions or desires, and by "reason" he means practical rationality for figuring out how to attain the object of desire.

Disunity and war are the natural state because in such a condition each individual strives to attain goals and recognizes no limitations; consequently, these goals are at odds, and conflict ensues. Given that the state of nature is a war of all against all, "in which case everyone is governed by his own reason, and there is nothing he can make use of that may not be a help unto him in preserving his life against his enemies, it follows that in such a condition every man has a right to everything."[6] However, humans can call on practical rationality to see that in a condition of peace they are more likely to satisfy a greater number of their passions then in a state of war. Therefore, the "natural laws" that Hobbes described are those rules for living that will best ensure peace for attainment of desire: "A 'law of Nature,' lex naturalis, is a precept or general rule found out by reason by which a man is forbidden to do that which is destructive of his life or takes away the means of preserving the same, and to omit that by which he thinks it may be best preserved."[7]

6 Thomas Hobbes, *Leviathan* (Upper Saddle River: Prentice Hall, 2000), 82.
7 Ibid., 82.

Humans leave this state of nature by agreeing to suspend some of their rights, which in nature are universal and unlimited. Hobbes noted the distinction between a natural law, which he calls an obligation, and a natural right, which he calls a liberty. By suspending some liberties and living according to the obligations of this natural law, humans are better able to attain their final goal which is self preservation: "A 'commonwealth' is said to be 'instituted,' when a 'multitude' of men do agree, and 'covenant, every one, with every one,' that to whatsoever 'man,' or 'assembly of men,' shall be given by the major part, the 'right' to 'present' the person of them all, that is to say, to be their 'representative.' "[8] This unlimited liberty is then translated to the state, the sovereign, which becomes the basic unit of interaction between humans both within and between states. This state is the individual in that it speaks for the individual as the representative:

> And because the end of this institution is the peace and defense of them all; and whosoever has right to the end, has right to the means; it belongs of right, to whatsoever man, or assembly that hath the sovereignty, to be judge both of the means of peace and defense, and also of the hindrances, and disturbances of the same; and to do whatsoever he shall think necessary to be done, both beforehand, for the preserving of peace and security, by prevention of discord at home, and hostility from abroad.[9]

On this basis the state can make laws for the preserving of the peace. These are called civil laws in contrast to the natural law, which is the dictate of practical rationality. These civil laws are in one sense arbitrary, or conventional, and can differ from state to state, but they must be obeyed by the citizens of a given state:

> But as men, for the attaining of peace, and conservation of themselves thereby, have made an artificial man, which we call a commonwealth; so also have they made artificial chains, called "civil laws," which they themselves, by mutual covenants, have fastened at one end, to the lips of that man, or assembly, to whom they have given the sovereign power; and at the other end to their own ears.[10]

There is no room in this system for religious wars or divisions within a state except by those who have abandoned reason and knowledge. Hobbes recognized that religious differences would persist, but these are based on ignorance and error, or at best are mere fideistic assertions. What is

8 Ibid., 91.
9 Ibid., 93.
10 Ibid., 97.

common to all must be governed by knowledge and can only proceed in the realm of what can be known (this world). This is a substantial reversal from the Medieval period, including the Renaissance and the Reformation, in which otherworldly concerns (whether Christian or Greek in origin) molded political life.

To go beyond a simple statement of what Hobbes contributed, I lay bare his beliefs about the good and how these shape the law, and also how these are based on a foundation of metaphysics and epistemology. Then I want to argue that his foundation is insufficient in a number of ways that had a dramatic effect on the modern world. Beyond the common assertion that Hobbes believed in law and order is a worldview about God, human nature, and the good. To begin, we can identify some distinguishing marks of his philosophy:

1. All knowledge begins in the senses.
2. We have no natural knowledge of what happens after death, which is the focus of religion.
3. Authority of scripture, including the Ten Commandments, can only be known by persons to whom it is given or must be established by the civil authority.
4. Good and evil are defined in relation to the appetites/desires/passions.
5. The state of nature is a perpetual war of all against all in which life is short, nasty, and brutish.
6. Our highest goal is survival, and natural laws aim at this goal.
7. The social contract gives the power to enforce laws to the sovereign.
8. The sovereign is supreme vis-á-vis religious factions.

I do not want to settle the personal religious beliefs of Hobbes here. It is enough to note that in *The Leviathan*, he speaks of God, but also rejects immaterial substance (whether for God or the human soul):

> But the opinion that such spirits were incorporeal, or immaterial, could never enter into the mind of any man by nature, because, though men may put together words of contradictory signification, a "spirit" and "incorporeal," yet they can never have the imagination of anything answering to them; and therefore men that by their own mediation arrive to the acknowledgement of one infinite, omnipotent, and eternal God chose rather to confess He is incomprehensible and above their understanding than to define His nature by "spirit incorporeal," and then confess their definition to be unintelligible; or, if they give Him such a title, it is not "dogmatically" with intention to make the divine nature understood, but "piously," to honor

> Him with attributes of significations as remote as they can from the grossness of bodies visible.[11]

Hobbes affirmed that God alone is eternal (without beginning) and is the creator of the world,[12] and the world is not co-eternal with God, God is not the spirit of the world, and the world is temporal (with beginning) and dependent on God. God can be known by considering causation and knowing that causation cannot regress into infinity but that there must be a first cause and this is what we call God.[13]

Hobbes noted that idolatry as false beliefs about God has been a significant hindrance to human society. These, like religion, are based on ignorance and rely on the fears of the masses. The religions that sprout from such fears are diverse and are the cause of great strife between persons:

> [In] these four things, opinion of ghosts, ignorance of second causes, devotion towards what men fear, and taking of things casual for prognostics, consists the natural seed of "religion: which, by reason of the different fancies, judgments, and passions of several men, hath grown up into ceremonies so different that those which are used by one man are for the most part ridiculous to another[14]

Hobbes asserted that human suffering is caused by God in order to manifest the power of God, and believed this is how the book of Job should be interpreted.[15] He spoke in general terms about heaven as the promise for those that obey God in this life where heaven is a place in which humans continue to fulfill their appetites.

Hobbes rejected the claim that there is a *summum bonum*, a highest and final good;[16] instead good and evil are an individual's appetites and disapprobations.[17] In rejecting the *summum bonum*, he says he is rejecting the medieval schoolmen and their old moral philosophy and replacing it with a moral philosophy, or science of virtue, which studies the natural laws that are immutable and eternal in that they are required for peace and their opposites produce war.[18]

11 Ibid., 79.
12 Thomas Hobbes, "Leviathan," in *Great Books of the Western World* 23, ed. Robert Maynard Hutchins (Chicago: Encyclopedia Brittanica, 1952), 78.
13 Ibid., 80.
14 Ibid., 79.
15 Ibid., 160.
16 Ibid., 76.
17 Ibid., 61, 96.
18 Ibid., 95.

And so, on these natural laws, which he says are really theorems guiding us to peace, rest all other laws, which are the word of him who has the right and power to issue laws.[19] He acknowledged that Scripture contains laws from God, yet to know that scripture is indeed the word of God, either God would have to speak to each of us, or it must be attested to through a prophet speaking in the name of the established religion and performing a miracle.[20] Because all miracles have now ceased,[21] any laws based on scripture and not attested to directly by God to us are given their authority by the legitimate law, given in the state as the one who has the authority to make laws and to decide what is the correct interpretation of scripture.[22]

Although the good for each individual is the satisfaction of desires, there is a final end for the state: "The final cause, end, or design of men, who naturally love liberty, and dominion over others, in the introduction of that restraint upon themselves, in which we see them live in commonwealths, is the foresight of their own preservation, and of a more contented life thereby."[23] This final end gives the context for the "natural laws" that Hobbes considers. We do not need to detail all of them here, and Hobbes summarized them as follows: "For the laws of nature, as 'justice,' 'equity,' 'modesty,' 'mercy,' and, in sum, 'doing to others, as we would be done to,' of themselves, without the terror of some power, to cause them to be observed, are contrary to our natural passions, that carry us to partiality, pride, revenge, and the like."[24]

If Hobbes is wrong about the goal of life being peace, then his natural laws are incorrect. He is correct that moral philosophy is the science of good and evil,[25] and that laws are meant to identify the means to good and protect against evil. Therefore, if the good is not properly identified, the rest of the system will be flawed. Hobbes claimed that ignorance of the natural law he articulates is inexcusable[26] because it has been made available in such a simple and clear formula that there is no excuse for failing to know it. But if he has himself failed to know what is good, then this same inexcusability will apply to him.

19 Ibid., 96.
20 Ibid., 166.
21 Ibid., 167.
22 Ibid., 171, 172.
23 Hobbes, *Leviathan*, 88.
24 Ibid., 88.
25 Hobbes, *Leviathan*, 96.
26 Ibid., 95.

Like Socrates, Hobbes said that all voluntary actions are done to attain what is believed to be good.[27] In asserting that there is no highest good, Hobbes wished to affirm that humans will always need to be growing and that there is no point where humans will have attained something and can stop being satisfied. There is here a rejection of the "beatific vision" as the *summum bonum*. There is, by implication, an affirmation that whatever is good must be continuing and inexhaustible. However, if the good is to be fulfilling, it must be connected to what is ultimate; anything less than what is ultimate will not provide the inexhaustible interest required for lasting fulfillment. Hobbes made reference to knowing God but it is a bare knowledge of God as creator and possibly judge. The creation is not a revelation of God's nature. Heaven is a conjecture and, if it exists, is more of the same appetite satisfaction as found on earth. Human existence, for Hobbes, is confined to the satisfaction of our appetites in this life, and this vision of the good is not continuing or inexhaustible.

There is, of course, a long tradition of discussion about whether the good is good because we desire it or if it is desired because it is good. I suggest an alternative analysis that in a way can affirm both sides of that debate in different senses. That is, I argue that our desires are the result of our beliefs about what is real and what is good. Because these beliefs come in a system, and because people are not always very conscious or consistent in the implications of beliefs they hold, there is not always a one-to-one correspondence between belief changes and desire changes. But even in such cases a shift in system does result in a shift in desires. And there are often many cases where there is a one-to-one correspondence. To consider a mundane example, a person's desire for a donut can change immediately upon finding out that the donut is poisoned.

The cases where a person seems to want something that the person also denies being good are indications of an internal struggle about what is actually good. The changeability of persons can be such that from moment to moment, competing beliefs about the good vie for acceptance; such a person is referred to as double-minded, or moveable, or inconstant.

How does this relate to Hobbes? He is right in a sense that the good is what is desired. He is also right that whenever we achieve what we desire we are happy for a time. However, he does not consider that any given individual may desire something, the desiring of which is based on a false belief about what is real and what is good. Consequently, because what the person desires is not actually good (something that is continuing, inexhaustible,

[27] Ibid., 87.

fulfilling, ultimate), it will not result in lasting happiness. Hobbes did not distinguish between happiness and lasting happiness.

The outcome is that the goal of the state is peace for the individual citizens to fulfill their desires within the bounds of the law. However, the satisfaction of our desires is limited to the satisfaction of our senses. Even knowledge is reducible to our senses and turns out to be a kind of practical rationality for improving our comfort. Hobbes did not identify for us anything that will provide lasting happiness, and so the citizens of his state will search for satisfaction of their burning desires without relief. Such a condition will of necessity tend toward excess as people yearn for satisfaction and do not find it. Needless to say, this has indeed been a characteristic of the Modern age.

Although Hobbes, like Socrates, saw that persons act for what they believe to be good, he overstepped himself in saying that all men desire peace. He could say this because he believed that peace is the highest end, the good. What he is saying is formally true – all men desire the good. But a peaceful condition is a means to the good; it is not the good itself. A person in a vegetative state has achieved peace, but such a person has not achieved the good life. Furthermore, we want peace to achieve the good, but we also want enmity with what is evil.

The existence of evil remains a problem. The solution that God causes suffering (natural evil) for the manifestation of his power is not a full solution. There are many other ways for God to manifest his power. Furthermore, it does not explain why there is moral evil. A mere reference to the will of man threatens how Hobbes construes the sovereignty of God. Hobbes argued that God is omnipotent and indifferent to our self-preservation,[28] and that God is not unchanging but that change is necessary to anything that exists.[29]

We will not find a solution to these problems in *The Leviathan*. Indeed, this is an important characteristic of Modernity. The good has not been correctly identified, and so law has no basis. Evil cannot be explained. God is allowed to hang around but only as a first cause and then as a judge after death. Knowledge is limited to this life, and it is a practical kind of knowledge for the increase of our comfort; nothing ultimate is revealed to us in the creation. It is not surprising that this bequeaths a tradition of debate

[28] Michael Allen Gillespie, *The Theological Origins of Modernity* (Chicago: Chicago University Press, 2008), 230.

[29] Ibid., 229.

and uncertainty about what law is and how to understand the foundation of law.

SAMUEL VON PUFENDORF

Samuel von Pufendorf has had considerable influence on modern legal theory, particularly because he furthered the removal of religious issues from the public sphere, which had begun at the Peace of Westphalia.[30] He is anti-metaphysical in his leanings and grounds the natural law in human sociability. He accepted the Lutheran framework of two kingdoms (church and state) and argued that religious beliefs are personal and should have no influence on state matters. As a voluntarist, he focused on the will as the primary causal factor in choice and law.

Rejecting the idea that there is no law and that humans can live by their impulses alone, Pufendorf argued that reason shows us there is a general and universal rule of human conduct that creates obligations for all.[31] This rule is unchangeable, in contrast to positive law, and is universal in that it applies to all persons as part of the human race.[32] In this sense he continues in the traditional understanding of the relationship between natural law and positive law. All civil laws presuppose the basic ideas of the law of nature and have as their aim the security of human life. The universality and perpetuity of the natural law is not threatened by the need for particular laws governing differing regions.[33]

This grounding of the law in human sociability and with the general goal of security carries with it the rejection of the idea of a final end toward which human life aims: "I question whether it can be said, with any tolerable sense, that God hath constituted any End, common to Man with himself, or that the Order prescribed by him to Man, that is, the Observation of the Law of nature doth produce the End for which God created the world."[34] Pufendorf rejected the idea of a final end because it brings theological beliefs into the consideration of natural law, and because it would require great deduction to show that honoring one's parents or some such law is related to the end appointed by God. He said that the laws of scripture are the same as those written on the heart, but this does not mean that

[30] Samuel von Pufendorf (1632–1694) was a German jurist who defended natural law.
[31] Samuel von Pufendorf, *Of the Law of Nature and Nations*, Eighteenth Century Collections Online ed. (Oxford: L. Lichfield, 1703), 92.
[32] Ibid., 92.
[33] Ibid., 103.
[34] Ibid., 104.

they are innate; rather, they are discoverable by reason. It is hard to believe that he means by this the entire *Decalogue*, but rather that he limits it to what he considers to follow from "loving one's neighbor."

This idea of deducing the law by reason means the use of practical rationality to solve disputes about common goods of this life in order to protect human society. This is a significant limitation of the idea of "reason"; it lumps theoretical rationality into the private sphere with an assumed skepticism about its powers. However, this is reflective of how "reason" was generally understood in Modernity, and unfortunately this limiting of reason led to the rejection of reason by those who saw that more was needed. This is unfortunate because reason incurred a negative connotation when really it is the limiting of reason to practical rationality that should be given a bad name. Consider these quotes:

> The dictates of right reason are true principles, which agree with the nature of things well observed and examined; and which are deduced from other true and first principles, by the rules of good consequence.[35]

and

> Therefore when we acknowledge the law of nature to be the dictate of right reason, our sense and meaning is this, that the understanding of man is endued with such a power, as to be able from the contemplation of human condition to discover a necessity of living agreeably to this law.[36]

A further tension that persisted in Modernity is, on the one hand, an emphasis on the universal rationality of all humans, but on the other it is the claim that much of what is most important is very difficult to know. For instance, he said that although there are some who cannot know the natural law from reason, it should be sufficient for them that their superiors practice it and that they cannot find any reason against it. Obviously this does little to solve the problem of knowledge because one needs to be able to know who counts as a "superior," and part of demonstrating this is showing that one knows what is good. It creates serious problems for responsibility because if the masses cannot know because it is too difficult, then their responsibility for being good is mitigated.

In attempting to respond to the critic who says none of these considerations matter, and that all that matters is pursuing whatever makes one happy, Pufendorf tried to argue that self-love requires society. And because

[35] Ibid.
[36] Ibid.

when an end is commanded, all the means are also commanded, so this natural sociableness also commands the means to society.[37] Therefore, the ethical egoist best serves himself/herself by submitting to the obligations created by social life. It is one thing to assert this, quite another to prove it, and still another to convince the ethical egoist. It is not enough to reply that consistent ethical egoists are few and far between, or to label them as sociopaths. What is desired is a sufficient reply to the skeptic in order to show that knowledge has been attained.

When pressed, Pufendorf fell back on appeals to voluntarism. A law is the command of a superior's will:[38]

> But man obtained a social nature from the good pleasure of God Almighty, not from any immutable necessity. And consequently the morality of actions agreeable or disagreeable to him as a social creature, must be derived from the same origin and spring, and must be attributed to man, not by an absolute, but by a hypothetical necessity, or upon supposal of that condition which God was pleasured freely to bestow on mankind above the privileges of inferior creatures.[39]

However, voluntarism leaves the will of God inscrutable. We cannot know why God wills something. God does not will it for some reason that we can ascertain, for this would threaten the omnipotence of God. What use then is the appeal to God and God's will? This challenge will press modern thinkers to become more and more consistent to the point that what cannot be known will no longer be appealed to as grounds for a theory of law.

CHRISTIAN THOMASIUS

Christian Thomasius's influence on Germany has been likened to Locke's influence on England.[40] One area of his importance was in stressing that the natural law can be known by reason and that religion brings division into political matters. He agreed with Pufendorf about the purpose of law, but he is of special interest to us because he represents the modern

37 Ibid., 107.
38 Ibid., 13.
39 Ibid., 15.
40 Christian Thomasius (1655–1728), was a German philosopher who argued for the independence of philosophy from theology, and for the freedom of rulers in religious matters.

approach to religious divisions. For our purposes, he is an example of how thinkers in this period viewed religion and knowledge of the law.

Thomasius began his *Essays on Church, State, and Politics* by affirming that all humans are in the same condition of misery. Everyone wants to live a long and happy life. However, because of some simple confusions, people actually bring more misery into their lives. The most important of these confusions is to misidentify natural and supernatural light. So, like other modern thinkers, he takes the Wars of Religion as an example of what must be avoided, and that a much happier life will be achieved if persons focus their attention on practical rationality to achieve the goods of this life.

While he did not believe that the natural and supernatural lights conflict in any way, he did argue that they are aimed at different goods. Indeed, Modernity kept this general Thomistic view of the good. There is a kind of happiness that can be achieved in this life by attaining natural goods; but there is an eternal happiness that can be achieved in the next life by keeping one's religious duty. Thomasius argued that this religious duty is very simple, teaching what man must do in his miserable condition after the Fall, that there is an immortal soul, and what means God has given to attain eternal happiness. These means are a kind of simple piety where one does one's duty in this life toward God and neighbor and is then given eternal happiness in the next life. This view of religion is characteristic of the minimal theology of Modernity, where theological divisions are seen as disputes about opinion and not necessary for eternal bliss. Later, it turns into a kind of individual piety that feels at home within, as well as outside of, theism.

In this same work, Thomasius gives an account of why Christianity has not kept this simple doctrine. In this history, he traces the confusion of the supernatural and natural light and argues that the introduction of Plato and Aristotle into Christianity caused no end to confusion. He identified the chief error of the "pagan natural philosophy" to be the eternity of the world and its coeternal origins, God and the prime matter. Although he asserted that these beliefs are contrary to plain reason, he seems to hold that they are best clarified by scripture. Furthermore, he does claim that it is not sufficient to know what is good, but that God's grace is also needed to uphold the will in order to do what is good. In this he does not seem to consider that God's grace is first given in order to know the good, not only to uphold the will. Like many others in Modernity, he seemed to think that knowing the good is universal, but doing what is good is hard.

This problem of grace helps bring a question into focus for us in our study. Modernity wrestled with the problem of scripture and its purpose.

Although many early modern thinkers affirmed the need for scripture, this was largely a soteriological need. Scripture supplies knowledge about how to get to heaven, which is not given in general revelation. Law and the good, as understood to apply to this world, had little need for scripture except as a background reference or to cite examples. Indeed, for persons like Thomasius, the belief seemed to be that if we can know the *summum bonum* without scripture, we would not need scripture and therefore we cannot know this from the natural light. Other Modernists seem to agree with this but take the other path, arguing that scripture is not needed. A third option is that although we can know the *summum bonum*, and ought to know it, from general revelation, it is precisely because we have not known it that we need redemptive revelation.

Thomasius traces the confusion of Greek philosophy and Christianity into the law. He argued that the Romans only rarely touched on actual natural law and instead usually confused natural law and the particulars of Roman society:

> Under these circumstances it is not surprising that the *Corpus juris* itself contains teachings which confuse the general law of nations with Roman law. This occurs, for example, in the chapters on paternal authority, on the authority of masters over their servants, on the ways of acquiring property according to law of nations, on imprisonment, and on the right [of exiles or refugees] to return.[41]

Although Thomasius wanted to move beyond the Wars of Religion, he did continually argue against the Roman Catholic Church. This included his belief that their canon law was not only insufficient but also subversive:

> Anyone who scrutinizes the secrets of the papalist clergy will quickly see that canon law aims only at subverting all principles of sound reason concerning the true difference between good and evil, as well as the fundamental principles of government and secular authority. Under the guise of zeal for the glory of God and with much chatter, clerical power attempts to arrogate these principles to itself. It is much to be wished that Protestant lawyers would show in even more detail the politically erroneous state-secrets of papalist law. I am certain that not a single title can be found in either Gratian's *Decretum* or in the *Decretals* to which such political maxims of the clergy have not been added.[42]

41 Thomasius, *Essays on Church, State, and Politics.*
42 Ibid.

Thomasius did not limit his criticisms to Roman Catholics, but also lamented at what he considered to be the miserable condition of Protestants. He traced this to the dispute between Luther and Zwingli over the nature of the Lord's Supper. According to Thomasius, Luther retained the same errors as had been present in Roman Catholicism. Furthermore, the two lights continued to be confused so that no progress could be made in understanding nature or revelation. All of this was remedied, Thomasius argued, by the work of Grotius, who properly kept each light in its own sphere and gave a foundation for understanding the law of nations.

This helps remind us what consequences followed from the Wars of Religion. They had solidified deep divisions within Christianity, which would only become less vociferous as religion itself faded into mere private opinion. However, another important result was that the law codes relied on by Europe for centuries could no longer be looked to for authority. Because nations were no longer all Roman Catholic, the laws of nations could not be referred to canon law or any other traditional law accepted by the Church. This forced Europeans to inquire into the natural law in order to get back to what is more universal to all persons.

Applying the ideas of the Peace of Westphalia, Thomasius argued that most of the issues that divided religious persons (Calvinist, Lutheran, and Roman Catholic) were not essential to the good life. He argued that many of the religious differences that had resulted in tension were actually areas of *adiaphora*, meaning not moral matters but matters of personal choice. He gives a brief description of the growth of Christianity from an early simple form to its more complex forms and seems to be indicating that the complex forms are mere human constructs. Indeed, he appeals to Acts 15 as an example of setting aside superfluous religious rituals.[43] It is fascinating that in this argument he is making the case that the first Christian council affirmed that the Holy Spirit is not given in sacraments, but had been given apart from circumcision and that circumcision never imparted grace (and, by implication, no sacrament does). He then makes the argument that the accumulation of rituals since that time is in violation of this conclusion at the Council of Jerusalem.

And yet, rather than see the growth of historic Christianity as expressed in the creeds of the faith based on Scripture, he affirmed that Christianity is only meant to teach a basic soteriological message. We need revealed religion, he says, because natural religion cannot provide us with a full account of our misery. Revealed religion provides us with the

[43] Ibid.

> special path to men by which [God] was to be reconciled to them, and by which he wanted to be revered by them. ... The Christian religion would thus appear to be content with an internal worship, that is, with the true humility of self-abnegating mind, which devotes itself entirely to God. And through the grace of the Holy Spirit, the disciples of Christ and the apostles devoted themselves to this practical religion with all their powers, in order to take part in the kingdom of Christ, which consists in justice, peace, and joy.[44]

Religion is meant to have this individual effect, but in fact religion has been used by "evildoers" to harm others and become an instrument in personal gain:

> Nevertheless, the experience of all centuries testifies that religion has such a perverse effect on many humans, that they use it as a sort of instrument for perpetrating the most awful crimes; and not only for causing unrest in the commonwealth in which they live, but also for threatening, disturbing, and overthrowing neighboring states. Therefore, the prince is obligated to take care that no damage is inflicted on the commonwealth by the religion of these evildoers.[45]

Thomasius accepted the view of Pufendorf that the purpose of law is peace within the state. Having just exited the destructive Wars of Religion, it is not surprising that a solution to such violence would be of top priority. However, note that the solution offered here as elsewhere in such modern thinkers is a practical solution built on skepticism about our ability to have knowledge in religious matters. Because knowledge is not possible in this area, it must be relegated to the personal and private and not allowed to threaten the public peace.

Like Locke's latitudinarianism, this view of religion emphasizes personal piety and otherworldliness, while giving the affairs of this world to the political realm. Even so, he does seem to strike on a solution to these differences in his appeal to Acts 15. If the Christian scriptures and first church council affirm that the sacraments do not impart grace, but that this is the work of the Holy Spirit, then later teachings of the Church must be consistent with this or be considered departures.

That he did not press this method is perhaps an indication of his view of the good life. Resolving such divisions is not necessary for achieving individual peace of mind or performing acts of practical piety and later going

44 Ibid.
45 Ibid.

to heaven. Although there are important differences in the medieval and modern worlds, one point of commonality is the belief that religion is otherworldly. Such a view does not require unity between persons except on very minimal points about how to get to heaven. The rest of life is spent enjoying the goods of this world. However, if the good is to know God, then unity between humans as we work together to more deeply understand what can be known of God is essential. In this sense, Thomasius is another example of how beliefs about the good shape beliefs about the purpose of law.

JOHN LOCKE

> The end of government is the good of mankind.[46]

Although I am not trying to measure specific influence of each thinker considered here on the world, Locke's influence, particularly on the development of the United States, was more substantial than that of Hobbes.[47] Like Hobbes he was an empiricist. Unlike Hobbes, his personal religious beliefs are more clearly stated, and a transition from orthodoxy to Socinianism is found in his text. Like Thomasius, he understands religion to provide a simple account of soteriology not accessible by the light of nature. Within such religion, however, is great "latitude" of belief about practice. He provides a civil solution to the problems of religious wars, but also a personal solution to what he considers the dangers of enthusiasm: "This I take to be properly enthusiasm, which, though founded neither on reason nor divine revelation, but rising from the conceits of a warmed or overweening brain, works yet, where it once gets footing, more powerfully on the persuasions and actions of men than either of those two, or both together."[48] Where Hobbes is said to focus on law and order, Locke is said to focus on the right to life, liberty, and property.

To help focus how Locke is similar to, and different from, Hobbes, we can articulate the following points:

1. All knowledge is from the senses.
2. There are two kinds of knowledge: knowledge of the relation of ideas (which originated in senses) and knowledge of the world from the senses.

[46] John Locke and Peter H. Nidditch, eds., *An Essay Concerning Human Understanding* (Oxford: Oxford University Press, 1979).

[47] John Locke (1632–1704) was an English philosopher who established empiricism and political liberalism. He argued for the origin of all knowledge in sense data, social contrast as the beginning of government, and religious toleration.

[48] Ibid.

3. Good and evil are nothing more than pleasure and pain.
4. The state of nature is one of freedom and has its pleasures, but greater pleasures particularly connected with property are only secured by a social contract.
5. The natural law is summarized as the preservation of life; the civil law is aimed at preserving life and property so that humans can increase their comfort.
6. God can be known with certainty; other religious differences are matters of personal preference.
7. The purpose of religion is to reveal a moral standard that, if kept, leads to heaven.
8. Religious disputes are never about anything important enough to justify civil division – they are to be kept in the private realm.

Locke provides a full theory of human knowledge and what can be known in his *Essay Concerning Human Understanding*. He proceeds along empiricist lines, but he claims that humans begin as a blank slate in contrast to how Hobbes understood humans as beginning selfish and nasty. The senses leave imprints on this blank slate, which become ideas and can be combined together into compounds, and this represents the building of knowledge of the world.

Locke clearly states his view of the good: Good and evil are nothing but pleasure and pain. This follows from the emphasis on the senses and gives shape to his view of how the state develops and of the role of laws in the state. The state not only protects the citizens on their way to the goal of peace; it also protects their property that is the result of their work in the pursuit of pleasure. The life and liberty of persons must be protected to make this work worthwhile and lasting, because no one would go through great exertion for what can only be temporary and fleeting. The freedom of the will is in the ability to use reason, and this is mostly a kind of practical rationality aimed at understanding how labor and private property contribute to achieving the goal of furthering life and comfort:

> The great end of men's entering into society being the enjoyment of their properties in peace and safety, and the great instrument and means of that being the laws established in that society, the first and fundamental positive law of all commonwealths is the establishing of the legislative power, as the first and fundamental natural law which is to govern even the legislative.[49]

49 Ibid.

The natural law is an eternal law: "The fundamental law of Nature being the preservation of mankind, no human sanction can be good or valid against it."[50] This law is the will of God, and as such is eternal and unchanging. This will of God is relatively bare in relation to the full work of the legislature to give the details of how human society will run.

A law is enacted through the power of the legislature and must be for the public good and must fit within the bounds of the law of nature.[51] Voluntary acts are done to achieve some perceived good, and so entering into a social contract is done in the belief that the individual's good will be advanced.[52] And so men leave the state of nature for the "great and chief end" of preserving their property.[53] God gave the world to humans to be used for their best advantage for life and convenience.[54] Private property is the result of adding labor to what was otherwise shared in common.

Unlike Hobbes, Locke endeavors to give a more developed proof of God's existence. Indeed, he asserts that we know God more certainly than anything else, with equal certainty to how we know ourselves. We know that God exists because we know that there are no uncaused events, and that if something now exists, something must have always existed. What is eternal cannot be the material world, and must be personal if it is the creator of the human person. At least this much Locke believes is knowable by all persons, although he gives the excuse to many of being too busy making a living to seek out knowledge.

From theism he gives a principle of latitudinarianism, which allows a broad group of religious beliefs to coexist without troubling the state. Indeed, what he rejects is the form of enthusiasm that, based on strong emotions, seeks to convert and condemn others on the basis of theological differences. The divisions about soteriology that led to Wars of Religion, or the enthusiasts of his day that in their passion promulgated divisions, were part of what humans cannot know about. If we cannot know, we should not take strong positions. We certainly should not go to war for these sorts of opinions. If there is conflict, it is redirected to what we can know about, as well as to the goods of this life, such as private property.

Thus Locke fits into, and refines, the picture of Modernity we saw in Hobbes. The accumulation of property through work under the general theme of pleasure as the good gives an added duty to the state of protecting

50 Ibid.
51 Ibid.
52 Ibid.
53 Ibid.
54 Ibid.

private property. He inadvertently expresses a problem that Hume latter makes more explicit (and which comes to be called Hume's Fork) which is that if all knowledge is through experience, then how can synthetic *a priori* knowledge be possible (how can we know about the world from reason alone)? This is one of the problems in the course of Modernity that will force a solution that in turn leads to the skepticism of Postmodernity.

Locke gives detailed consideration of the nature of reason in his *Essay*. He ascribes to intuition the highest degree of certainty.[55] This is knowledge of ideas that present themselves to us immediately, and he illustrates it with geometrical examples. This is a feature of Modernity: mathematics is the most certain, followed by reasoning about our sense of the natural world, and least knowable are the objects of religious disputes. Faith is the assent to some claim on the basis of authority derived from God.[56]

Nevertheless, the differences between Locke and Hobbes are not significant enough to protect Locke from similar criticisms of his view of the good. Although he develops a more robust vision for use of the creation (private property), he invests more time in thinking about religion and even claims to justify a form of moral religion relying on Christianity, with which he shares the same definition of the good. This leads naturally to the utilitarian perspective that the maximization of pleasure is the goal of human life and law.

However, clarification requires that we draw a distinction between pleasure and happiness, and that we distinguish between the good as an end in itself and happiness and the effect of possessing the good. Once this distinction has been made, Locke's definition is seen to be empty. The good cannot be the effect of possessing the good. Simply focusing on happiness does not tell us what will bring lasting happiness. In Locke, we are no closer to having a statement of the good, or an explanation of law grounded in the good, than we were in Hobbes.

CHARLES DE MONTESQUIEU

Montesquieu also related positive law to natural law.[57] For Montesquieu, the natural law begins with a law about man's duty to God. Evil results

[55] Ibid.

[56] Ibid.

[57] Charles-Louis de Secondat, baron de La Brede et de Montesquieu (1689–1755) was a French political philosopher and author of *The Spirit of Laws*. Some of his other works, like *The Persian Letters*, are satirical in nature and attempt to point out the cultural relativity in matters of morals and taste.

from human freedom to transgress the laws established by God.[58] The other natural laws are derived from the human frame and existence.[59] The first of these laws is peace, because in the state of nature, every person would consider oneself inferior to all others and seek out peace. The next law is the prompting for nourishment, and the third is the natural inclination of male and female for each other.[60] The fourth is for life together in society, and on these rest the positive laws.

Montesquieu is best known for his study of different kinds of laws, and how the positive laws of a society are an expression of the unique life of that society. "The law of nations is naturally founded on this principle, that different nations ought in time of peace to do one another all the good they can."[61] The state of war arises after nations are formed, when competing nations come into conflict and seek to incorporate the benefits of the other society. The best government is "the government most conformable to nature is that which best agrees with the human and disposition of the people in whose favor it is established."[62] He defines law, in general, as "human reason, inasmuch as it governs all the inhabitants of the earth: the political and civil laws of each nation ought to be only the particular cases in which human reason is applied."[63] It is these particular conditions that Montesquieu calls the spirit of laws.

Montesquieu notes the relativity of what is considered "virtuous" depending on the kind of government (republic, monarchy, or despotism), and that the role of education differs within each. This anticipates some of the insights of Alasdair MacIntyre in *Whose Justice Which Rationality?*

The laws of nature are practical laws because in the state of nature, humans are inclined toward the practical and not the speculative. This is another example of the division between the practical and the speculative, and the reversal of the two where the practical is viewed as easier and more accessible. In contrast, I argue that how a person interprets the practical depends on answers given to "speculative" questions about what is good and what is real.

For Montesquieu, we can note:

58 Montesquieu, *The Spirit of Laws*, trans. Thomas Nugent, ed. J. V. Prichard (Chicago: Encyclopedia Britannica, 1980), 2.
59 Ibid., 2.
60 Ibid., 2.
61 Ibid., 3.
62 Ibid., 3.
63 Ibid., 3.

1. Natural law begins with a person's relationship to God.
2. Natural law is predominately about human survival.
3. Positive law is based on natural law and differs in relation to what is best suited to a given environment; law is to command the will.
4. Governments are not equal in their development of human potential.
5. The state of war begins after nations are formed as they compete.
6. Religion is given for moral purposes (Christianity is about love whereas Islam is despotic).
7. An externalist description of law formation relies on geographic and cultural factors.

Montesquieu is known for having wondered why the laws of physics are inviolable, whereas the laws of nature for human conduct are violated numerous times each day. He references free will as the solution. However, J. S. Mill argued that in this question Montesquieu collapsed or overlooked the distinction between descriptive and normative laws. The laws of physics are descriptive, whereas the laws of human conduct are normative. Part of the problem of Modernity has been to explain the meaning and binding character of normative laws. Practical rationality requires that we have already identified our goal, and now we are reasoning about how best to get there. But if the goal is nothing more than my individual pleasure, on what basis can the skeptical critique of social norms be answered? Indeed, postmodern thinkers like Foucault and Derrida will point out that these early modern thinkers simply replaced medieval superstition with their own myth to justify social power. Montesquieu is relied on by such thinkers in showing the relativity of social laws.

JEAN-JACQUES ROUSSEAU

An even more important thinker both for Modernity and for Postmodernity is Rousseau.[64] Following the model already used by others, Rousseau grounded human law in society that was constructed out of the state of nature. However, unlike others who viewed the state of nature as unpleasant, Rousseau viewed it as total freedom. The individual left alone is not evil; rather, in this original state, all humans are good. Humans gather to

64 Jean-Jacques Rousseau (1712–1778) was a Swiss-born French philosopher. He is considered the father of the French Revolution. He is considered to have brought an end to the age of reason, and instead emphasized intuition and nature. He believed that humans are basically good but are corrupted by their environment.

form society only because it can increase their happiness. This is a social contract where equals willingly bind themselves together:[65]

> I suppose men to have reached the point at which the obstacles in the way of their preservation in the state of nature show their power of resistance to be greater than the resources at the disposal of each individual for his maintenance in that state. That primitive condition can then subsist no longer; and the human race would perish unless it changed its manner of existence.[66]

Because human cultivation and civilization cannot be shown to have increased either virtue or happiness, Rousseau argues that we will need to look elsewhere than these to explain the origin of society. Society is not needed to protect us from unlawfulness like Augustine claimed, nor is it needed to guide us toward the highest happiness as Aquinas maintained. It is needed for this-worldly survival.

Rousseau recognized that this viewpoint is contrary to what is taught by Scripture.[67] He argued that it is religion that has perpetuated the idea of inequality, and that religion has appealed to some kind of original creation ordinance to justify this inequality.[68] Therefore, in considering the origins of law, we must set aside religion, which is shrouded in the unknowable, and rely on what Rousseau believed is common sense. This is naturalism, which is neutral with respect to religious claims (according to Rousseau), rather than revealed religion, which is biased in favor of the reigning power structures.[69]

As with all of the other modern thinkers we have considered, Rousseau argued that natural man is only concerned with survival and that this is the basis of the law.[70] However, in contrast to Hobbes, he believed that the state of nature was one of peace, and that in this state there is no good or evil.[71] Also in contrast to Hobbes, he says that evil arises after the creation of society, whereas Hobbes understood it to lie in the lack of knowledge that could be present before society. "Since no man has a natural authority over his fellow, and force creates no right, we must conclude that conventions form the basis of all legitimate authority among men."[72]

65 Jean Jacques Rousseau, *A Discourse on the Origin of Inequality*, trans. G. D. H. Cole (Chicago: Encyclopedia Britannica, 1980), 334.
66 Jean Jacques Rousseau, *The Social Contract*, trans. G. D. H. Cole (Chicago: Encyclopedia Britannica, 1980).
67 Rousseau, *A Discourse on the Origin of Inequality*, 333.
68 Ibid., 334.
69 Ibid., 334.
70 Rousseau, *The Social Contract*.
71 Rousseau, *A Discourse on the Origin of Inequality*, 343.
72 Rousseau, *The Social Contract*.

The most basic and influential feature of human nature, according to Rousseau, is the feelings, particularly of compassion.[73] Feelings are the source of morality, but our feelings are shaped by the society in which we live and therefore can be corrupted by society. Indeed, society creates inequalities, and it is in this sense that people are, everywhere, in chains. Even thought itself is a construct because it is based on language, and language is a construct of society.[74] So whereas Rousseau spoke about finding the laws of nature, what he did (in the eyes of postmoderns at least) was to show the constructed nature of all human thought, worldviews, and therefore laws.

In his *Social Contract*, Rousseau provides the groundwork for these ideas. All rights are based on social convention.[75] The first law of nature is the law of survival.[76] This naturalist outlook provides the groundwork for much of later thought in the biological sciences. Human survival is enhanced by creating a society, and therefore the social contract is constructed in that context.[77] "The passage from the state of nature to the civil state produces a very remarkable change in man, by substituting justice for instinct in his conduct, and giving his actions the morality they had formerly lacked."[78]

However, it would be incorrect to get the idea that it is each and every individual that constructs this or gives consent. Rather, it is the product of the "general will." Problematically, this general will is created by the social contract but also presides at the creation of the social contract. The General Will gets capitalized, as it is the highest source of authority. The General Will is always correct, and any apparent mistake on its part is only owing to someone else having withheld information:

> It follows from what has gone before that the general will is always right and tends to the public advantage; but it does not follow that the deliberations of the people are always equally correct. Our will is always for our own good, but we do not always see what that is; the people is never corrupted, but it is often deceived, and on such occasions only does it seem to will what is bad.[79]

73 Rousseau, *A Discourse on the Origin of Inequality*, 344.
74 Ibid., 340.
75 Ibid., 387.
76 Rousseau, *The Social Contract*, 388.
77 Ibid., 387.
78 Ibid.
79 Ibid., 396.

Furthermore, the General Will holds the life and property of each individual at its disposal as it understand these in relation to the common good: "In order then that the social compact may not be an empty formula, it tacitly includes the undertaking, which alone can give force to the rest, that whoever refuses to obey the general will shall be compelled to do so by the whole body."

Law is created in order to join rights and duties; it is articulated by the general will and always toward the advance of the common good.[80] Because humans are the product of their environment, if you change the environment you will change the person. A more just society will create a more just person:

> Each member of the community gives himself to it, at the moment of its foundation, just as he is, with all the resources at his command, including the goods he possesses. I shall end this chapter and this book by remarking on a fact on which the whole social system should rest: i.e., that, instead of destroying natural inequality, the fundamental compact substitutes, for such physical inequality as nature may have set up between men, an equality that is moral and legitimate, and that men, who may be unequal in strength or intelligence, become every one equal by convention and legal right.[81]

Each person gives himself/herself totally to the society, but because everyone does this, no one wants the demands of the society to become harsh: "These clauses, properly understood, may be reduced to one – the total alienation of each associate, together with all his rights, to the whole community; for, in the first place, as each gives himself absolutely, the conditions are the same for all; and, this being so, no one has any interest in making them burdensome to others.[82]" This idea of alienation figures prominently in Marx's thought.

Rousseau does speak often of the Creator, although as a deist he denies that God rules in history. He makes a nod toward Christianity but argues that it is spiritual, about heaven and not about this world.[83] Rousseau's philosophy is what can guide us in this life, whereas religion at best plays a private and otherworldly role. In this sense he is an example of growth in consciousness and consistency from some of the earlier thinkers. God, as the object of opinion, not knowledge, plays an

80 Ibid., 399.
81 Ibid., 399.
82 Ibid., 391.
83 Ibid., 437.

increasingly minor role. The object of knowledge, the good of this life, and especially survival are all that needs to be appealed to in order to explain human law.

DAVID HUME ON MORALITY

Hume is perhaps the most important figure considered here because he offers arguments against the medieval viewpoint particularly as it is intertwined with Aristotle, and he fits in with those who argue that society is formed by humans for natural purposes, but he also offered a devastating critique of earlier Enlightenment figures such that most of what is said later by Postmodernists can be found in some form or another in Hume.[84] Specifically, Hume argued about the powers of reason, rejecting the view that reason can discover the good or God. He followed earlier thinkers in dividing all thinking into either matters of fact or relations of ideas, but he gets the distinction of having this named Hume's Fork because he takes the step to show that by reason alone we cannot know what exists. One implication of this is that we do not know causation by reason; rather, what we call causation merely refers to constant conjunction in experience. It was the implications of this for both science and religion that led Kant to reject his previous rationalism and look for a way to justify the synthetic *a priori*.

We can call Hume a naturalist in that he traces law to a natural feature of human survival and psychology, a moral sense that responds to actions with approbation or disapprobation. He rejects any view that attempts to find eternal and unchanging forms of justice and virtue, or that seeks to reduce morality to rationality or to discover virtue and vice through reason alone. With this broad stroke he rejects medieval debates about voluntarism, intellectualism, and divine command, along with both Plato and Aristotle. He also rejects his closer contemporaries who have claimed to find morality in a kind of rationality and calculated self-preservation, or those who have sought to discover virtue and vice through reason alone.

Hume can work in such broad strokes because of the division of all knowledge into matters of fact or relations of ideas. If morality is a kind

[84] David Hume (1711–1776) was a Scottish philosopher who emphasized radical empiricism and philosophical skepticism. His rejection of causation as anything more than constant conjunction in experience caused Immanuel Kant to rethink his early rationalism. His book, *Dialogues Concerning Natural Religion*, demonstrated the problems and invalidity of the traditional proofs for God's existence. This is consistent with his empiricism, which claims that we can have no knowledge of anything outside experience.

of knowledge, it must fit into one of these categories. It does not, however, fit into one of these categories. Therefore, morality is not a kind of knowledge. He uses an argument similar to that which he gives for thinking about causality. When we observe a scene, we do not observe something called "virtue" or "morality"; rather, we observe various activities and objects. It is our response that adds the category of virtue, when we respond to an activity as noble or generous.

Like so many before him, Hume also distinguishes between speculative and practical rationality. Morality and moral science are said to fall under the latter. This is especially true when morality is construed to be about ends and the means to those ends. But practical reason alone cannot excite us to action; we must first find some given end desirable. Moral passions produce or prevent actions because of desire to attain or avoid something. Therefore, morality is not the conclusion of reason, nor can reason alone move us to moral action (Hume said reason is perfectly inert).

One of the enduring problems articulated by Hume is called the "fact/value dichotomy." He asserted that what we call crime is not a matter of fact; instead, it is something that arises from a set of circumstances that excite the sentiment of blame. Hilary Putnam tells us that "Hume's metaphysics of 'matters of fact' constitute the whole ground of the alleged underivability of 'oughts' from 'ises.'"[85] Although Putnam points in the direction of Dewey and fallibilism for a solution, we can concur that the problem is with incorrect metaphysical assumptions in Hume, which need to be brought to the surface and critically analyzed for meaning. This particularly involves his form of empiricism and naturalism.

This division between speculative and practical rationality, hardly questioned by those who make it, and given all the power of the apparently obvious, leads for Hume, as it does for others, to the claim that knowing what is good does not preclude acting against what we know. His assertion is that we can know what is virtuous without being able to conform our will to it. This is a different claim than that we can act against what we know to be good; virtue is defined as the means to what is good, and therefore a person could act against what is considered virtuous in the pursuit of another good. However, the essence of the claim remains: Speculative reason is ineffectual with regard to action. At best it informs practical rationality, but because this information can be ignored, it is a weak function at best.

[85] Hilary Putnam, *The Collapse of the Factvalue Dichotomy: And Other Essays* (Cambridge, MA; London: Harvard University Press, 2002), 190.

Not surprisingly, Hume argues that all persons are moved by self-interests. But this is not the Socratic claim that all persons act for what they believe to be good. Rather, Hume argues that whatever good appears to be the strongest is the good that is the nearest and that is what will motivate to action. So, some distant but greater good will be set aside for an immediate but lesser good. Hume does not believe that humans are mere egoists, and he found natural virtues existing in places like the family where genuine generosity is found. But he did find the origin of the state in this weakness of humans to choose the immediate good. To protect ourselves, we develop the state and set up impartial judges and magistrates who can remind us of the greater good and adjudicate in a disinterested manner.

The philosophical skepticism of Hume shaped the intellectual world after his time. He is more consistent in his empiricism than those that came before, and he used this to undermine categories that had been taken for granted, like causation. In that sense, his philosophy is the consistent outworking of the empiricist tradition of which he is a part. His philosophy gives voice to the conviction of Modernity that human reason is limited to what can be experienced, and that all else is mere opinion and construct.

There are notable patterns in these Enlightenment thinkers (Hobbes, Locke, Rousseau, Montesquieu, and Hume) about the nature of morality and the origin of the state and law. The purely natural or this-worldly concern for self-preservation and the attainment of greater material goods and worldly comforts is the origin of the state. Although there may be some disagreement about the actual condition of the state of nature, there is agreement that greater security and goods can be obtained in corporate unity working in common with others. Although God may appear here or there, his role is specifically that of a creator and perhaps distant lawgiver, but the immediate origin of law and the state is man.

THOMAS REID AND SCOTTISH COMMON SENSE

A formative influence for law, especially in the United States, was the Scottish Enlightenment.[86] Despite the skeptical conclusions of Hume, or perhaps because of these, thinkers like Thomas Reid sought to provide

[86] Thomas Reid (1710–1796) was a Scottish philosopher who helped invigorate the Scottish Enlightenment. He rejected David Hume's philosophical skepticism and empiricism, and instead sought to replace it with an appeal to common sense as the basis for the rest of knowledge.

an explanation of human knowledge that could support all areas of human study. Reid's particular target was Hume, and specifically what he considered to be the absurdities to which Hume had taken empiricism. In this sense, Reid is analogous to Kant, and I believe they share some important insights, although Kant's mention of Reid is not flattering (as if Reid merely appealed to the vulgar common sense of the uneducated masses). Here I would like to make the case that one of Reid's most important insights can be taken in two ways – as an externalist or as a form of transcendental argument – and that he is read today exclusively in the first way, even though the second way is much more promising.

In his introduction to *Selections from Scottish Common Sense Philosophy*,[87] G. A. Johnston argued that Reid occupied one of three possible positions given the parameters set by Locke. Locke explained human knowledge as a relationship between things, the perception of the thing, and the mind. According to this view (which has shaped Modernity), knowledge begins with the "ordinary objects" of sense experience, and from there it can attempt to build to high subjects like God's existence. Although Locke himself argued that we know God with certainty, his arguments came under serious criticism by Hume, using Locke's own principles.

Not only did Hume follow out the implications of this epistemology to skepticism; he also rejected part of the three pieces that Locke suggested. Hume affirmed things and ideas, but rejected the mind, saying that when he looks within, all he sees are a bundle of mental images. On the other hand, Berkeley affirmed ideas and the mind but rejected the things. The third position was taken by Reid, who argued that there are things and minds, but no ideas along the lines understood by these others. Reid argued that there are some judgments, or principles, that precede experience and which are necessary to understand experience:

> If there are certain principles, as I think there are, which the constitution of our nature leads us to believe, and of which we are under a necessity to take for granted in the common concerns of life, without being able to give a reason for them – these are what we call the principles of common sense; and what is manifestly contrary to them, is what we call absurd.[88]

87 G. A. Johnston, ed., *Selections from Scottish Common Sense Philosophy* (London: Open Court, 1915).
88 Ibid.

One example he gives is the claim just mentioned by Hume about the mind. To claim that there are sensations or beliefs, but not a mind that has these, is, according to Reid, absurd.

Reid gives a history of why philosophy, particularly modern philosophy, had failed up until his time. The essence of this failure is in postulating a world of ideas intermediate between the knower and the object that is known. This necessarily raised the problem of appearance and reality: How do we know we are getting it right, that there is not a mistake in the intermediate portion of our sensing? Whereas Berkeley had argued that there is mind plus ideas, Reid argued that there is mind plus matter, and both thinkers believed this relationship to be immediate.

Two examples of these commonsense judgments are the existence of mind (and that our individual mind persists in time) and extension. When Reid begins to become specific about common sense, problems also begin to arise as to the validity of his claims. He often speaks in a way that leads contemporary externalists to embrace him. He speaks of beliefs that are required by the composition of our nature. There are two problems here: (1) How does he know the composition of our nature in a non-question-begging manner? (2) The beliefs he posits to fit the standards of common sense are in fact rejected by entire civilizations.

For instance, it is an important part of the Four Noble Truths that the individual is not real, and so there is not a mind that persists in time. Similarly, it is an important part of Advaita Vedanta to claim that the individual is not real but is a fiction owing to ignorance about the nature of reality. To simply claim that these beliefs are contrary to our nature is mere table pounding. Perhaps these are the beliefs that are in accord with our nature and not commonsense realism.

Contemporary externalists, such as the "Reformed" Epistemologists, claim that such civilizations are not properly functioning. But of course, this claim can be made in return about the West, and we are faced with the need for internalist justification to determine who is correct. This focuses the problem for Commonsense Philosophy: It relies on assumptions about what is real that are not (and, it claims, cannot be) proven. However, any other philosophical system can also anoint its starting principles as "commonsense" and therefore not in need of proof.

It is for this reason that I do not think the externalist reading of Reid is the best reading, although it is the most popular today. It may be that this was Reid's view, but also that his thinking suggests another approach. Here is an example of a passage that certainly gives credence to the externalist reading:

I am aware that this belief which I have in perception stands exposed to the strongest batteries of scepticism. But they make no impression upon it. The sceptic asks me, Why do you believe the existence of the external object which you perceive? This belief, sir, is none of my manufacture; it came from the mint of Nature; it bears her image and superscription; and, if it is not right, the fault is not mine: I even took it upon trust, and without suspicion. Reason, says the sceptic, is the only judge of truth, and you ought to throw off every opinion and every belief that is not grounded in reason. Why, sir, should I believe the faculty of reason more than that of perception? – they came both out of the same shop, and were made by the same artist; and if he puts one piece of false ware into my hands, what should hinder him from putting another?[89]

Here the problems I mentioned earlier manifest themselves. The assumption is that there is some "Nature" that gave humans faculties like reason and sense. Many philosophical systems doubt this, so why should we accept Reid's account? The overall attitude of this quote is part of Reid's claim that perception is not entirely passive, that it is true that we are affected by the world but also that we can decide how to direct our attention. However, he sometimes seems to hint in another direction, the one that was more fully taken up by Kant:

Simple perception has the same relation to the conclusions of reason drawn from our perceptions, as the axioms in mathematics have to the propositions. I cannot demonstrate that two quantities which are equal to the same quantity, are equal to each other; neither can I demonstrate that the tree which I perceive, exists. But, by the constitution of my nature, my belief is irresistibly carried along by my apprehension of the axiom; and, by the constitution of my nature, my belief is no less irresistibly carried along by my perception of the tree. All reasoning is from principles. The first principles of mathematical reasoning are mathematical axioms and definitions; and the first principles of all our reasoning about existences, are our perceptions. The first principles of every kind of reasoning are given us by Nature, and are of equal authority with the faculty of reason itself, which is also the gift of Nature.[90]

Kant also wanted to find the necessary preconditions for human thought and rationality. Needless to say, there is in Reid a whole assumed framework here about nature and human faculties, which is merely assumed. Furthermore, there is a projection from Reid's own case to all of humanity – a problem that often occurs in natural law.

89 Ibid.
90 Ibid.

However, we could also understand Reid to be claiming that there are some beliefs that are necessary to make sense of any other belief. For instance, that I exist is required to discuss further matters of what I should believe. Similarly, extension is presupposed by material objects. Reid uses this kind of thinking when he discusses the good and human society. "We cannot live without the society of men; and it would be impossible to live in society, if men were not disposed to do much of that good to men, and but little of that hurt, which it is in their power to do."[91] This comes close to what Kant later articulates concerning society, duty, and the categorical imperative.

Reid takes the standard modern approach to the good, although in a way that responds to Hume's division of reason and desire. "Whatever makes a man more happy or more perfect, is good, and is an object of desire as soon as we are capable of forming the conception of it. The contrary is ill, and is an object of aversion."[92] So, even though we may find our current desires directed in one way, once our beliefs change about what will make us happy, so too will our desires change. I think this overall framework has some promise, although I do not believe we should confuse the good and happiness. Indeed, it seems in some places that Reid does not either: "Every deliberate human actions must be done either as the means, or as an end; as the means to some end, to which it is subservient, or as an end, for its own sake, and without regard to anything beyond it."[93] Furthermore, he affirms that it is the office of reason to understand what can and cannot be sought as an end in itself. As has already been noted, happiness is not something sought directly, but indirectly as an effect of attaining the end in itself. On identifying this we do not find much in Reid.

Reid's influence has been significant in the United States, which shares the attitude that some things are "self-evident" even if in fact they are doubted by many. Obviously, Thomas Paine relied on the term "common sense" to explain his arguments against the British government, and this kind of appeal has been important in almost all areas of American education. Given that appeals to common sense are made by persons in competing camps, and that it has not brought about greater unity and insight, it seems we will need to look elsewhere if we are to find a basis for the law and the good.

[91] Ibid.
[92] Ibid.
[93] Ibid.

IMMANUEL KANT

Kant's influence on all subsequent philosophy is immense.[94] Here it will only be possible to highlight the most notable aspects of his philosophy that shaped his legal and ethical theory. He claims to have been awakened from his dogmatic slumbers (adherence to the rationalism of Christian Wolff) by David Hume's skeptical critique. Kant saw the need to respond to this challenge, and did so by limiting the powers of pure reason and arguing that the mind of man shapes all information it receives from the world. Because of this filter, pure reason cannot tell us anything about being in itself, but we are limited to practical rationality shaped by transcendental requirements of immortality, freedom, and God. I believe the insight that something must be transcendental is important, although I do not go in the same direction as Kant with this. Furthermore, I also believe Kant's focus on a moral law that has universal application is important, and although I may disagree otherwise with his approach to the moral law, I think this is a more helpful phrase than "natural law" and will return to it in my response to Postmodernity.

Kant responds to Hume's Fork by arguing that there are some *a priori* beliefs that tell us about matters of fact. One example he gives is mathematics. Unfortunately for Kant, he relied heavily on Euclidean geometry for examples of the synthetic *a priori*, and it was not long after him that non-Euclidean geometry was discovered. Nevertheless, his claim is that the human mind shapes experience of the world by adding qualities like space and time. The world in itself is never known, but only the world as shaped and perceived by the human mind. So what is necessary as a precondition for human knowledge are these transcendentals. How well he identifies these is an important question that I discuss later. For now, we can note that he carries this kind of thinking into his study of the good and obligation.

Kant famously begins his discussion of morality by stating his view of the good. The only thing that can be called good without qualification is a good will. What this means is that moral value is determined by intentions,

94 Immanuel Kant (1724–1804) was a German philosopher. In his earlier career, he subscribed to the rationalism of Christian Wolfe, but was "awakened from his dogmatic slumbers" by the skepticism of David Hume. In his books, like *The Critique of Pure Reason*, he attempts to explain how knowledge is possible by distinguishing between the world in itself and the world as experienced. The latter is shaped by the human mind, which imposes categories necessary for human experience. Representing the peak of the Enlightenment, his limitations on reason also can be traced to the end of Modernity and are relied on by postmodern thinkers.

and these are good when they are determined by a general maxim guided by reason alone. By "reason alone" Kant means a contrast with both other sources of authority, like scripture, and with the goal of personal gain. Reason alone tells us that we should act only in a way that we could will to become universal. If universalizing our act would mean the end of society (like universal theft), then we must refrain from that act. A categorical imperative is therefore a direct command that ought to be done from the perspective of reason alone.

This formulation of law allows us to be autonomous rather than fall into heteronomy. We keep the law because it is in accord with our own will, not because we were told to do so by another. However, it also elevates the survival of society. We are obligated, or duty-bound, to act only in ways that preserve society. In this sense, Kant follows earlier thinkers in setting social survival as the goal of law, and he also thinks of rationality in terms of its practical powers while limiting its theoretical powers.

Kant saw the problem that this focus on duty created. Those who are dutiful in this life are rarely the most happy in this life. Consequently, the skeptic will ask Kant why duty is so important. Kant's reply is that all of morality requires that we presuppose the existence of God and the next life, and that in the next life duty is perfectly connected to happiness. This otherworldly solution might shock us given Kant's position as a modern thinker. But we must be reminded that Kant is in keeping with the modern outlook that knowledge about God or the afterlife is impossible, and rather we must simply keep these beliefs around for practical purposes.

Kant's focus is on duty that has shaped subsequent thinking. Obligation is at the heart of much of legal theory all the way to the twenty-first century. However, a significant problem remains that keeps such discussion from attaining the status of knowledge. If my duty is based on my thinking about the categorical imperative, and the categorical imperative is an expression of what I would will, then duty is directly based on my will. Kant valued the survival of society, but what about those who do not? Why should I (the skeptic asks) act only in ways that preserve society when this is not what I want (what I will)? Apologists for this perspective will appeal to common sense and moral intuition, but because these can also be questioned, they are not a final or highest source of authority. This failure to provide an account of duty that can withstand these criticisms is quickly pointed out by postmodern thinkers.

MODERNITY AND THE DIVISION BETWEEN PRACTICAL AND THEORETICAL RATIONALITY

Before concluding, I am going to distinguish what can be set aside as helpful discoveries by modern thinkers and then sift out weaknesses noted by Postmodernity. One strength is that these thinkers are looking for an explanation of the state from general revelation alone – that is, what can be known about morality, the state, and law from general revelation (and is therefore accessible by everyone) and without appeal to special revelation (which was supposedly the cause of the Wars of Religion). Problematically, they limit knowledge to this world and the goods of morality and law to material and psychological goods. Thus, the corporate endeavors of humans are in relation to such goods, and all of the discourse about work ethic, distribution of goods, retributive justice, and oppression is limited to these kinds of good. The good, the *summum bonum*, is marginalized as part of opinion discourse and considered either unknowable or unreal. Where it does make an appearance, it is projected into the next life as a continuation of the medieval beatific vision or as a state of heaven where one enjoys material and psychological goods forever.

Furthermore, for all of its lofty praise of knowledge, Modernity tended to minimize "theoretical" knowledge as ineffectual, and its praise of reason was really praising practical rationality. The new science argued that the Aristotelian worldview was based on speculation and assertion about the nature of things, which had no basis in experience (consider Aristotle's claim that heavier objects fall faster than lighter objects), and thus had very little practical application. When the Enlightenment thinkers did delve into what might be considered theoretical rationality, it was to support practical rationality. Descartes appealed to God to justify believing the report of our senses and guarantee the relationship between appearance and reality to support the new science.

For all of its changes from the medieval worldview, Modernity accepted the division between theoretical and practical rationality. I believe this is the case in part because of the belief that in general, humans know what is good, and the problem facing them is not a matter of knowing the good, but of practical rationality about how to best achieve the good. By way of contrast, I argue that in general, humans do not know the good, or that they are very often inconsistent and changeable in their beliefs (again, indicating that they do not actually know). Such a view does away with the division between theoretical and practical rationality and instead affirms that the problem for humans is one of not knowing what is clear, and this is a result of not seeking to know. This not seeking to know grows out of the belief that one already knows, and that one does not need to seek.

Can knowledge of the good be ineffectual with respect to choice? In making a choice, a person is choosing what is believed to be the best option, all things considered. Thus, the choice is only as accurate about what is best as are the beliefs it is based on. A person might accidently get the choice correct (actually choose what is indeed best), but not know this and so not benefit from it. Such situations are exemplified in numerous Socratic dialogues, including that with Thrasymachus in the *Republic*, who believed the best choice is the one that brings immediate happiness. A person might have a correct belief about what is good, but not have knowledge because the belief is based on insufficient proof (such as intuition or common sense).

It is popular in contemporary epistemology to attempt an externalist description of how knowledge is warranted. Something like this: Owen is warranted in his belief that *x* is the good because he formed that belief under reliable mechanisms of belief formation. Needless to say, this only moves the debate up a notch, because what counts as "reliable mechanisms" is the question needing to be answered, and generally an empiricist or intuitionist answer is given. These are insufficient if what is desired is certainty. The externalist still must answer the internalist question: How do you know your description of warrant and knowledge is correct? Here is where Modernity and Postmodernity meet in that, over time, modern thinkers had to abandon claims about certainty and become skeptics about its possibility.

If a person's choices reflect that person's beliefs about what is good, then we are responsible to the extent that we can know what is good. If the good is unknowable, or there is no good, then there can be no responsibility. If the good is knowable, and failure to know is a result of not seeking, then we are responsible for this ignorance. For instance: Owen did not know the good and therefore Owen did not choose what is good; Owen did not know the good because Owen was not seeking to know the good (he was content with what he already believed and did not think further seeking was necessary).

CONCLUSION

In light of these considerations, Modernity faces a problem that has resulted in widespread skepticism. Because modern thinkers made lofty claims in the name of reason, and because these claims were shown to be unjustified, reason and the pursuit of knowledge have been defamed. I suggest a clarification. Perhaps the problem is not with reason, but with the partial and limited use of reason – that is, a constructive use of reason where implications are drawn out from unsupported premises, as well as a continued division of reason into the practical and theoretical, with the practical viewed as the source of the good life. So whereas modern thinkers wanted to focus on general revelation to avoid bloody feuds over special revelation, it is a very limited and sparse view of general revelation that is offered. The problem of Modernity is thus affirming human reason to know general revelation (setting aside special revelation as mere opinion and divisive), yet limiting human knowledge to the practical (if God exists, we cannot know it or we must merely affirm it to support practical rationality). This limitation of rationality and general revelation had disastrous consequences for modern Europeans as they engaged with each other and those they encountered from around the world on purely practical terms while rejecting the work of critically analyzing basic beliefs to come to unity.

5

The Challenges of Naturalism

Legal Realism or Natural Law?

Smerdyakov articulated. ... "For if there's no everlasting God, there's no such thing as virtue, and there's no need of it. You were right there. So that's how I looked at it."
"Did you come to that yourself?" asked Ivan, with a wry smile.
"With your guidance."
"And now, I suppose, you believe in God, since you are giving back the money?"
"No, I don't believe," whispered Smerdyakov.
"Then why are you giving it back?"
"Leave off... that's enough!" Smerdyakov waved his hand again. "You used to say yourself that everything was lawful, so now why are you so upset, too?"[1]

In *The Brothers Karamazov*, Dostoyevsky famously deals with questions about law and morality from the perspective of those who reject God. Ivan Karamazov adopted a naturalistic philosophy because he was unable to believe in God given the amount and kind of evil in the world. However, he was not able to act on his beliefs; he merely discussed them and tried to persuade others. One of those he tried to persuade was Smerdyakov, who was able to act more consistently and, after adopting Ivan's perspective, killed Fyodor Karamazov. Can metaphysical naturalism support the idea of law as anything more than culturally or individually relative? Does the scientific method require naturalism, and is not the lesson of Modernity that in matters of knowledge we need to rely on the scientific method? This is the approach that many modern thinkers take, and it has important implications for law and jurisprudence.

1 Fyodor Mikhailovich Dostoevsky, *The Brothers Karamazov*, trans. by Constance Garnett (Chicago: Encyclopaedia Britannica, 1980), 335.

INTRODUCTION

Until now, this book has studied the relationship between God and the natural law. Can a theory of the world and of the natural law be constructed that does not rely on the idea of God? Can the justice of a law be determined apart from an appeal to a Creator? In this chapter, we study the rise of naturalism as a development toward the end of the Enlightenment. Where the early Enlightenment sought for a foundation for knowledge that was common to all humans and included in this some rather limited knowledge of God as creator and/or designer (but leaving redeemer for private beliefs in particular churches), naturalism continued the emphasis on the material world but rejected God as useless for any description of the world. It was asserted that "laws" were being discovered to explain causal processes that before had been attributed to God – for instance, laws concerning origins and design, such as the survival of the fittest.

Epistemologically, this naturalism is expressed in positivism that argues that only facts about the world known through sense data count as knowledge. This is an application of "Hume's Fork," which says that there are only matters of fact and relations of ideas, the latter never telling us about what actually exists. In this formulation, religious beliefs about what is not seen are considered mere opinions, and harmful opinions at that, because they have led to significant divisions and warfare. Therefore, the solution to this is to keep what is personal and opinion-based out of the realm of the public and to consider as public only what is accessible by all. Formally, as a rule about the public and private, this seems true. In detail, naturalism must prove its claim that all knowledge is limited to sense data of the material world, and therefore all belief about God is private.

With respect to the good, naturalism gives a positivist account of the origin of law based on these worldly, bodily concerns like safety and sustenance. Its enduring description of law is that of a mechanism for a stable society that maximizes access by all individuals to the goods of this life, which in turn results in happiness. Natural law is dismissed as an antiquated notion that relies on supernatural accounts of the purpose of life and an essentially "conservative" attempt to justify social hierarchies as based on "the nature of things." Thus, natural law makes sense for Cicero or Aquinas, who accepted a stratified society, but not for the modern individual world made up of changing particulars. Natural law liberalism attempts to address this and argues that in fact all law, including the liberalism of the Enlightenment era, relies on a kind of natural law thinking, and I believe there is much of importance in this claim. However, I take a slightly different approach in considering naturalism.

Although it rejects the idea of "natures," positivism relies on metaphysical naturalism to make the assertion that only the material world exists (nature). Clearly this indicates an ambiguity with respect to the term "nature." It seems that "nature" always refers to "what is," or "what kind of being something is." In this sense, the use of the word is not essentially different in these cases, but it is given competing content depending on the worldview of the user. So, the Greeks can argue that law should maintain the nature of things, and they believe the nature of things is a particular kind of stratified society. The Romans adopt this view and continue with the same purpose for law, as does medieval Europe. The Enlightenment introduces a changed view of "what is," and naturalism furthers this process.

So naturalism is affirming the formal relationship between law, the good, human nature, and what is real. The difference from Ancient or Medieval natural law is that naturalism denies that there is anything real beside the material world. Law and the good must be explained within those confines. If those confines are based on an incorrect belief about what is real, then they are distorting law and the good, and legal positivism will have those errors in all of its conclusions about law.

To consider the historical development from Enlightenment Deism to Naturalism, I look at some of the history of thinking about "law" as causal order. This is a broader sense of "law" than merely the moral law, but the moral law is itself part of such thinking about the causal order between choice and the good. We will see that naturalism arose out of a belief that God has no causal relationship to the world, or that the material world can be explained in law like fashion, apart from appealing to anything else. Of course, this is itself a belief about what is real. It is not self-evidently true, nor can it be proven true by its own standards.

The increasing success of natural science to explain the laws of nature became especially controversial in the nineteenth century with Darwin's explanation of the origin of species. This was quickly turned into a kind of natural law, sometimes called Social Darwinism, where the facts of Darwinism were used to give the *ought* of a moral system. Using naturalistic methodology, Marx sought to give a materialist account of human economy and civilization, which also inspired a natural law. Indeed, I argue that it is through Marxist metaphysics and existentialism's denial of essences that Modernity is finally challenged and overcome by postmodern thinkers. This is true in the case of Derrida's rejection of the logos and Foucault's reduction of law to power, but also many other attempts to develop natural law without a metaphysical absolute. If law is power, then in what way can a law be tested to determine if it is just or unjust? Foucault's solution is a brand of antinomianism.

It is here that the case for natural law after Modernity becomes most pronounced: If there are no natures, no essences or universals, there can be no natural law; the denial of natures is initially a metaphysical claim, but ultimately an epistemological claim, and a solution requires that both problems be addressed. This chapter bridges the periods of Modernity and Postmodernity in its study of how the problem of epistemology and essences led from one to the other. Although it is not only in science that final causes have been rejected, science is generally appealed to (in a circular manner) to justify this change. Indeed, final causes are still formally present in moral thinking, but Modernity has put individual desire in the place of the final cause. This chapter explains some of the metaphysics behind that change.

ARISTOTLE'S SOLUTION TO BEING AND BECOMING

Although we have already considered Aristotle's influence on natural law thinking, and how his belief about what is eternal shaped his belief about the good, it is worthwhile here to understand how these beliefs also shaped his thinking about the four causes and therefore the final cause (teleology). The influence of Aristotle with respect to science is typically taken to be negative. It will be helpful to consider how Aristotle came to develop his view of the unmoved mover as a response to specific problems that arose in Greek philosophy and that continue to pose problems for making sense of the scientific worldview. In the *Physics*, Aristotle said that to have knowledge, one must know the four causes: "Now, the causes being four, it is the business of the physicist to know about them all, and if he refers his problems back to all of them, he will assign the 'why' in the way proper to his science – the matter, the form, the mover, 'that for the sake of which'."[2] These causes relied on Aristotle's analysis of potentiality and actuality as a solution to the skepticism that arose in earlier Greek philosophy because of the impasse between appearance and reality, change and permanence. How can there be both being and becoming, and what is their relation? The difficulties in solving this problem lead to an impasse in Greek philosophy that Plato and Aristotle attempted to solve.

[2] Aristotle, "Physics," in *Aristotle: 1*, trans. R. P. Hardie and R. K. Gaye, Vol. 86 (New York: Encyclopedia Britannica, 1952), II.7.

Aristotle's solution involved an analysis of potentiality and actuality. Aristotle defined "nature" as the "principle of motion and change."[3] It has reality but is also becoming – it is changing from potentiality to actuality. To understand motion and change, more than a description is necessary – one must understand what is changing, how the change is affected, the formal essence of the change, and that toward which it is changing (the *telos*). This introduces the idea of a "primary cause," which plays an important role in later thinking about the God and the good. Aristotle said that "knowledge is the object of our inquiry, and men do not think they know a thing till they have grasped the 'why' of it (which is to grasp its primary cause). So clearly we too must do this as regards both coming to be and passing away and every kind of physical change, in order that, knowing their principles, we may try to refer to these principles each of our problems."[4]

The problem of motion is a problem of being and becoming. How can change occur and yet something still be? The acorn changes into an oak tree, but in the process, before it is an oak tree, it is no longer an acorn – so, what is it? Earlier Greek philosophy divided between saying there is only being and saying there is only becoming (both assumed something is and so assumed being in some sense). Aristotle's analysis of potentiality and actuality was an attempt to resolve the impasse. Aristotle said that no one doubts that there is motion,[5] which implies that no one doubts there is being and becoming. Therefore, according to Aristotle, there has always been being and becoming: "Let this conclude what we have to say in support of our contention that there never was a time when there was not motion, and never will be a time when there will not be motion."[6] But Aristotle distinguished between motion that is secondary – and hence derived – and that is primary. "We have argued that there always was motion and always will be motion throughout all time, and we have explained what is the first principle of this eternal motion: we have explained further which is the primary motion and which is the only motion that can be eternal: and we have pronounced the first movement to be unmoved."[7] Thus, the primary cause of motion and change is itself eternal and unmoved by anything else.

Aristotle's form of dualism differs from Plato's, where there is a clear distinction between spirit and matter. For Aristotle, the distinction is between

3 Ibid., III.1.
4 Ibid., II.3.
5 Ibid., VIII.1.
6 Ibid., VIII.1.
7 Ibid., VIII.9.

form and matter, and the forms are known through the material world. Thus, the unmoved mover is in motion, and from this Aristotle constructs his view of the solar system, based on his understanding of this eternal motion rather than observation. Such motion must be "rotatory" and must be at the circumference of a circle rather than at the center.

> So, too, in order that the motion may continue to be of the same character, the moved must not be subject to change in respect of its relation to the movement. Moreover the movement must occupy either the centre or the circumference, since these are the first principles from which a sphere is derived. But the things nearest the movement are those whose motion is quickest, and in this case it is the motion of the circumference that is the quickest: therefore the movement occupies the circumference.[8]

It is simple for the contemporary mind to dismiss this view of the solar system, but what is more difficult is to dismiss it and yet also offer a solution to the problems that Aristotle addressed: change and motion – being and becoming.

NEW SOLUTIONS TO THE SAME PROBLEMS: GALILEO, DESCARTES, NEWTON

The shift away from Aristotle included a shift away from the idea of final causes.[9] This had a significant effect on legal philosophy and natural law. It was Aristotle's framework that Galileo challenged, a framework that said the heavenly bodies were eternal and unchanging while the earth was undergoing change as it moved from potentiality to actuality and the final cause. By noting change in the sun, Galileo argued that the sun is not eternal and changeless and therefore challenged the foundation of Aristotelianism. He also distinguished between the kinds of questions asked by different fields, between the questions of science and the questions of religion: "Can an opinion be heretical and yet have no concern with the salvation of souls? Can the Holy Ghost be asserted not to have intended teaching us something that does concern our salvation? I would say here something that was heard from an ecclesiastic of the most eminent degree: 'That the intention of the Holy Ghost is to teach us how one goes to

8 Ibid., VIII.10.

9 Galileo Galilei (1564–1642) was an Italian natural philosopher who is best known for his work in astronomy. He noted inconsistencies in the Ptolemaic view of the solar system and in Aristotle's analysis of bodies in motion. He believed the book of nature was written in the language of mathematics.

heaven, not how heaven goes'."[10] Religion has to do with revealed knowledge and redemption, science with the mechanism of the universe – two different spheres that need not compete.

There was still a need to respond to the problems of change and permanence (this is one of the problems that Postmodernity is responding to as well), and this was done by abandoning the Aristotelian model in favor of a mathematical one. It has been said that Descartes is responsible for the shift to naturalism, based on his claim that God's immutability keeps him from acting in the creation, and his philosophy certainly did raise questions about the causal relationship of God to the world. I think Descartes contributed in a different way to the eventual rise of naturalism, in that his solution to the problem of knowledge and sense data, which relied on God's assurance that appearance tells us about reality, was insufficient and gave fuel to the empiricists whose explanation of sense data did not need to refer to God for support. Descartes said, "All science consists in sure and evident knowledge,"[11] and "in treating of the objects proposed for investigation what we have to examine is not what others have opined, nor what we ourselves may conjecture, but what we can clearly and evidently intuit, or can deduce with certainty: knowledge is not obtainable in any other way."[12]

Where Aristotle required the four causes to have knowledge, Descartes focused on intuition and ideas. "No paths leading to certainty in the knowledge of truth are open to men save self-evidencing intuition and necessary deduction. ... And it is evident that the mind's intuitive power extends to all those simple natures and to the knowing of the necessary connections between them."[13] Here we have a solution to the problem of change and permanence in a different form: Mathematical truths are thought to be eternal and changeless and are applied to explain the changing world. Descartes appealed to God to solve the problem of appearance and reality.[14] As a theist, Descartes distinguished between God, who is a spirit, and the created, material world – God is unchanging, the material world is changing. He appealed to God to solve the problem of appearance and

10 Galileo, "Letter to the Grand Duchess Christina of Tuscany," http://www.fordham.edu/halsall/mod/galileo-tuscany.html (accessed March 12, 2008).

11 Rene Descartes, "Rules for the Guidance of our Native Powers," in *Descartes: Philosophical Writings*, ed. Norman Kemp Smith (New York: Random House, 1958), 4.

12 Ibid., 8.

13 Rene Descartes, "Meditations on First Philosophy," in *Descartes: Philosophical Writings*, ed. Norman Kemp Smith (New York: Random House, 1958), 65.

14 Ibid., IV.

reality – God assures that there is a relationship between our ideas and the world.

However, Descartes's appeal has been rejected as circular: Proof for God's existence is based on clear and distinct ideas,[15] and we can trust these clear and distinct ideas because they are given by God.[16] This appeal to God is different than Aristotle's appeal to an unmoved mover in that God is a spirit, and the material world (and therefore physical motion) is created by God and not eternal. Furthermore, Descartes did encourage investigation into how the world works through an experiment method. This was lacking in Aristotle, who, although he gathered data about animals, plants, and stars, was limited by his notion of the formal cause from the kind of experimental investigation that we consider to be "scientific."

Descartes's influence affected a change from Aristotelianism to "modern science" where mathematics plays a central role, and where mechanism (Aristotle's efficient cause) is isolated from other types of causes. Francis Bacon[17] also played a central role, and perhaps a more important one, because his approach did not rely on an appeal to God in the way that Descartes did. He rejected both rationalists and empiricists: "Those who have treated of the sciences have been either empirics or dogmatical. The former like ants only heap up and use their store, the latter like spiders spin out of their own webs. The bee, a mean between both, extracts matter from the flowers of the garden and the field, but works and fashions it by its own efforts."[18] He proposed an investigative method and a modified form of induction:

> In forming axioms, we must invent a different form of induction from that hitherto in use; not only for the proof and discovery of principles (as they are called), but also of minor, intermediate, and, in short, every kind of axioms. The induction which proceeds by simple enumeration is puerile, leads to uncertain conclusions, and is exposed to danger from one contradictory instance, deciding generally from too small a number of facts, and those only the most obvious. But a really useful induction for the discovery and demonstration of the arts and sciences, should separate nature by proper rejections and exclusions, after collecting a sufficient number of negatives. Now this has not been done, nor even attempted,

15 Ibid., III.

16 Ibid., IV.

17 Sir Francis Bacon (1561–1626) was a lawyer and philosopher. He wrote in defense of the scientific method, and distinguished the book of nature and the book of scripture.

18 Francis Bacon, "Novum Organum," in *Francis Bacon*, Vol. 30 (Chicago: Encyclopedia Britannica, 1952), 126.

> except perhaps by Plato, who certainly uses this form of induction in some measure, to sift definitions and ideas. But much of what has never entered the thoughts of man must necessarily be employed, in order to exhibit a good and legitimate mode of induction or demonstration, so as even to render it essential for us to bestow more pains upon it than have hitherto been bestowed on syllogisms. The assistance of inductions is to serve us not only in the discovery of axioms, but also in defining our notions. Much indeed is to be hoped from such an induction as has been described.[19]

Bacon's system did have a reference to God, but I argue that his system is the one that comes down to us in modified form. Descartes's system was influential in its appeal to mathematics, but other systems can also support the need for mathematics (consider Pythagoras). Bacon encouraged an investigation of the world, gave a bifurcation between the world of revealed religion and the natural sciences, and while making mention of God, he did not do so in a way that is essential to his theory – in other words, the investigative method can proceed without mention of God:

> For certain it is that God worketh nothing in nature but by second causes: and if they would have it otherwise believed, it is mere imposture, as it were in favour towards God; and nothing else but to offer to the author of truth the unclean sacrifice of a lie. But further, it is an assured truth, and a conclusion of experience, that a little or superficial knowledge of philosophy may incline the mind of man to atheism, but a further proceeding therein doth bring the mind back again to religion. For in the entrance of philosophy, when the second causes, which are next unto the senses, do offer themselves to the mind of man, if it dwell and stay there it may induce some oblivion of the highest cause; but when a man passeth on further, and seeth the dependence of causes, and the works of Providence, then, according to the allegory of the poets, he will easily believe that the highest link of nature's chain must needs be tied to the foot of Jupiter's chair. To conclude, therefore, let no man upon a weak conceit of sobriety or an ill-applied moderation think or maintain that a man can search too far, or be too well studied in the book of God's word, or in the book of God's works, divinity or philosophy, but rather let men endeavour an endless progress or proficiency in both; only let men beware that they apply both to charity, and not to swelling; to use, and not to ostentation; and again, that they do not unwisely mingle or confound these learnings together.[20]

19 Ibid., 128.

20 Francis Sir Bacon, "Advancement of Learning," in *Francis Bacon*, Vol. 30 (New York: Encyclopedia Britannica, 1952), 4.

Here we have mention of secondary causes and their grounding in the highest cause, the primary cause. This solves the problem of change and motion by locating these in the secondary causes of the created order, and permanence in God who is eternal. This is also provides a look at empirical and logical gaps; knowledge of the secondary causes is an empirical matter, whereas their relationship to God is a logical relationship.

NEWTONIAN DESCRIPTION OF PHENOMENA AND LOCKE'S EMPIRICISM

Newton's natural philosophy follows this method. Indeed, Newton's gravitational theory was criticized by Cartesians for not supplying a mechanism and for involving "action at a distance." Newton was aware of this criticism and responded:

> Hitherto we have explained the phenomena of the heavens and of our sea by the power of gravity, but have not yet assigned the cause of this power ... hitherto I have not been able to discover the cause of those properties of gravity from phenomena, and I frame no hypotheses; for whatever is not deduced from the phenomena is to be called an hypothesis; and hypotheses, whether metaphysical or physical, whether of occult qualities or mechanical, have no place in experimental philosophy. In this philosophy particular propositions are inferred from the phenomena, and afterwards rendered general by induction. Thus it was that the impenetrability, the mobility, and the impulsive force of bodies, and the laws of motion and of gravitation, were discovered. And to us it is enough that gravity does really exist, and acts according to the laws which we have explained, and abundantly serves to account for all the motions of the celestial bodies, and of our sea.[21]

This represents a shift as important as the change from Aristotle to Galileo. Abandoned altogether is the attempt to solve the problem of change and motion, being and becoming, and instead Newton is content with describing the phenomenon of motion. This description relies on mathematics (indeed, Newton invented calculus as an aid in such description), because physical motion can be quantified. But this quantification tells us nothing about being in itself, or motion in itself, nor does it address the problems that occupied Aristotle.

Newton appealed to God in the same way that Bacon did:

[21] Isaac Newton, "General Scholium," in *Newton, Huygens*, Vol. 34 (Chicago: Encyclopedia Britannica, 1952), 371.

> This most beautiful system of the sun, planets, and comets, could only proceed from the counsel and dominion of an intelligent and powerful Being. And if the fixed stars are the centres of other like systems, these, being formed by the like wise counsel, must be all subject to the dominion of One. … This Being governs all things, not as the soul of the world, but as Lord over all. … The Supreme God is a Being eternal, infinite, absolutely perfect.[22]

God is the explanation of the design and beauty of the universe, but is not required for a description of the motion of the universe. This is still one of the most popular appeals to God: God explains design, or irreducible complexity. Bacon and Newton speak of God as the primary cause, and state that the natural sciences are concerned with the secondary causes created by God. Human law falls entirely into this level of secondary causation.

To defend this approach, Locke wrote in his *Essay*:

> The commonwealth of learning is not at this time without master-builders, whose mighty designs, in advancing the sciences, will leave lasting monuments to the admiration of posterity: but every one must not hope to be a Boyle or a Sydenham; and in an age that produces such masters as the great Huygenius and the incomparable Mr. Newton, with some others of that strain, it is ambition enough to be employed as an underlabourer in clearing the ground a little, and removing some of the rubbish that lies in the way to knowledge. … Vague and insignificant forms of speech, and abuse of language, have so long passed for mysteries of science; and hard and misapplied words, with little or no meaning, have, by prescription, such a right to be mistaken for deep learning and height of speculation, that it will not be easy to persuade either those who speak or those who hear them, that they are but the covers of ignorance, and hindrance of true knowledge.[23]

What must be cleared to make way for the work of Newton is not just Aristotle, but the innate ideas of the Cartesians. In contrast to Descartes, Locke argued that there are no innate ideas, and that all knowledge is from the senses: "Whence has it [the mind] all the materials of reason and knowledge? To this I answer, in one word, from experience."[24] What appear to be innate ideas are really intuitions based on the strength of our perceptions. Understanding comes when we know the meaning of a statement, and even though we may quickly assent to the truth of supposed innate ideas, this is really because we have come to understand what they mean through experience. "The different clearness of our knowledge seems

22 Ibid., 369.

23 Locke and Nidditch, *An Essay Concerning Human Understanding* (Locke 1952, 89).

24 Ibid. (2.2).

to me to lie in the different ways of perception the mind has of the agreement or disagreement of any of its ideas. For if we reflect on our ways of thinking, we will find that sometimes the mind perceives the agreement or disagreement of two ideas immediately by themselves, without the intervention of any other: and this I think we may call intuitive knowledge."[25] But much knowledge cannot be attained this way, and instead must be attained through investigation in the world and demonstration through experiment.[26] This demonstration still relies on perception, but connects perceptions the connectedness of which we do not readily see by relating them to other perceptions.

Like Bacon and Newton, Locke did appeal to God. Indeed, he said we have certain knowledge of God's existence, and God's existence is one of the first things we come to know. "We have an intuitive knowledge of our own existence, and a demonstrative knowledge of the existence of a God: of the existence of anything else, we have no other but a sensitive knowledge; which extends not beyond the objects present to our senses."[27] Locke distinguished between reason and faith in a way that reason can operate independently of faith or belief in God (compared to Descartes). Faith is needed, according to Locke, to confirm certain beliefs that are difficult to know through reason – like the immortality of the soul, or moral systems – or to reveal other truths not knowable from reason that God wants us to know.

I argue that this bifurcation between knowledge derived from the senses and knowledge from scriptures, called faith, established a line of development that ends in the rejection of knowledge of God (although many still believe in God) and any need to appeal to God in understanding the operations of the physical world (no longer understood as secondary causes because the idea of "secondary" implies there is a primary cause). Appeal can be made to the senses, to the quantification of motion, without any appeal to God. Indeed, appeals to God can appear superfluous to any explanation of the natural world, whether to describe motion or human law.

THE CHALLENGE OF HUME AND SUCCESS OF NATURALISM

I do not think that naturalism is traced directly to Descartes (although perhaps it is indirectly), in that his system relied on God to give assurance of the relationship between appearance and reality; instead, naturalism can

25 Ibid. (2.1).
26 Ibid. (2.3).
27 Ibid. (2.21).

be traced to Hume's criticism of the empirical method found in Bacon and Newton, and defended by Locke. Hume's criticism is of other empiricists, like Locke, but in his work he challenges the idea of causation that is the central piece of Descartes's philosophy as well. His challenge is essentially to renew the ancient problem of appearance and reality. What is the basis for the appearance of causation? Hume's analysis of causation is important for the discussion about God and the natural law. Hume limits the sources of knowledge to sense data and the relationship between ideas.[28] According to Hume, as we experience change, we begin to notice patterns and regularities, and we call these causation. But because this is based on our extremely limited experience, we cannot say we have knowledge about causation, or that we know what to expect tomorrow. Applied to law as the means to the good, this claim about causation would undermine any moral law.

Hume noted that we never experience causation itself, only two events that we link together as regularities.[29] These are not linked by necessity but only in our limited experience. This is by implication a rejection of Descartes' method of knowing, and a reject of the appeal to God made by Descartes. But this also opens up troubling problems about appearance and reality, and about change and permanence for Locke. Indeed, Hume harkens back to one of the views that led to ancient skepticism when he said: when I look inside all I see are mental images – all is change, all is becoming.[30]

> What will suffice to prove this hypothesis to the satisfaction of every fair enquirer, is to shew from daily experience and observation, that the objects, which are variable or interrupted, and yet are suppos'd to continue the same, are such only as consist of a succession of parts, connected together by resemblance, contiguity, or causation. For as such a succession answers evidently to our notion of diversity, it can only be by mistake we ascribe to it an identity; and as the relation of parts, which leads us into this mistake, is really nothing but a quality, which produces an association of ideas, and an easy transition of the imagination from one to another, it can only be from the resemblance, which this act of the mind bears to that, by which we contemplate one continu'd object, that the error arises. Our chief business, then, must be to prove, that all objects, to which we ascribe identity, without

[28] David Hume, *Hume's Enquiries*, ed. L.A. Selby-Bigge (New York: The Clarendon Press, 1966), 371.
[29] Ibid., 75.
[30] David Hume, A Treastise of Human Nature (Mineola: Dover Publications, Inc., 2003). (Hume 2003, IV.VI).

> observing their invariablness and uninteruptedness, are such as consist of a succession of related objects.[31]

Hume applies this to the rejection of miracles as divine acts, given that our knowledge of these is limited to our sense data (we cannot appeal to scripture/testimony to justify calling an event a divine act since these are simply further instances of sense data). Furthermore, Hume argues that there is overwhelming (if not universal) confirmation that "miracles" are explainable through natural causes. Indeed, this tension between scientific knowledge and revealed knowledge has been summarized in the question "what has Jerusalem to do with Athens" by Tertullian, and continues to be explored by thinkers like John Caiazza ("The Athens/Jerusalem Template") and Paul Moser.

Hume began his study on morals by noting that the recent (relative to his time) debate focused on whether morality was grounded in human nature or in changing custom and education. Hume came down on the side of human nature.[32] For us this is another reminder of the formal relationship between beliefs about human nature, the good, and law. Hume accepted a naturalistic account of human nature, and therefore conceived of the good as pleasure, and thus law relates to what is useful for pleasure. Hume injected a moral psychology here that fits into the Scottish Enlightenment debates. However, such discussions are only as good as his presuppositions about human nature.

Hume is influential today because he provides positivists with an account of why law is not the product of command alone, and how law changes and adapts to human needs. What is not obvious is that Hume's assertions can survive his own epistemology and academic skepticism. I will turn to a consideration of skepticism in a moment.

KANT'S TWO-WORLD SOLUTION TO THE PROBLEM OF APPEARANCE AND REALITY IN CAUSATION

This skepticism about causation troubled Kant and was the impetus for awakening him from his dogmatic slumbers. However, Kant was also troubled by the idea of causation/determination, especially in the area of the will. His resulting system distinguishes between the phenomenal world of

[31] Ibid. (Hume 2003, IV.VI).

[32] David Fate Norton, "Hume and the Foundations of Morality," in *The Cambridge Companion to Hume*, ed. David Fate Norton (Cambridge: Cambridge University Press, 1993).

experience and change and the noumenal world of things in themselves.[33] Causation applies to the world of experience, but not to the things in themselves. The problem for this explanation is the following: Is there a causal relationship between the things in themselves and the phenomena? If not, then the noumenal realm serves no purpose in the system and cannot be intelligibly spoken of. If so, then causation does apply to the noumenal realm. Kant appealed to God in order to justify morality – this continues to be one of the most popular and most used examples of appeals to God. It is said that science tells about how things are, and religion/belief in God gives values and morals (not much different than Galileo's solution).

The problem of change and permanence, being and becoming, is addressed by the model that being in itself is unchanging, and we attempt to make sense of changing appearances through the use of mathematics, which is also eternal and unchanging. Thus, reality is only approximated by scientific models, which are increasingly improved and modified (C. S. Peirce). In this model, there is no room for appeals to God as such appeals literally serve no purpose: we do not need God as the eternal, final cause toward which all things are striving; we do not need God to assure us that appearances match reality; and we do not need to appeal to God to explain anomalies in appearances because these will eventually be explained through empirical research. Changes in the world are explained through efficient/natural causes through the use of mathematics.

DARWINISM AND NINETEENTH-CENTURY EVOLUTIONARY LEGAL THEORY

> The second half of the 20th century witnessed a resurgence of evolutionary theory in both the natural sciences and the social sciences. The most significant feature of this movement has been the extension of the Darwinian theory of evolution – or, more accurately, the neo-Darwinian synthesis – to human culture.[34]

Although likely the most famous of the naturalists, Darwin is nested within a century of attempts to explain origins by appealing only to forces now seen and projecting these into the past at magnitudes currently observed.[35]

33 Immanuel Kant, *Critique of Pure Reason*, trans. Norman Kemp Smith (New York: Palgrave Macmillan, 2003), A251.

34 Suri Ratnapala, *Jurisprudence* (Cambridge: Cambridge University Press, 2009).

35 Charles Darwin (1809–1882) is best known for his law of the survival of the fittest. Relying on work by earlier naturalists such as his grandfather and Charles Lyell, as well

Suri Ratnapala points out that English Common Law provided Darwin with a context of thinking about how law grows, and seems to contradict the Enlightenment claim that law begins after the Social Contract.[36]

Like Hobbes, Darwin began with the war of nature, and argued that from this "the most exalted object which we are capable of conceiving, namely the production of the higher animals, directly follows."[37] He argued that this accords more with his view of God, and that it gives a beauty to life he does not see in competing theories. Of course, these are not scientific arguments.

His empirical arguments require the acceptance of Uniformitarianism,[38] which claims that the present can be entirely explained in terms of the now observable forces projected into the past. He affirms this in saying:

> As all the living forms of life are the lineal descendants of those which lived long before the Cambrian epoch, we may feel certain that the ordinary succession by generation has never once been broken, and that no cataclysm has desolated the whole world. Hence we may look with some confidence to a secure future of great length. And as natural selection works solely by and for the good of each being, all corporeal and mental endowments will tend to progress towards perfection.[39]

And:

> To my mind it accords better with what we know of the laws impressed on matter by the Creator, that the production and extinction of the past and present inhabitants of the world should have been due to secondary causes, like those determining the birth and death of the individual. When I view all beings not as special creations, but as the lineal descendants of some few beings which lived long before the first bed of the Cambrian system was deposited, they seem to me to become ennobled. Judging from the past, we may safely infer that not one living species will transmit its unaltered likeness to a distant futurity.[40]

as economists like Thomas Malthus, Darwin suggested a natural explanation of the origin of species. While this theory fit in with the intellectual climate of the day (which was drifting toward naturalism away from theism), it also is thought to explain why nature is full of waste, suffering, and death.

36 Ibid.

37 Charles Darwin, "The Origin of Species by Means of Natural Selection," in *Darwin*, ed. Robert Maynard Hutchins, Vol. 49 (Chicago: Encyclopedia Britannica, 1952).

38 Owen Anderson, "Charles Lyell, Uniformitarianism, and Interpretive Principles," in *(Re) Creating Science in 19th Century Britain*, ed. Amanda Caleb (Newcastle upon Tyne: Cambridge Scholars Press, 2007).

39 Darwin, *The Origin of Species by Means of Natural Selection.*

40 Ibid.

Perhaps, if Uniformitarianism is true, then so is Darwinism. Further, why not limit our studies to secondary causation; perhaps this is the only kind of causation? If God bears no causal relationship to the world, then in what sense is God real?

Darwin was confident that this method could be applied also to the study of human moral psychology and origins. "Psychology will be securely based on the foundation already well laid by Mr. Herbert Spencer, that of the necessary acquirement of each mental power and capacity by gradation. Much light will be thrown on the origin of man and his history."[41] This history is governed by natural selection, which operates along utilitarian lines in governing each species.

> Natural selection will never produce in a being any structure more injurious than beneficial to that being, for natural selection acts solely by and for the good of each. No organ will be formed, as Paley has remarked, for the purpose of causing pain or for doing an injury to its possessor. If a fair balance be struck between the good and evil caused by each part, each will be found on the whole advantageous.[42]

With respect to our current study, we can understand Darwin to have given expression to the origin of life within naturalism. This explanation operates on the utilitarian claim that changes occur to benefit a species, and that by projecting current forces into the past we must appeal to great spans of time to explain what we now see. Darwin himself noted that any problems with utilitarianism will translate into problems with his theory:

> The foregoing remarks lead me to say a few words on the protest lately made by some naturalists, against the utilitarian doctrine that every detail of structure has been produced for the good of its possessor. They believe that many structures have been created for the sake of beauty, to delight man or the Creator (but this latter point is beyond the scope of scientific discussion), or for the sake of mere variety, a view already discussed. Such doctrines, if true, would be absolutely fatal to my theory.[43]

Darwin noted the formal relationship between his beliefs about reality and what these beliefs entail about human nature, and from here to the good and law. The debate is not whether such mechanisms as described by Darwin produce new species or merely variation within a species (as has been the focus of the past 150 years), but rather whether his presuppositions are in

[41] Ibid.
[42] Ibid.
[43] Ibid.

fact true. Obviously naturalists believe they are true, and just as obviously non-naturalists will find them false.

This is not a debate between science and religion, but between presuppositions. Because these presuppositions shape how empirical data is interpreted, empirical data cannot be appealed to in order to adjudicate between presuppositions. Rather, we must consider the meaning of the claim that only matter exists and matter is not created. Although Darwin retained references to the Creator, evolutionary theory has quickly jettisoned such appeals and limited study to secondary causes as truly scientific. Can this be successful in the realm of human moral laws? Can these be explained and legislated only with reference to evolution and utilitarianism? I argue in the following sections that such claims do not have the support of rational justification.

THOMAS HUXLEY AND HERBERT SPENCER

Evolutionary legal theory begins its consideration of ethics and law within the context of beliefs about what is real and the human condition.[44] Here I want to consider Thomas Huxley and Herbert Spencer as examples of how ethical theory was developed along evolutionary lines closely after Darwin's time. These retain the utilitarianism of Darwin and its claim that happiness is the good and law should maximize happiness for as many as possible while minimizing harm. Furthermore, both illustrate how these claims are set within a worldview about what is real and how humans fit into the cosmos. Consider Huxley's view of the human condition:

> The motive of the drama of human life is the necessity, laid upon every man who comes into the world, of discovering the mean between self-assertion and self-restraint suited to his character and his circumstances. And the eternally tragic aspect of the drama lies in this: that the problem set before us is one the elements of which can be but imperfectly known, and of which even an approximately right solution rarely presents itself, until that stern critic, aged experience, has been furnished with ample justification for venting his sarcastic humour upon the irreparable blunders we have already made.[45]

44 Thomas Huxley (1825–1895) is known for having coined the word "agnosticism" to describe his approach to religion. He gave vigorous support to Darwinism and natural explanations of life.

Herbert Spencer (1820–1903) was an English philosopher who applied the theory of evolution to the study of morality and society.

45 Thomas Henry Huxley, *Evolution and Ethics and Other Essays*, Authorized ed. (New York: D. Appleton and Company, 1896), 334.

Humans can hardly know anything, and are part of larger cosmic drama that they can never understand. He begins his work on evolution and ethics by setting the human condition into the vast amounts of time needed by naturalism to account for the evolutionary process.

Spencer began his *The Principles of Ethics* by stating that this field is the study of conduct, and to understand conduct we must understand how it evolved. The individuals of the human race must be thought of in relation to the whole of the human race. Spencer accepts this kind of utilitarian thinking and essentially gives a utilitarian ethical theory based on Darwin's naturalism. He viewed humans as just one more kind of animal, and therefore believed that his many analogies from the animal world were relevant for considering human conduct. If humans are different from animals, then these examples are not analogous.

Spencer's utilitarianism uses a means/ends thinking that is appropriate for consequentialism but should not be confused with teleology. Evolution guides conduct so that more and more of the type of conduct aimed at a worthless end is cut out of the species. Conduct becomes more efficient and more focused on survival. This is not simply survival of an individual or a race, but of life in a larger sense. He argues "that perfect adjustment of acts to ends in maintaining individual life and rearing new individuals, which is effected by each without hindering others from effecting like perfect adjustments, is, in its very definition, shown to constitute a kind of conduct that can be approached only as war decreases and dies out."[46] From here he argues that the word good means, "above all other things, the conduct of one who aids the sick in reacquiring normal vitality assists the unfortunate to recover the means of maintaining themselves, defends those who are threatened with harm in person, property, or reputation, and aids whatever promises to improve the living of all his fellows."[47] While these are acts of kindness and should be encouraged as such, for Spencer they are the means to achieving the good because a peaceful society in which everyone can do as they please without interfering with what others are doing is the highest good.

I agree with Spencer that a peaceful society of all humans is a wonderful condition. However, I believe it is the effect of pursuing the same good, not the good itself. If man does not live by bread alone, what else has Spencer and the naturalists offered? If the material world has not existed from eternity, why should we limit our inquiry to the natural world, and why should

[46] Herbert Spencer, *The Principles of Ethics, Vol. 1* (Indianapolis: Liberty Classics, 1978).
[47] Ibid.

we assume that all aspects of reality are explained in terms of secondary material causes?

EMPIRICISM AND PRAGMATISM LEADING TO SKEPTICISM

Empiricism and pragmatism limit explanation to efficient causes and the immediate workings of physical processes ("how" questions, rather than "why," "what is it," "where did it ultimately come from," "where is it going," or "for what ultimate purpose" questions). Some speculative or abstract physical sciences address "larger" questions, but they are generally seen to be nonempirical and to not produce the same results as their more empirical cousins. This limits the natural sciences as well as the rest of the academy. Significant energy is put into explaining immediate physical processes, and significant success is attained. "Success" is defined in terms of accurate prediction, and "fit" within the rest of the system (does the hypothesis require significant change to what is already assumed, or does it "fit" nicely in the existing system?). This success was, and is, used as further confirmation that the right path has been chosen, and this reduces to naturalism.

With respect to laws of human morality or society, these same methods are applied. Human society as a compromise of competing individual wills, or competing individual desires and interest groups, requires law to limit friction and so maximize stability and contentment in pursuit of individual/group goals, all in the setting of survival. This affirms the formal relationship between law, the good, and human nature in that this view of law is founded on a belief about "how things are" and what is worth pursuing. Laws of human conduct relate merely to the physical world, and an appeal to God is not needed to explain how human society can maximize compromise between competing desires.

Rejecting Any Appeal to God in Explanation

Given this historical context, appeals to God as an explanation for the immediate workings of physical processes are viewed as problematic for a number of reasons:

1. They are nonempirical, non-verifiable, and non-repeatable. This means there is no place for them as an object of sensory investigation, given that knowledge has been limited to the empirical. As explanations, they "don't make sense."

2. As explanations, they are unnecessary. The same physical process can be explained through physical efficient causes without appeals to God. Where this explanation is not yet available, there is trust that greater empirical investigation will eventually yield the explanation. This trust is based on (a) success thus far achieved and (b) the fact that it is the only viable option given the nature of knowledge (sense data).
3. As explanations, they are unhelpful. They do not add anything to the explanation and raise greater questions that have not – and perhaps cannot, within empiricism – be answered. The appeal to sense data by Bacon, Newton, and Locke can be kept, and their view of, and reliance on, God can be jettisoned.
4. As explanations, they are anachronistic. They come from a time when the systems of Aristotle and Descartes limited science or relied on appeals to God, and are therefore out of place with subsequent development. Their use indicates that the person making the appeal is not "up to speed" on developments, discoveries, and successes of the past three centuries.
5. As explanations, they commit the fallacy of "appeal to ignorance." For many, God continues to be important. But as an explanation, God tends to be left to areas of the "unknown," the distant past, distant future, or afterlife. But these areas are simply gaps that can be filled through greater empirical investigation. Design, values, beauty, and so on can be explained as empirical gaps, or as part of the appearance/reality problem.

Thus, methodological naturalism emerges as the only reliable theory of knowledge and as a solution to the problem of change and permanence. This view claims to make no comment about being (metaphysical atheism), but it does imply that nothing can be known about what is nonmaterial (where the material world is the world of extension that can be measured and quantified), and therefore if God exists, God cannot be known (and therefore need not be posited at all). It is also a direct influence on postmodern thinking in that while postmodern thinkers take time to show naturalists that their view is not interpretation-free, Postmodernity accepts many of the limitations on knowledge claims given by naturalism.

I argue that a proper understanding of logical and empirical gaps can also help in solving problems about being and becoming, change and permanence. This will be helpful in understanding the conflict between science and religion because these often involve conflicts about the domain of knowledge between what are empirical and logical matters.

Having given an overview of the problem, I now argue that an important but little recognized contributor to the problem is a difference in kinds of gaps, and that this difference has hindered the pursuit of explanations. Noting the difference between empirical gaps and logical gaps is therefore important for the discussion about appeals to God, and also important for understanding what constitutes a scientific worldview and how to address ancient problems that continue to affect the search for knowledge.

Two Kinds of Gaps in Explanations

The kinds of gaps considered thus far in this chapter have been empirical gaps, such as design, change, values, and meaning. Greater empirical investigation can help explain these, or at least explain why they are important to the human (although not part of reality).

> Newton and other scientists used God to fill gaps in their scientific accounts – until better data or new theories made divine intervention unnecessary. The 'God of the gaps,' invoked as a hypothesis to account for scientifically unexplained facts, or introduced as a cause producing effects on the same level as natural causes, retreated further as each of the gaps in human knowledge was closed.[48]

Is there a role left for God in the halls of academia or the research labs? In his article, "What Is a Scientific Worldview, and How Does It Bear on the Interplay of Science and Religion?", Matthew Orr discusses the difference between unscientific and non-scientific components of worldviews. Although he dismisses the personal creator of Genesis as facing empirical problems, he states that science is amoral and a full worldview must contain nonscientific components to fill the gaps. This is not unlike my distinction between empirical and logical gaps, although rather than calling them nonscientific, I believe they are meta-scientific (assumed by empirical investigation, transcending – in the Kantian sense – scientific investigation). But here I am speaking about something more basic than these, about being itself, and putting this in the historical context of how thinkers have tried to defend or explain what Carvalho says science must presuppose. This applies to scientific laws, but also to human law. Is there a law-like way to organize society, and how do we understand such laws? What do they presuppose?

[48] Ian Barbour, *Issues in Science and Religion* (New York: Harper & Row, 1971), 1.

Logical Gaps – Being and Non-Being

The most basic gap is a logical gap, and it has to do with being. Aristotle tried to solve the problem of being and becoming, which is one step removed from the most basic, the problem of being and non-being. This is a logical gap in that it cannot be addressed empirically; indeed, being is assumed in all sense experiences – there can be no experience of non-being. All scientific investigation relies on sense data, and therefore assumes being – it would beg the question to use sense data to investigate the difference between being and non-being. No laws can be applied to non-being, no tests done, no observations made – it is nothing. The most basic question, slightly more basic than being and becoming (although related), is "is some (all) being eternal, or was there ever only non-being?" Empirical scientists do not hesitate to weigh in on this question, and as we will see, they come down on all three sides (all is eternal, only some is eternal, none is eternal).

Carl Sagan began his influential work, *Cosmos*, by saying "The Cosmos is all that is or ever was or ever will be."[49] By way of contrast, Alan Guth says that the universe sprang into being from absolutely nothing, nada, zip (on the cover of April 2002 *Discover* magazine).[50] The origin of being is not an empirical gap but a logical gap. Once there is being, the laws that govern that being can be understood in increasing detail through empirical investigation. But the origin of being itself cannot be empirically investigated because it cannot be experienced. Nor can a greater understanding of the laws of being explain the origin of being in that these laws presuppose being; the existence of these laws must be explained, and it cannot be the explanation of their own existence. If the material universe is eternal, then the laws that govern it are also eternal and could be said to be "brute facts," but in such a case there is no origin that needs explaining.

Guth makes the mistake of using the laws to explain their own existence: "If the creation of the universe is to be described by physical laws that embody the conservation of energy, then the universe must have the same energy as whatever it was created from. If the universe was created from nothing, then the total energy must be zero."[51] Apparently these laws are uncreated and govern matter but are not explained by matter (i.e., are

49 Carl Sagan (1934–1996), an American astronomer.

50 Alan Guth (b. 1947), an American physicist.

51 Alan Guth, *The Inflationary Universe: The Quest for a New Theory of Cosmic Origins* (Reading: Helix Books, 1997), 9.

not owing to the nature of matter, which would mean they are cocreated with matter). Guth wants his theory to appear empirical, but his claim that these laws are eternal is not an empirical claim. There simply is no way to empirically fill in this gap – it is a logical gap.

However, failure to note this logical gap has led some cosmologists to assert that being came from nothing, or from non-being. Alan Guth has said: "Conceivably, everything can be created from nothing. And 'everything' might include a lot more than what we can see. In the context of inflationary cosmology, it is fair to say that the universe is the ultimate free lunch."[52] Of course, everything should mean everything, which means all being came into being from non-being. Stephen Hawking[53] affirms that "energy cannot be created out of nothing"[54] and explains what Alan Guth might be speaking of when he uses the term "nothing":

> What we think of as "empty" space cannot be completely empty because that would mean that all the fields, such as the gravitational and electromagnetic fields, would have to be exactly zero. However, the value of a field and its rate of change with time are like the position and velocity of a particle: the uncertainty principle implies that the more accurately one knows one of these quantities, the less accurately one can know the other. So in empty space it would have both a precise value (zero) and a precise rate of change (also zero). There must be a certain minimum amount of uncertainty, or quantum fluctuations, in the value or the field.[55]

Some scientists suggest that the universe is without beginning, eternal, and they offer an oscillating picture to explain this. Hawking once suggested such an oscillating system, but has since come to reject it. The implication is that all that exists has always existed, there was no creation, and therefore another gap filled by God is closed. In discussing the possibility that the universe is oscillating between the Big Bang and the Big Crunch, Hawking says: "if the universe is really completely self-contained, having no boundary or edge, it would have neither beginning nor end: it would simply be. What place, then, for a creator?"[56] More recently, Hawking has claimed:

52 Ibid., 15.
53 Stephen Hawking (b. 1942) is an English theoretical physicist.
54 Stephen W. Hawking, *A Brief History of Time* (New York: Bantam Books, 1988), 106.
55 Ibid., 105.
56 Ibid., 141.

> [B]ecause there is a law like gravity, the universe can and will create itself from nothing. ... Spontaneous creation is the reason there is something rather than nothing, why the universe exists, why we exist. It is not necessary to invoke God to light the blue touch paper and set the universe going. Why are the fundamental laws as we have described them? ... We've seen that there must be a law like gravity. ... For these reasons M-theory is the *only* candidate for a complete theory of the universe. If it is finite – and this has yet to be proved – it will be a model of a universe that creates itself. We must be part of this universe, because there is no other consistent model ... the fact that we human beings – who are ourselves mere collections of fundamental particles of nature – have been able to come this close to an understanding of the laws governing us and our universe is a great triumph.[57]

Note how in this passage Hawking links his beliefs about laws to his beliefs about human nature and all of this to his beliefs about the nature and origin of the universe. Why begin with his belief that only the material world exists and must be explained in material terms? Isn't invoking a material law to explain the origin of all material things a self-contradiction? Or perhaps he is falling back on a kind of Platonism, and the law of gravity is part of the ideal realm. In this case he can no longer consistently make claims that only the material world exists, and he is stepping into a history of philosophical discourse that prevents him from making simple assertions about how his theory is "scientific." Indeed, his reliance on a certain view of mathematics is reminiscent of the Pythagoreans and is more akin to rationalism than empiricism. The tendency of the naturalist is to not notice the influence of commonsense realism on their belief system and to assert conclusions from these presuppositions as if they were agreed on by all competent thinkers.

Popular science fiction writer Isaac Asimov rejects the idea of creation and instead seems inclined toward the view that the universe is eternal. Of those who believe in God the Creator he says: "Until quite recently in time, most people in the West thought the Earth and sky was [sic] formed by supernatural creation about six thousand years ago. (Many people today still earnestly believe this, though their intellectual achievement in doing so is about on a par with those who still believe the Earth is flat)."[58] Asimov also looks to Guth's theory to fill in the gap of God the Creator:

57 S. W. Hawking and Leonard Mlodinow, *The Grand Design*, 1st ed. (New York: Bantam Books, 2010), 198.

58 Isaac Asimov, *Isaac Asimov's Guide to Earth and Space* (New York: Random House, 1991), 258.

> Must we assume that if there was a beginning to the universe this was caused by a supernatural being? Not necessarily.... In 1980, an American physicist, Alan Guth, took up the problem of the origin of the big bang. ... The pre-universe had energy, and since all of its other properties resemble those of a vacuum, it is called a false vacuum. From this false vacuum, a tiny point of existence appears where the energy just happened, by the blind forces of random changes, to have concentrated itself. ... Of course, even if some version of Guth's theory is right, we might simply take a further step backward and ask where did the energy of the false vacuum come from in the first place.[59]

Asimov does note that the existence of quasars might indicate that the universe had a beginning. He appeals to quasars to make the point that the universe cannot have always existed: "This alone [the nature of quasars] would show that the universe in its youth was quite different from what it is now and that there has been an evolutionary process. This tends to disprove competing theories that would have the universe possess no true beginning and that describe it as having had the same overall appearance at all times in the indefinite past."[60] This empirical consideration does not settle the matter for those who limit knowledge to empirical investigation, because some other observation might be made tomorrow. To say that the universe was quite different in its youth does not rule out Guth's theory of the oscillating universe. But being coming from non-being is a logical gap, not an empirical gap. Can the universe, which is changing toward sameness (burning out), but has not yet reached sameness, have always been changing toward sameness?

The fundamental mistake in this area would be to assert that being (what exists, including energy or matter) came from non-being. This is not the same as the problem of being and becoming in that this problem assumes existence, whereas non-being is neither being nor becoming. Being coming from non-being is a contradiction because it fails to uphold the distinction between being and non-being and therefore reduces one to the other. If being can come from either being or non-being, then there is no distinction (in this sense) between them – in other words, being is non-being (eggs are non-chickens, but both are material objects). Instead, non-being is that which can do, and is, nothing; non-being cannot produce being, and nothing can come from non-being. Remember that Aristotle was concerned about this problem of being and becoming, but knew that

59 Ibid., 259.
60 Ibid., 256.

if there is now being, then there must have always been being because being cannot arise from non-being. This observation does not of necessity lead to Aristotle's physics, because Galileo, Bacon, Descartes, and Newton also believed that there was an eternal being (God), although not an eternal material being.

This is an important implication of the insight that there is no being from non-being. If there can be no being from non-being, then if something now exists, something has always existed. What it is that has always existed is not a gap that can be filled through empirical investigation. This involves two parts: (1) it cannot be empirically determined if all being is eternal or only some is eternal; (2) it cannot be empirically determined what kind of being –matter or spirit – exists and is eternal (matter is that which has extension; spirit is that which is conscious). The latter is an issue of the problem of appearance and reality – does the material world exist apart from ideas, or is it only an appearance? Conversely, does the mind exist, or is there only the appearance of the mind while the reality is the material brain? If only God is eternal and is the Creator of all else, then this has relevance for the human good.

Two Parts of the Most Basic Logical Gap

The first part involves the distinction between unchanging being (and therefore eternal/without beginning), and changing/temporal being. Was some being created by another being, or has all being (in one form or another) existed from eternity? This is not something that can be empirically investigated because it involves the origin and nature of the being that can be empirically investigated and the being doing the investigating. It involves the difference in kind between changeable being and unchangeable being. It requires answering the question: Is there unchangeable being, or is all being changeable? That there is or is not unchangeable being cannot be empirically confirmed, because all empirical investigation is temporally situated. Alan Guth notes that the possibilities are: (1) unchangeable being (and therefore eternal/without beginning) brought into existence changeable being (temporal); (2) all being is unchangeable, and no being was brought into existence; (3) all being is changeable, and all being is brought into existence.[61] Which of these is the case cannot be determined through greater empirical information. These involve logical differences. For contemporary cosmologists, working empirically (or as rationalist

[61] Guth, *The Inflationary Universe: The Quest for a New Theory of Cosmic Origins*, 9.

mathematicians), to affirm one or the other is to go beyond empiricism and encounter the problems of change and motion, being and becoming, and appearance and reality.

The second part of this logical gap involves the question of the nature of being; this is the difference between material and spiritual being. Material beings have extension whereas spirits and ideas have no extension but are conscious or objects of consciousness. Empirical investigation can get no further than perception and appearance. Is this perception of an extended being or of an idea? What is appearance, what is reality? Is change/becoming real, or does it only appear to be real? And if material being exists, has it existed from eternity or was it brought into being? If it was brought into being, was it brought into being by another material being or by a spirit? On the other hand, if spirit exists, has it existed from eternity, and is all spirit one or are there separate consciousnesses/selves? These are not questions that will be answered through further empirical investigation because they involve issues that go beyond empirical perception and encounter the problem of appearance/reality. A quick response might be to say that on these matters empirical science is silent, but that would not be correct. The contemporary materialist cosmology assumes that matter exists, and includes schools of thought that affirm either that matter has always existed or that it came into being from non-being. The failure to notice the difference between empirical gaps and logical gaps leads to the appearance of empirical knowledge in an area of study that cannot yield empirical knowledge. When this is pointed out, the response is often skepticism, the claim that we cannot have knowledge of these matters. Historically, the result of this kind of uncritically held assumption has been widespread skepticism with damaging effects on human advancement.

I offer two arguments here to support appeals to God for the remainder of this book. The first has a shared premise with thinkers like Hawking and Guth. It is that the universe is tending toward sameness (burnout, heat death, whatever the term). If the universe has always existed, it must be self-maintaining, but if it is tending toward sameness, it is not self-maintaining and therefore has not always existed. Attempts to explain an oscillating universe have failed (read Hawking's rejection of these in *A Brief History of Time*) and represent attempts to find a perpetual-motion machine (which is rejected by physics). On this basis we can conclude that the material world has not always existed but came into being. This is contrary to both Naturalism and Dualism (neither Plato nor Aristotle considered that perhaps the material world was brought into being).

My second argument is that Naturalism is not sufficient to explain thought. Such arguments have been advanced by thinkers like C. S. Lewis and Alvin Plantinga,[62] but are also behind the Platonic and Aristotelian turn away from Greek materialism. If thought is reducible to the brain, then it is essentially the motion of atoms. However, the motion of atoms does not capture the qualities of thought, which are true/false. No amount of motion qualities (up/down, left/right, fast/slow) end up with true/false. Nor is thought explainable as an emergent property in that emergent properties (like "wet" from hydrogen and oxygen becoming water) are of the same kind as their constituent parts ("wet" is a physical descriptor), whereas true/false is not made up of motion descriptions.

I present these two arguments to make the case that naturalism, as the claim that only matter exists and it has always existed, is not meaningful when its basic beliefs are analyzed. It makes claims about matter and mind that are contradictory. Matter (which is not self-maintaining) is eternal (self-maintaining). In other words, all that exists can be reduced to material parts, and this is true (where "true" is not something that can be reduced to material parts). I offer this as an example of using reason critically. When we analyze Postmodenrity and schools like Critical Theory, we are justified in asking if this school really uses reason critically, or if it has adopted these naturalistic assumptions.

I believe there is another kind of worldview that still needs to be addressed, and it is the one asserting that only the mind exists and that the mind is eternal (either individuals are eternal or they are illusions in the mind of the eternal one). This can be addressed along the same lines as demonstrated earlier, through the critical analysis of basic beliefs (for instance, if the individual has always existed and is pursuing knowledge/enlightenment, then the individual should have infinite knowledge).

However, for our purposes here, we can make the case that naturalism, as a challenge to theism, can be demonstrated to have no meaningful foundation. If we are forced by this insight to maintain that the material world – and human beings – has been created, then we must also conclude that what is good and evil for human nature is determined by the creator of human nature. To attempt a legal theory without this metaphysical absolute is to repeat the mistakes of Modernity.

62 C. S. Lewis (1898–1963) was a British scholar, author, and Christian apologist.
Alvin Plantinga (b. 1932) is an American philosopher, best known for his work arguing for the warrant of Christian belief and his development of Reformed Epistemology.

Skepticism and the Overextending of Naturalism

Two issues should be addressed before leaving our study of naturalism. The first is that empirical investigation – that is, science – never claimed to give this kind of knowledge, and therefore citing it for failing to do so is unfair. It is true that many scientists do not make such claims, but it is also true that many do (think of the claims of scientists like Alan Guth or Richard Dawkins), and that many nonprofessionals look to science as the body of all knowledge. This leads to the second problem, which is that what I have described is not a problem for science, but a problem for human limitations. This is skepticism. It is the claim that we cannot know the answers to these kinds of questions. A skeptic might affirm that we can know some things, and these things are what can be known empirically, but we cannot know the answers to questions that are outside of the empirical domain. This is not simply a discussion of the "limits of science," where science is said to study the material world and religion provides values, morals, meaning, and hope in a next life. Instead, what is being asked are the traditional questions about motion and change, being and becoming, and appearance and reality. The skeptic is asserting that there is no solution to these problems. The implication is that while we may have some current success in quantifying motion and predicting future motion, we have no certainty that this will last or that it actually tells us anything about what is real. We may have the appearance of success without real success, the appearance of correct quantification and prediction without the reality of such. The mechanism of change and motion is still a mystery, and we are no closer than before to explaining the process of being and becoming.

It is here that methodological naturalism overextends itself. While it maintains that explanations can only be given if they limit their appeals to what is available to sense data, it is a theory that is not itself limited to sense data. This is the well-known criticism of logical positivism, and it applies to methodological naturalism as well. The alternative it does not consider, and which has been relied on by many throughout the history of thought without falling into superstition, is that there is a difference between primary causes and secondary causes, the latter being material and the former being nonmaterial and intelligent. To avoid this discussion by only studying secondary causes is a metaphysical viewpoint, not a conclusion of empirical research. While the problems of superstition have been discussed earlier, the problem noted here with methodological naturalism is sufficient to rule it out and make it worthwhile to explore a method that relies on primary and secondary causes.

PRIMARY AND SECONDARY CAUSES IN HISTORIC CHRISTIANITY

Because methodological naturalism is most often leveled against Christians, and explanations involving the theistic God (it is not so often used to root out Aristotelians anymore), it is worthwhile to note that the distinction between primary and secondary causes is made in historic Christianity, in the Westminster Confession at the beginning of Modernity. Consider the following: "God, from all eternity, did, by the most wise and holy counsel of his own will, freely, and unchangeably ordain whatsoever comes to pass: yet so, as thereby neither is God the author of sin, nor is violence offered to the will of the creatures; nor is the liberty or contingency of second causes taken away, but rather established."[63] Similarly: "Although, in relation to the foreknowledge and decree of God, the first Cause, all things come to pass immutably, and infallibly; yet, by the same providence, he ordereth them to fall out, according to the nature of second causes, either necessarily, freely, or contingently."[64]

Here, historic Christianity has not made appeals to God where empirical research could fill the gap. Physical events are explained by secondary causes, as are human actions. Research in physics explains how contingent events come to pass, and research in psychology explains human actions. But the Confession also avoids the mistake of philosophical naturalism in limiting all knowledge to the empirical and material and reducing all to secondary causes, and allows that God as the primary cause can work through, against, or without secondary causes. There is a logical gap between the primary and secondary causes. This distinction between primary and secondary causes has much promise in solving ancient skeptical problems, explaining the relationship between science and religion and protecting both.

SKEPTICISM AS THE PROBLEM

Skepticism is the true problem. Modernity, for all of its lofty claims, limited knowledge and imported a kind of fideism not dissimilar to what it rejected in the medieval world. If the skeptic is correct and we cannot know, we cannot have certainty about the kinds of questions discussed earlier, nor can we do more than describe what we experience, without knowing if this

63 (3.1).
64 (5.2).

applies to our future experiences. This does not help in knowing the primary cause (in developing a full worldview), or in solving the appearance/reality or being/becoming problems. However, progress can be made in logical gaps, and it is made, well, logically. The progress must be made logically, not empirically, and it must be made presuppositionally, not intuitively. To say that it must be made logically and presuppositionally is to say that the most basic (logically basic) aspect of reality must be understood before other aspects of reality can be understood. This is in contrast to proceeding empirically and intuitionally, which means seeking to fill empirical gaps to problems that strike us as personally important. We can get some insight about how this can work from Hume.

Making Progress with Logical Gaps

Hume pointed out that logic cannot tell us about existence, and I think he was partially correct in this. Logic can only give hypotheticals about existence, such as "for all 'a' (without saying there are any), if 'a=b' and 'b=c,' then 'a=c'." But Hume also pointed out, I think correctly, that what is self-contradictory is meaningless and cannot be. This means that if we have but two options, 'a' and 'non-a', and one is self-contradictory and thus cannot be, then the other must in fact be. Earlier I quoted Guth, who points out that there are only three options: all being has always existed, only some being has always existed and created the rest of what exists, or being came from non-being. If the last is logically impossible, then we are left with only two options. If one of these proves to be logically impossible, then we are left with one – we have filled a gap in knowledge about being and becoming through logic. This is progress, and it is progress that meets the desired requirements of science mentioned at the beginning of this chapter – it is able to be duplicated and confirmed by others (it is universal).

Only God Is Eternal

If our options can be narrowed down from "none is eternal," "all is eternal," and "only some is eternal" to just the last one, then we can do the work of showing that this eternal creator is God, who has the incommunicable attributes of *infinite*, *eternal*, and *unchanging* and the communicable attributes of *knowledge*, *power*, and *goodness*. The three incommunicable attributes hold together logically: Whatever has existed from eternity is also infinite and unchanging. Knowledge, power, and goodness follow from being the creator and the foundation for personhood. These qualities are what God has eternally, infinitely, and unchangeably, and what forms the basis for humans being the image of God, albeit temporal, finite, and changeable.

The long history of theistic proofs does not progress along this path. In general, these: (1) did not affirm that it is clear that God exists, but instead that proofs are nice for some but not necessary for the good life; (2) overextended from premises to conclusion (necessary being, therefore theism; first cause, therefore theism; designer, therefore theism); and (3) looked to find God among the list of things that exist, rather than distinguishing between eternal and temporal being and affirming that eternality can only be attributed to God.

The turn from God to only considering temporal being is an instance of ignoring and neglecting the question "What is eternal?"; it is not an actual sound conclusion (nothing is eternal). When questioned, this neglect defends itself through self-justification. Rejecting all belief in eternal being by attacking the failings of Platonism is also not sufficient. Plato was a dualist, not a theist, and attributed eternality to the material world and the individual self. It is not that Modernity has deeply wrestled with the question of what is eternal, and that the study of metaphysic has come up empty. Rather, it is either that "metaphysics" has meant scholastic acceptance of Plato and Aristotle, or the study of metaphysics has been neglected. In contrast to those two options, I argue that we must study metaphysics to know what is eternal in order to make progress about human nature and the good.

The challenges of Modernity about both the human ability to know God and God's existence are important because they expose the insufficiency of the traditional proofs. I discussed this in more detail in my 2008 book, *The Clarity of God's Existence*, but it is worth noting here that the traditional proofs : (1) fail to show that it is clear that God exists and (2) overextend themselves from premises to conclusion (there is a highest being, therefore theism; there is a first cause, therefore theism; there is a designer, therefore theism). This was not viewed as much of a problem, because such proofs were not necessary to go to heaven. However, if the good is knowing God, then proof becomes necessary.

Modernity has challenged the idea of knowledge itself. This has occurred when knowledge has been limited to empirical data, or when knowledge has been equated with common sense, intuition, or the ordinary opinions we use to get through the day. Indeed, much of contemporary epistemology takes it for granted that we "know" our ordinary opinions, and then tries to explain what it means to know in this way. Philosophically, the question of what counts as knowledge began by noting that knowledge is different from opinion, because when we have knowledge, we can prove that we are correct and the other options are incorrect, whereas when we merely have an opinion (even if it is correct), we cannot do this.

There is no reason to abandon this definition of knowledge. The tendency to do so is rooted in skepticism, which assumes we cannot have this kind of knowledge and so renames various kinds of opinion "knowledge." If we are going to rethink the skeptical underpinnings of Modernity and Postmodernity, we need to reexamine the possibility of knowing God.

If the distinction between knowledge rests on being able to give proof that a belief is correct and its alternatives are not, then in applying this to knowing God we must be able to show that only God is eternal. This is different from the way God's existence is usually phrased, which is more like trying determine if God is on the list of existing things. Rather, we are asking if anything has existed from eternity, and whether anything beside God can be said to have existed from eternity. This involves proving:

1. Something has existed from eternity versus being coming from non-being.
2. What is eternal is God (as defined in theism), and eternality cannot be attributed to:
   A. the material world (as claimed by Lucretius and many contemporary materialists);
   B. the individual soul/self (as Plato claimed in Book 16 of the *Republic*).

It also involves rejecting attempts to deny that there is a material world or an individual self (as do some pantheists, or philosophers like Shankara and Nagarjuna).

Earlier I considered why being coming from non-being is impossible. However, to cover each of these steps would take us too far afield from our current topic. Arguments along these lines have been given in other work.[65] The approach there is to use the ontological, cosmological, and teleological arguments in a cumulative manner, taken step by step. So, the ontological argument can be relied on to show that something has existed from eternity, and the cosmological to show that what is eternal is not material, and the teleological to understand the nature of God. This is not a cumulative case argument that says there are many plausible but no conclusive

[65] Surrendra Gangadean, *Philosophical Foundation: A Critical Analysis of Basic Beliefs* (Lanham: University Press of America, 2008).

arguments. Instead, at each point the impossibility of the opposite can be established.

Some of the most famous thinkers of Modernity attained that rank in part by claiming to have shown that knowing God is impossible. Hume did this, and Kant did this. However, Hume's case relies on his empiricism, and Kant's case relies on his division of the world into the noumenal and phenomenal realms and limitation of knowledge to the latter. These are the views that flowered in Modernity's soil and led to the more radical skepticism of Postmodernity. There is no reason we must accept either empiricism or Kant's two-world approach.

In a way this requires us to think about a genealogy of "reason." The empiricism attempts to take the high ground and claim rationality. "Science" is today equated with using reason. However, I have meant something very different by the use of reason. I take "reason" to be the laws of thought (identity, excluded middle, and noncontradiction) by which we form concepts (a), judgments (a is b), and arguments (a is b, b is c, therefore a is c). On this account of reason, empiricism must give arguments in its support, rather than being taken as the default view. Epistemology in Modernity has tended to mean "human psychology," beginning with the British empiricists like John Locke who studied how people formed beliefs (in his view), rather than asking if indeed we know this. It continues to be so with contemporary epistemologists who say "the ordinary man knows he had breakfast, let's explain how he knows it." Much has been taken for granted and assumed. All that has been built on faulty assumptions is in danger of toppling.

A genealogy of reason would show how the critical use of reason to expose unproven assumptions is used to make breakthroughs that then, in turn, repeat this process. Socrates, Plato, and Aristotle questioned the earlier Greek materialists and exposed faulty presuppositions, but then replaced materialism with dualism. Some Christian philosophers attempted to integrate Greek dualism with Christian theism; others noted their incompatibility. Descartes critically examined Aristotelian assumptions and replaced these with his method and the new science. Locke built an edifice for the new science on an empirical foundation. Hume challenged this less consistent empiricism and replaced it with a radical empiricism that led to philosophical skepticism. Kant replied with a solution that accepted the limitations of reason to what can be experienced after it is shaped by the human mind. Precursors to Postmodernity like Nietzsche and Heidegger relied on Kantian skepticism to reject the life of the mind in finding universals (Nietzsche) and limit thinking to temporal and changing being (Heidegger).

In each case we can find that "reason" is used constructively to build a worldview (Platonic worldview, Aristotelian worldview, Cartesian and Kantian worldviews), and to be "rational" means consistent with that worldview. Without the critical use of reason, "reason" becomes relative to each of these worldviews, and what counts as rational depends on one's perspective. The constructive use of reason is necessary, but only after the critical use of reason. I have been using reason critically in this study to examine various beliefs about the good. I believe we can do this same thing with the idea of eternal existence, and critically examine those who deny there is anything eternal, as well as those who attribute eternality to something beside God. Beliefs about what is eternal are basic to the rest of a given worldview's picture of what is real. A mistake there ripples throughout the system.

Although the discipline of philosophy is often derided by its more pragmatic cousins in the academy for having made no progress over the centuries, we can discern progress and a pattern. The progress comes in exposing presuppositions and testing them for meaning. Where they are found to involve a contradiction they have been rejected. It takes time for their replacement to come to expression but it too must be critically examined and tested for meaning. And so we have progressed from Greek materialism to Postmodernity. We are now at a global age unlike any other, so that the consequences of building on a faulty presupposition will be more devastating than in the past, and past devastation has been significant. For humans to unite at a global level on a foundation of false presuppositions will allow for unprecedented harm.

Just as what is considered "rational" is relative to the system making the judgment, so too what counts as "human flourishing" is relative. However, within any system it is formally true that knowing the highest reality is good. This is even true in those systems that consist of knowing that we cannot know – this is taken to be the highest truth, and all else is organized around it.

CONCLUSION

The desire to make progress in knowledge and avoid false explanations is noble and should be encouraged. Limiting all explanation to an empirical explanation ignores logical gaps that cannot be filled through greater empirical research. This kind of limitation is as much a hindrance to gaining knowledge as is ignoring efficient or secondary causes in favor of final or primary causes. Noting these distinctions in kinds of gaps can be helpful in making progress when considering law and the good. Methodological naturalism makes the same mistake as superstition – both fail to give an adequate explanation of reality. Limiting explanations to efficient causes is not an advancement and is not helpful in the pursuit of knowledge; it is a kind of skepticism about ultimate questions, questions that must be answered in order to understand all the implications of empirical research. Proofs that involve showing the logical impossibility of a conclusion (and therefore the necessity of its opposite) are equally universal and are able to be duplicated by all who think. Such work involves filling logical gaps in knowledge, which goes beyond efficient causes. It is my hope that sufficient foundation has been given for increased work in this area.

I believe we can use this method in our thinking about God and the good. God, as the creator of human nature, is the determiner of good and evil for human nature. Postmodernism argues that all is change, all is impermanence, and postmodern legal theory presupposes this metaphysical claim. If it can be shown that not all is change, then we must look elsewhere for a metaphysical foundation to support law. The postmodern critique of Modernity correctly indicates that Modernity itself made assumptions about what *is*, and these in turn have shaped modern law. We can build on this critique and move beyond postmodern metaphysics of change and impermanence to argue that something must be eternal, and that only God is eternal.

6

Objectivity without a Metaphysical Foundation

Edm. This is the excellent foppery of the
world, that, when we are sick in fortune – often
the surfeit of our own behaviour – we make guilty
of our disasters the sun, the moon, and the stars,
as if we were villains by necessity, fools by heavenly
compulsion, knaves, thieves, and treachers,
by spherical predominance, drunkards, liars, and
adulterers, by an enforced obedience of planetary
influence, and all that we are evil in, by a divine
thrusting on. An admirable evasion of whoremaster
man, to lay his goatish disposition to the
charge of a star! My father compounded with
my mother under the dragon's tail; and my
nativity was under Ursa major*; so that it follows,*
I am rough and lecherous. Tut, I should have
been that I am, had the maidenliest star in the
firmament twinkled on my bastardizing.[1]

INTRODUCTION

As part of the subplot in *King Lear*, Edmund is plotting the destruction of his father. Although here Edmund is rejecting astrology, he illustrates how modern thinkers have characterized the study of "metaphysics." Indeed, it is not uncommon to find books about astrology in a section titled "metaphysics" in bookstores. Whether the study of metaphysics is understood as the superstitious and fallacious thinking behind astrology or the more refined work of the scholastic philosophers, modern thinkers turned away

1 William Shakespeare, *King Lear*, Act 1 Scene II.

from metaphysics to practical rationality and the individual's desires or will in search of explanations about morality and law. I choose this passage because much of the twentieth century has been spent trying to ground objectivity, where it was sought at all, in the individual's idealized desire. This was a reaction to the metaphysical errors of the nineteenth century, yet neither century offered a clear definition of the good. By way of contrast, I argue that the study of metaphysics is presupposed in any moral or legal theory, and that it must not be identified with scholastic thinking but understood more generally as the study of what is real. What Edmund does is substitute one metaphysical theory for another, but the study of metaphysics as the study of what is real is present in the form of presuppositions.

Modern thinkers quickly fell into the same problems as their ancient counterparts. A false dichotomy arose about the good as either pleasure or duty. This period is marked by disputes between utilitarians and deontologists. Alasdair MacIntyre's famous book, *Whose Justice Which Rationality*, exemplifies how Modernity limited reason to practical rationality within one or the other of these systems. Epistemologically, they emphasized empiricism and self-evident principles. However, their appeals to the self-evident amounted to little more than appeals to common sense. We will need to examine their attempts at consistent empiricism in more detail and how radically consistent empiricism is an important part of Postmodernity. For now it is also worth noting that modern thinkers increasingly relied on the avoidance mechanisms regarding relating the law to the good. I provide a few examples from the twentieth century to illustrate that things did not improve in this regard as modernity matured. Inevitably, these developments must be linked to the "modern self," particularly as developed by David Hume who was more consistent than most in drawing out the implications of empiricism.[2]

G. E. Moore[3] set the tone for the twentieth century in his *Principia Ethica*. In his study of the twentieth century, Paul Johnson notes Moore's participation in the secret society at Cambridge, known as The Apostles, and its relationship to the Bloomsbury group, with all the political and social concerns that this entails. This helps put Moore in a historical context, namely that he is actively responding to specific religious, political, and ethical systems that he rejects. Johnson says:

2 Parts of this chapter are based on my research which appeared in "Moral Objectivity: A Socratic Response to Hume." *Heythrop Journal*. Vol. 51.No. 2 (2010): 178–191.

3 G. E. Moore (1873–1958), a professor at Cambridge, defended ethical non-naturalism and sought to ground moral claims in the preferences of the individual.

> Its [*Principia Ethica*'s] last two chapters, "Ethics in Relation to Conduct" and "The Ideal," were, by implication, a frontal assault on the Judaeo-Christian doctrine of personal accountability to an absolute moral code and the concept of public duty, substituting for it a non-responsible form of hedonism based on personal relationships. "By far the most valuable things which we know or can imagine," Moore wrote, "are certain states of consciousnesses which may be roughly described as the pleasures of human intercourse and the enjoyment of personal objects. No one, probably, who has asked himself the question, has ever doubted that personal affection and the appreciation of what is beautiful in Art and Nature are good in themselves."[4]

Apart from considerations about Moore's relationship to the Judeo-Christian tradition, he is offering a view contrary to the Socratic position that states that the good is knowledge of the highest reality, and instead relies on Humean skepticism about the human ability to know highest reality. His "naturalistic fallacy" is meant to expose as incomplete any attempt to define "the good":

> When a man confuses two natural objects with one another, defining the one by the other, if for instance, he confuses himself, who is one natural object, with "pleased" or with "pleasure" which are others, then there is no reason to call the fallacy naturalistic. But if he confuses "good," which is not in the same sense a natural object, with any natural object whatever, then there is a reason for calling that a naturalistic fallacy; its being made with regard to "good" marks it as something quite specific, and this specific mistake deserves a name because it is so common ... even if it [the good] were a natural object, that would not alter the nature of the fallacy nor diminish its importance one whit. ... Why, if good is good and indefinable, should I be held to deny that pleasure is good? Is there any difficulty in holding both to be true at once? On the contrary, there is no meaning in saying that pleasure is good, unless good is something different from pleasure.[5]

If pleasure, or happiness, or knowledge, is said to be "good," Moore says, the follow-up question of why is it so good cannot be answered. Some things (beauty, relationships) are good in themselves, and one must simply "see" this. Here is the influence of Hume: Moral claims cannot be said to be more or less rational; one simply sees them. But, of course, if the individual is the final arbiter of what is good, then disagreements about beauty or relationships are incommensurable – there is no hope for a universal moral

[4] Paul Johnson, *Modern Times: The World from the Twenties to the Eighties* (New York: Harper & Row, 1983), 167.

[5] G. E. Moore and Thomas Baldwin, *Principia Ethica*, Rev. ed. (Cambridge; New York: Cambridge University Press, 1993), 12.

law based on a universal good grounded in a universal human nature. This sets the problem of objectivity for the twentieth century and attempts to give a subject relative account (mind dependent) of morality within the framework of Moore's ethical philosophy.

In a recent book, Hilary Putnam gave voice to this perspective in saying:

> It is not that I possess a metaphysical story that explains how I know, for example, that concern for the welfare of others regardless of national, ethnic, or religious boundaries, and freedom of speech and thought are better than the alternatives except in the sense of being able to offer the sorts of arguments that ordinary nonmetaphysical people with liberal convictions can and do offer. The very idea of explaining how ethical knowledge is possible in "absolute" terms seems to me ridiculous ... but recognizing that our judgments claim objective validity and recognizing that they are shaped by a particular culture and by a particular problematic situation are not incompatible. ... The solution is neither to give up on the very possibility of rational discussion nor to seek an Archimedean point, an "absolute conception" outside of all contexts and problematic situations, but – as Dewey taught his whole life long – to investigate and discuss and try things cooperatively, democratically, and above all *fallibilistically*.[6]

My goal is to help identify how many metaphysical assumptions there are in a statement like this or an approach like Dewey's.

COGNITIVISM AND NONCOGNITIVISM

Cognitivists and Noncognitivists work within the intellectual context established by Moore. Rather than seeking to ground morality in an objective reality such as God or the good, these thinkers dispute how morality is related to the individual's mind. A noted member of this discussion is Gilbert Harman.[7] Harman gives an account of morality, which focuses on subject dependent attitudes. Harman describes the problem of objectivity that concerns both cognitivists and noncognitivists. In his work, "Ethics and Observation," Harman asks: "Can moral principles be tested and confirmed in the way scientific principles can?"[8] His answer is "no." Objectivity requires a subject-independent standard that can be

6 Putnam, *The Collapse of the Factvalue Dichotomy: And Other Essays*, 190.

7 Gilbert Harman is a professor of philosophy at Princeton University. His ethical theory is that moral claims are actually statements about the speaker's preferences. Consequently, his work falls into the intellectual tradition traced here to Moore and Hume.

8 Gilbert Harman, "Ethics and Observation," in *Moral Discourse and Practice*, eds. Stephen Darwall, Allan Gibbard, and Peter Railton (Oxford: Oxford University Press, 1997), 83.

confirmed by others. Whereas scientific observations can be confirmed by others, it does not seem that moral observation can be confirmed by others. "In the moral case, it would seem that you need only make assumptions about the psychology or moral sensibility of the person making the moral observation. In the scientific case, theory is tested against the world."[9] Here is the problem of objectivity: If objectivity means "mind independent," yet moral sensibility can be explained in light of the person making the moral observation, then moral sensibility is not objective.

Gilbert Harman

Harman gives an example of a person observing a group of children setting a cat on fire. "In one sense, your observation is that what the children are doing is wrong. In another sense, your observation is your thinking that thought."[10] He claims that moral principles can help explain the first sense, but not the second. That is, the fact that I think the action of the children is wrong can account for my moral declaration about the observation, but it cannot account for my thinking that this action is wrong.[11] "In the second sense of 'observation,' moral principles cannot clearly be tested by observation, since they do not appear to help explain observations in this second sense of 'observation'."[12]

Harman considers the differences with this example and that of observing a proton passing through a cloud chamber. The scientist sees a trail in the cloud chamber and concludes that a proton has passed through. This does not seem to be a claim about the scientist, but about the cloud chamber and the impact of a proton. What explains the wrongness of the children's act is not that it is wrong, as if there were some object in the world called "wrong," but that the person who observes it believes it is wrong. In contrast, what explains the scientist's belief about a proton is not something about him, but about the effect a proton will have on a cloud chamber. Therefore, "the scientific realm is accessible to observation in a way the moral realm is not."[13]

Accordingly, moral claims are not objective: Their explanation only needs to include an explanation of the observer's beliefs, and not anything independent of the observer. However, even if there might not be an

[9] Ibid., 85.
[10] Ibid., 86.
[11] Ibid., 86.
[12] Ibid., 86.
[13] Ibid., 87.

independent object/quality in the world called "wrong," is there something objective about human nature that makes an action wrong? And is it precisely the diversity of beliefs about human nature that results in the diversity of beliefs about morality? To answer these questions, we turn now to the cognitivist/noncognitivist search for objectivity through the ideal self.

Allan Gibbard

In contrast to Harman, but still illustrative of twentieth-century presuppositions, Allan Gibbard[14] attempts to give an account of how moral claims can be mind-independent from a noncognitivist perspective.[15] His solution is that "morally right action simply is action that is truly rational."[16] "Wrongness" depends on the feeling of guilt. For Gibbard, "what a person does is morally wrong if and only if it is rational for him to feel guilty for having done it, and for others to be angry at him for having done it."[17] This is the noncognitivist perspective, but it also searches for an objective standard for morality. It implies that there is a subject-independent standard for moral claims that is related in an essential way to rationality. Thus, a claim may be relative to a subject, but the justification for the claim can be objectified by an appeal to what is rational.

But what does it mean to say that something is rational? Gibbard says "that to think something rational is to accept norms that, on balance, permit it."[18] But if my claim that an action is rational depends on what norms I accept, is this not still subject-dependent, and therefore not objective? Is there an objective way to determine which norms we should accept? Gibbard thinks that there is in that the correct definition for an action being rational, meaning that if a person thinks there is a reason for an action, that person thinks this would be a reason even if he did not actually consider it a reason; these are the norms that an ideal self would accept, or would have the nonideal self accept.

14 Allan Gibbard is the Richard B. Brandt Distinguished University Professor of Philosophy at the University of Michigan. Intellectually, he is also heir to Hume and Moore in grounding the meaning of moral claims in preferences, although he gives an account of how these can be objective. In his research he seeks to understand the meaning of moral statements, doing so within the confines of analytic philosophy and linguistic theory.

15 Allan Gibbard, "Wise Choices, Apt Feelings," in *Moral Discourse and Practice*, eds. Stephen Darwall, Allan Gibbard, and Peter Railton (Oxford: Oxford University Press, 1997), 181.

16 Ibid., 181.

17 Ibid., 181.

18 Ibid., 182.

Peter Railton

Peter Railton[19] also provides a naturalist account of how moral claims can be objective. Specifically, he posits an idealized self whose desires for the real self constitute objective moral claims: "Let us introduce the notion of an objectified subjective interest for individual A."[20] If we equip an actual individual with unqualified cognitive and imaginative powers, as well as full factual and nomological information about himself, this person A will become A+.[21] We are not interested in what A+ wants for himself, but what A+ wants for A. We can interpret Railton's view as positing an ideally rational self, a self who is rational to the extent of having all relevant knowledge with respect to himself so that he can make the correct decisions for his nonideal self. So again, objectivity is connected to rationality, which is an objective standard. It is hard to see how a "naturalized" self could have this kind of knowledge without really just being a description of God who is the creator of nature and the self. In a strange way, these thinkers are slouching toward God as the source of objectivity but unable to go there because of their presuppositions.

The ideal self as a ground for objectivity is also developed by Michael Smith,[22] who attempts to establish objectivity in the postulation of a fully rational self. Smith articulates a view where if a person values a specific action, then that person would desire to perform that action in his/her actual situation if he/she were fully rational.[23] Smith believes that there are normative reasons for action that can be objectively grounded in a fully rational self.[24] His definition of a normative reason is: "[T]o say that we have a normative reason to φ in certain circumstances C is to say that we would want ourselves to φ in C if we were fully rational."[25] This establishes the objectivity of moral claims, because what is fully rational is not dependent on the subject. This is a Kantian approach in that it focuses the

19 Peter Railton is the John Stephenson Perrin Professor of Philosophy at the University of Michigan. His research involves how empirical data can be used to understand the meaning of morality.

20 Peter Railton, "Moral Realism," in *Moral Discourse and Practice*, eds. Stephen Darwall, Allan Gibbard, and Peter Railton (Oxford: Oxford University Press, 1997), 142.

21 Ibid., 142.

22 Michael Smith is professor of philosophy at Princeton University. Although Smith's research recognizes the relationship between reason and objectivity, he fits within the intellectual history traced here because he seeks to ground what is rational in what an ideal person would do.

23 Michael Smith, *The Moral Problem* (Cambridge: Blackwell, 1994).

24 Ibid., 143.

25 Ibid., 182.

morality of an object in the will (nothing is good without qualification but a good will), yet directs the will through universal, objective principles (only act on what can be universalized).

REASON AND THE IDEALIZED SELF

Both cognitivists and noncognitivists appeal to reason as the foundation for moral objectivity. Whereas there are important differences between Gibbard, Railton, and Smith, the similarity is that rationality plays the central role in determining what is objective. In the one case, it has to do with what norms I would want myself to accept even if I did not in fact accept them (determined by the ideal self); in the other, it is what my ideally rational self would desire for my nonideal self. The ideal self replaces Kant's categorical imperative without explaining how this would be different. What imperatives would the ideal self apply? If we can know such imperatives, do we really need to mediate our knowledge of them through the ideal self?

For these thinkers, rationality means a claim is based on norms I would accept, on objectified self-interest, or what I would accept if I were fully rational. Nevertheless, these accounts of objectivity retain an element of the subjective (self-interest) and encounter the is/ought problem. Norms that I accept, and the idealized self, continue to be mind-dependent and so do not attain what is required for objectivity. Objectified self-interest leaves unanswered the most important question: What is it that is in my self-interest, what is good? None of these approaches actually answers the question about what is good. Indeed, they are kept from doing so by the constraints of their twentieth-century analytic philosophy presuppositions: They are explaining what people mean when they speak about morality without actually knowing what is good. In other words, even if they have helped us with the question "What do people mean when they make 'ought' statements?" they have not helped us answer the question "What ought I to do?"

This is illustrated by the is/ought problem. Even if my idealized self would do x in situation y, this does not tell me that I ought to do it. What is true for my idealized self does not translate to an ought for myself without adding in an explanation about the good. The Socratic approach does not encounter this same problem, because for Socrates, ought-claims are statements about what must be done to achieve the good given the nature of a thing. The *is* of human nature requires specific kinds of actions to achieve the good, and so one ought to do these. For Socrates, desire enters the equation in that all humans desire what is good. Whereas a particular conception of the good is mind-dependent for a given person, desire for the good is mind-independent in that it is the nature of the good to be desirable. Thus, these twentieth-century examples of attempts to respond to subjective moral theories do not advance the discussion as much as would an application of insights given by Socrates.

From these thinkers we can formulate a claim about finding objectivity: An action is right if I would judge (believe, desire) it to be so were I fully rational and in possession of the relevant knowledge. This addresses the problem as stated by Harman. Harman's example of a scientific and therefore objective claim was that a proton passed through a cloud chamber when a vapor trail is seen. We can reword this to say that if a scientist is fully rational, then that scientist will conclude that a proton is present in a cloud chamber when a vapor trail is present, given the relevant knowledge about this experiment. A less then fully rational scientist might not reach this conclusion. Similarly, a fully rational person will accept certain moral claims. Reason provides a foundation for objectivity. As stated, however, this definition is not very helpful because of the need to define the term "reason," and the need to understand the relationship between reason/knowledge and desire. What if the reasonable is not the desirable, or if reason is not valued by some people?

RICHARD HOLTON'S OBJECTION

An objection to Smith's approach is given by Richard Holton[26] in his "Reason, Value, and the Muggletonians." Holton summarizes Smith's view as stating that "An individual X values her potential action φ iff X believes that were she fully rational, she would desire that she perform φ if she were situated as she actually is."[27] To fill out Smith's view, he adds that the fully rational person would have no false beliefs, have all relevant true beliefs, and deliberate correctly.[28] To object to this position, Holton presents some claims about reason from a seventeenth-century thinker named Ludowick Muggleton: "It was the Spirit of Reason in Man that always blasphemed and fought against God, and persecuted and killed the Just and Righteous. Rational Truth is not the Truth of Christ but of Pilate. It is the Tree of Knowledge of

26 Richard Holton is professor of philosophy at the Massachusetts Institute of Technology. Although what is considered here are his objections to grounding morality in an ideally rational agent, his own research fits within this intellectual history in that he also grounds morality in the psychology of the agent.

27 Richard Holton, "Reason, Value and the Muggletonians," *Australasian Journal of Philosophy* 74, no. 3 (September, 1996), 484.

28 Ibid., 484.

Good and Evil."[29] Would the followers of Muggleton, called Muggletonians, accept Smith's standard for objectivity? Apparently, the Muggletonians do not value being rational, and therefore would not want to do what their fully rational self would prescribe. Holton's argument is that our conceptions about the ideal self are still mind-dependent, and claims about what constitutes the ideal self are relative to the speaker's values.

Holton considers three possible solutions, each of which he believes fails, and then concludes that the "attempt to analyze value in terms of rationality" must be abandoned.[30] Most of us value rationality, but not everyone does. Using the fully rational self as a standard for objectivity is still subject-dependent: It is dependent on the fact that most people value rationality. Holton's criticism is important because he raises a question about the relationship between reason and desire. Can a person use reason to know what is good and yet not desire the good? Before this can be addressed, it is worth noting that Holton and the Muggletonians have an insufficient understanding of reason, perhaps more akin to "common sense" or "thinking apart from God's plan," than the formative and critical functions of reason defined earlier.

According to the Muggletonians, the kind of thinking displayed by the serpent in Eden, or Pontius Pilate, are attempts to arrive at knowledge apart from special revelation. But this is not the most basic definition of "reason," as was given earlier. Even though Muggletonians reject thinking apart from scriptures, when a Muggletonian comes to the scripture, he/she must engage the mind to understand what is written. Furthermore, a Muggletonian would give various arguments to show that a person should accept what is written in the scriptures. This might involve an argument about regeneration: The unregenerate do not reason correctly and therefore would not listen even if a reasonable argument was given in support of scripture; what is required is the work of the Holy Spirit in regeneration. In such a situation, the unregenerate are shown to be exemplars of irrationality (as inconsistency): They reject reason and the conclusion of rational arguments, but continue to think (which is a function of reason). The Muggletonians are using reason as defined here (it is inescapable), but are rejecting a certain kind of reasoning, what might be called "worldly reason," which must be distinguished from reason. To give an argument about why reason should be rejected is self-referentially absurd; to use reason critically to analyze unbeliever's reasons is to use reason

29 Ibid., 484.
30 Ibid., 487.

presuppositionally. Therefore, although Holton may be correct that many constructions of what counts as the ideally rational self are constructs based on unproven premises, this is not enough to deny that there is a mind-independent standard of rationality/laws of thought. What Holton's observation should move us to do is take care in identifying what is universal, and come to recognize what counts as the laws of thought, but not to abandon such work.

THE IDEALIZED SELF AND OBJECTIVITY

There are two significant problems with grounding objectivity in an ideal self. The first is that it is simply unhelpful. It answers the question "what ought I to do" with "I ought to do what my ideal self (fully rational self) would have me do." This is because the ideal self knows what is good for me to do in the circumstances. Therefore, the answer becomes: I should do what I would have myself do if I knew what is good in these circumstances. Either I do know what is good, and therefore do not need to posit the ideal self, or I do not know what is good, which also means I do not know what the ideal self would have me do. The ideal self is unhelpful, and instead what is important is knowing what is good in my circumstances.

Second, it is often claimed that reason does not motivate.[31] This is sometimes called philosophical incontinence, and is described phenomenologically when a person says, "I know what is good/right but I don't want to do it." In his discussion with Socrates, Meno reports it this way: "There are some who believe that the bad things benefit them, others who know that the bad things harm them."[32] It is said that learning facts, or growing in knowledge, does not help motivate a person to do what is good. "Abstract or demonstrative reasoning, therefore, never influences any of our actions, but only as it directs our judgment concerning causes and effects."[33] I might believe something is good without desiring it, and "since reason alone can never produce any action, or give rise to volition, I infer, that the same faculty is as incapable of preventing volition, or of disputing the preference with any passion or emotion."[34] I might learn the facts of the matter without changing my values, or I might know what is the case

[31] Simon Blackburn, *Ruling Passions: A Theory of Practical Reasoning* (Oxford: Clarendon Press, 1998), 238.

[32] Plato, "Meno," in *Plato: Complete Works*, ed. John Cooper (Cambridge: Hackett Publishing Company, 1997).

[33] Hume, *A Treatise of Human Nature*, 87.

[34] Ibid, 88.

without knowing what I ought to do. "Satan and other fallen angles, for example, presumably know a good deal about God's commands; however, they are not motivated to act in accordance with them."[35] Milton portrays Satan saying: "Evil, be thou my good."[36] Therefore, I might know what the ideal self would have me to do without wanting to do it.

This also applies to practical rationality. Objectivity is sometimes sought by grounding it in the relationship between ends and means. To achieve a given end/goal, I must act in specific ways. This is phrased as a hypothetical imperative: If I want *x*, I must do *y*. But the problem is that a person could claim to know that *x* is good without wanting it, and therefore the hypothetical imperative is unhelpful. Reason tells us about the relationship between cause and effect and means/ends, but not which ends to desire. This is more than being practically irrational.[37] The problem is not in knowing the means/ends relationship, but in knowing which end to pursue. The person suffering from philosophical incontinence will say: "I know that *x* is good, and that to achieve *x* I must do *y*, but I want *a* and therefore I'm going to do *b*." Hume says:

> 'Tis not contrary to reason to prefer the destruction of the whole world to the scratching of my finger. 'Tis not contrary to reason for me to chuse my total ruin, to prevent the least uneasiness of an Indian or person wholly unknown to me. 'Tis as little contrary to reason to prefer even my own acknowledg'd lesser good to my greater, and have a more ardent affection for the former than the latter. A trivial good may, from certain circumstances, produce a desire superior to what arises from the greatest and most valuable enjoyment; nor is there any thing more extraordinary in this, than in mechanics to see one pound weight raise up a hundred by the advantage of its situation.[38]

If there is no connection between belief and desire, then it appears that motivation requires an affect, or change, of the desires rather than a change of belief. This is the critical objection to the use of an ideal self as the ground for objectivity, as well as the use of reason as a foundation for objectivity. To provide a moral law grounded on human nature, it must be shown that there is a direct relationship between human nature, reason, and desire.

35 Kyle Swan, "A Metaethical Option for Theists," *Journal of Religious Ethics* 34, no. 1 (2006), 3.

36 Great Books of the Western World. Encyclopaedia Britannica in collaboration with the University of Chicago, directed by Robert Maynard Hutchins (Chicago: W. Benton, 1952), Paradise Lost IV.110.

37 David Copp, "Belief, Reason, and Motivation: Michael Smith's 'the Moral Problem,'" *Ethics* 108, no. 1 (1997), 33.

38 Hume, *A Treastise of Human Nature*, 90.

KNOWINGLY DOING EVIL: SOCRATES VERSUS HUME

Socrates rejected the claim that persons knowingly do evil or that they knowingly choose the lesser good. "Socrates: And do you think that those who believe that bad things benefit them know that they are bad? Meno: No, that I cannot altogether believe. Socrates: It is clear then that those who do not know things to be bad do not desire what is bad, but they desire those things that they believe to be good but that are in fact bad. It follows that those who have no knowledge of these things and believe them to be good clearly desire good things."[39] This is relevant here because Socrates connects belief and desire in a way that avoids the problems raised by Hume.

Hume's analogy of a 1-pound weight lifting a 100-pound weight by the advantage of its situation sheds light on the solution. The desire of a trivial good in place of the one that will bring extraordinary enjoyment must be put in context. Just like the 1-pound weight does not lift the 100-pound weight in general, but only when placed in the right situation in relation to pulleys or a lever, so too a trivial good does not override a greater good in general, but only in a specific context. Once the context has been filled in, it is difficult to see how the "trivial good" remains trivial to the person in that context. Socrates is correct in that the person desires what they believe to be good in the context (although hindsight is often 20/20), and they do not know it to be evil.

Hume's contention is that it is not contrary to reason to desire a trivial good over a greater good. But is it contrary to reason to choose a trivial good over a greater good? In other words, while I may prefer the destruction of the whole world to the scratching of my finger, my preferences do not necessitate an action. That I prefer/desire it does not mean that I ought to choose it. In other words, what is interesting is not that I prefer, but that I choose to act on that preference. This reveals my thinking process in making decisions, and such a thinking process can be objectively evaluated (this is the basis for all pedagogy).

It has been objected that in the Socratic picture, it seems beliefs and desires are connected in a way that is not found in life. Hume's view, that reason and desire are disconnected, has the appearance of being more consistent with ordinary experience. However, I believe the Socratic picture is more robust because it describes the inconsistency and tension that exists within a person better than Hume does. Hume notices the tension between a desire and a belief. Socrates notices that behind this desire is another

39 Plato, *Meno*.

belief, so that the real tension is between two beliefs. I may desire to satisfy my immediate impulse through gluttony, but I also recognize that this is temporary and not as important as self-discipline and health. Behind this desire is the belief that the pleasure from gluttony is good. The real conflict, as Socrates notes, is over what I believe to be good and evil.

The problem of motivation is solved by noting that persons always do what they believe to be good: Tension between belief and desire is only seeming, and a more robust analysis shows that the real tension is between beliefs about what is good. Reason motivates in the sense that people desire to do what they believe will make them happy. When something is believed to be nonsense, meaningless, a contradiction, it will also be rejected as not bringing happiness. The problem is therefore not a conflict between belief and desire, but "what do I believe to be good," and the tension that arises between conflicting beliefs about the good. For instance, Milton portrays Satan not as pursuing evil, but as calling evil good: "Evil, be thou my good."[40]

Finding objectivity in a rationally ideal self is insufficient to help us know what we ought to do. But I asserted earlier that objectivity can be found in the concept of human nature and human flourishing. Two problems remain, namely how can we know what is flourishing and what is not, and how does this solve the problem of motivation – I may know what it is to flourish but not desire to do so. Having solved these problems, I then argue that the problem of objectivity as posed by Gibbard can also be solved.

HAROLD PRITCHARD

Harold Pritchard competed with Moore to explain moral philosophy.[41] In his "Does Moral Philosophy Rest on a Mistake," he agreed about the problem of is/ought, but argued that moral philosophy is simply the pressure to give arguments that justify our normative claims that we have already accepted. In contrast to Moore, he argued that the right is not to be understood in light of the good. It is obligation (duty) that is most basic, and we immediately apprehend that our obligations are self-evident.

I can appreciate this approach in that descriptively it captures the unexamined life that is so prevalent, or even universal in varying degrees. Persons are generally not aware of their assumptions and argue not to

40 John Milton, Encyclopaedia Britannica and University of Chicago, Great Books of the Western World. Encyclopaedia Britannica in collaboration with the University of Chicago, Paradise Lost, IV.110.

41 Harold Arthur Pritchard (1871–1947) was an English philosopher and advocate of the Oxford intuitionist approach to ethics and morality.

discover the truth, but to justify themselves. When they are questioned about their assumptions, they resist critical examination through this process of self-justification. Nevertheless, I do not believe this requires that we make the move to intuition about obligation. As with Moore, this provides us with no means of solving problems resting on competing intuitions.

Rather, we can agree that much of moral philosophy is self-justification resisting critical examination of assumptions. Furthermore, what Pritchard is calling apprehension is the relationship between beliefs and what they entail, about which any given person is more or less conscious. So a person might simply find themselves believing a given action is an obligation (such as "keep your promises"), but as we begin to question that person and search for an explanation, we discover that these intuitions rest on a whole worldview with beliefs about how we know, what is real, and what is good. Pritchard's claim that moral common sense is sufficient bears the same problem as all appeals to common sense – it is culturally relative. What he takes to be moral common sense can be seen to bear certain English attitudes. Appealing to this will do nothing to answer the objections of an Albert Camus or Jean-Paul Sartre.

W.D. ROSS

Even in light of these problems, the twentieth-century thinkers continued to embrace intuition. W. D. Ross's *The Right and the Good* also located the right in *prima facie* obligations.[42] He explains:

> The general principles of duty are obviously not self-evident from the beginning of our lives. How do they come to be so? The answer is, that they come to be self-evident to us just as mathematical axioms do. We find by experience that this couple of matches and that couple make four matches, that this couple of balls on a wire and that couple make four balls: and by reflection on these and similar discoveries we come to see that it is of the nature of two and two to make four. In a precisely similar way, we see the prima facie rightness of an act which would be the fulfillment of a particular promise, and of another which would be the fulfillment of another promise, and when we have reached sufficient maturity to think in general terms, we apprehend prima facie rightness to belong to the nature of any fulfillment of promise. What comes first in time is the apprehension of the self-evident prima facie rightness of an individual act of a particular type. From this we

42 Sir William David Ross (1877–1971) was a Scottish philosopher, best known for his work in ethics. He developed a deontological form of intuitionalism in response to thinkers like G. E. Moore.

> come by reflection to apprehend the self-evident general principle of prima facie duty.[43]

This approach is more akin to human psychology, asking how do humans learn, than it is to moral epistemology, which asks how we can know what is good. This is consistent with Pritchard's analysis that we develop our moral philosophy after having come to specific moral convictions. The theory is a justification of those convictions. Ross represents the turn to ordinary language, looking at how the "common man" comes to hold beliefs. This is not different from an appeal to common sense. What it gives us is a look at how the "common man" of Ross's time and culture came to hold beliefs. It does not tell us what the examined life is like. Ross partially addressed this:

> In what has preceded, a good deal of use has been made of "what we really think" about moral questions; a certain theory has been rejected because it does not agree with what we really think. It might be said that this is in principle wrong; that we should not be content to expound what our present moral consciousness tells us but should aim at a criticism of our existing moral consciousness in the light of theory. Now I do not doubt that the moral consciousness of men has in detail undergone a good deal of modification as regards the things we think right, at the hands of moral theory. But if we are told, for instance, that we should give up our view that there is a special obligatoriness attaching to the keeping of promises because it is self-evident that the only duty is to produce as much good as possible, we have to ask ourselves whether we really, when we reflect, are convinced that this is self-evident, and whether we really can get rid of our view that promise-keeping has a bindingness independent of productiveness of maximum good.[44]

This appeal to "incorrigible beliefs" is akin to appeals to the self-evident. When critics show that what a thinker says is self-evident is not actually self-evident, the thinker can respond that the belief is incorrigible, saying it is not possible for this thinker to deny the truth of that belief.

As in the case with Pritchard, we must analyze this in terms of the relationship between a given "incorrigible" belief and the worldview that the thinker assumes. Given premises 1-n, it is true that the thinker cannot reject this belief in duty. However, others do not find themselves in the same relationship to that duty. Upon examination, we find that these differences are a result of not sharing premises 1-n. The difference may be entire or only partial, but it accounts for the supposedly incorrigible belief about duty.

43 W. D. Ross, *The Right and the Good* (Oxford: Clarendon Press, 1955; 1930), 1, 176.
44 Ibid., 39.

Change the worldview assumptions, and this incorrigibility goes away. This occurs throughout the Socratic dialogues. Meno begins by asserting something to be true, and through a process of questioning what Meno means and what he takes for granted, this original assertion loses its strength.

Ross gives a clear statement of how to evaluate the rightness of an act:

> The more correct answer would be that the ground of the actual rightness of the act is that, of all acts possible for the agent in the circumstances, it is that whose prima facie rightness in the respects in which it is prima facie right most outweighs its prima facie wrongness in any respects in which it is prima facie wrong. ... Our duty, then, is not to do certain things which will produce certain results.[45]

However, this fits into the larger framework of confusing the good with either duty or happiness. It leaves unanswered how to evaluate what outcome is indeed good, or its answer amounts to circularity and table pounding about intuitions. If this is the best expression of modern thinking about moral philosophy, or at least the moral philosophy that has all of Modernity to reflect on before the horrors of World War II, should we be surprised that Modernity failed?

A thinker who continues to do work in contemporary philosophy but who also consciously seeks to further and defend a view related to Ross is Robert Audi. Although his work considered here dates to a 2004 book, he is working within the framework that I consider to be part of the end of Modernity. He fits into the false dichotomy of duty versus happiness, and attempts to justify a system based on a twentieth-century analysis of duty that subordinates the good to the right.

ROBERT AUDI

In his book, *The Good in the Right*, Robert Audi's purpose is to defend intuitionism against its philosophical critics and to develop an intuitionist position that goes beyond W. D. Ross's while relying on its basic framework.[46] He looks closely at Ross's position and some of the main concepts in this position such as *prima facie* duty and self-evidence. He also deals with the standard criticisms against Ross, which are the disagreement of

45 Ibid., 46.

46 Robert Audi (b. 1941) is an American philosopher who works in many areas, including the epistemology of ethics and defending ethical intuitionalism. He is a professor at the University of Notre Dame. Robert Audi, *The Good in the Right: A Theory of Intuition and Intrinsic Value* (Princeton: Princeton University Press, 2004).

intuitions, incommensurability, and dogmatism. He then considers Kantian intuitionism and intrinsic value. He attempts to show that "Kant and other philosophers who have produced major ethical theories built around a master principle have had too little faith in intuitive everyday moral judgment; Ross and other intuitionists have had too little faith in comprehensive ethical theory."[47] The result of Audi's approach is a moral theory that uses axiological integration of intuitionist's principles that, when acted on, add to human flourishing and thus to the value of everyday life.

What Audi specifically wants to do is develop Ross's position in a way that addresses its critics and yet keeps the ability to be responsive to everyday life. The three main challenges to Ross are that there is widespread disagreement about which principles count as being self-evident, the incommensurability problem that arises from positing irreducibly different kinds of moral grounds for action, and the charge of dogmatism on the part of intuitionists by those who do not intuitively arrive at the same guidelines for moral conduct. Audi offers strong responses to these challenges, but his position remains unconvincing, because behind the intuitionist approach is the assumption that human intuitions are morally ideal as opposed to fallen and corrupted, and that they can provide a basis for knowledge rather than being mistaken or in need of interpretation to be meaningful. Hence, even if the intuitionists can address the three standard challenges to their position, this does not prove that human moral intuitions are as they should be or that they have been correctly interpreted.

Part of what Audi wants to show is that adhering to such a principle is conducive to human flourishing. This idea of human flourishing is central to the "new natural law" thinkers. Audi's use of the idea shows that it can be approached from differing theories and that people can disagree about the particulars of "flourishing." In chapter 5 of his book, Audi gives the reader ten rules that can serve as intermediate-level principles for moderating choices. These include the prohibition of harm, veracity, fidelity, justice, and beneficence. Each sounds good, but they are too ambiguous to be helpful. What exactly does it mean to harm another? Western secularism may have one answer, the Hindu caste system will have another, and Buddhism still another. If death is the end of existence, then "human flourishing" means one thing, whereas if at death the soul reincarnates based on past karma, then "human flourishing" is something different. It is fine to say that we should act with beneficence, but this begs the question, because just what it is to act in a way that is good is the problem at hand when discussing divisions between worldviews about the moral law.

47 Ibid., 120.

This concern is not the same as the "difference" or "incommensurability" objections that Audi tries to answer. What Audi does not consider is that the intuitions of any given person are part of a worldview that must be critically examined before the intuitions can be relied on. The major worldviews that have developed the civilizations of world history have significant, long-term differences of intuition that cannot be ignored, and which give differing answers to questions such as "What is it to harm?" or "What is the good?" The need to take into account the variety of worldviews does not necessarily entail relativism, but nor can they be ignored when the meaning of key terms such as "good" vary between them.

Audi summarizes his approach when he says "moral intuition has an authority of its own; but it can be refined, and must sometimes be corrected, by theoretical reflection. Intuition must also respond both to the pressure of obligation and to the incentive of ideals."[48] Although his book offers a very informative survey of intuitionist thought, and is written in a clear style, it does not give an adequate explanation of why human moral intuition should be assumed to be morally ideal as opposed to flawed or fallen. Audi is a thoughtful writer and responds cogently to the standard criticisms of intuitionism, but there are assumptions behind his position that need to be addressed.

In basing his system on intuition, he is continuing the modern problem of asserting that in general, people seem to know the good, and the problem is one of practical rationality in making a system to explain these moral intuitions. However, to make real progress on the fact that moral intuitions differ between worldviews, we must critically examine the basic beliefs of worldviews. This critical use of reason is different than the constructive use of reason to build a worldview, and requires identifying the logically most basic beliefs of worldviews. If worldviews are examined at all, it is usually at less basic levels, such as how they measure up in practical ways. I argue that moral objectivity in law requires that we know what is real and discussions about intuitions do not make progress on this front.

CHARLES STEVENSON

Before turning from these examples of twentieth-century thinking, I want to consider Charles Stevenson.[49] Another analytic philosopher, he accepted Ayer's logical positivism and gave a noncognitivist analysis of

48 Ibid., 202.

49 Charles Stevenson (1908–1979) was an American philosopher who defended emotivisim.

ethical assertions. These are merely assertions of attitude with the goal of altering behavior. What is clear for Stevenson is that it is difficult to answer what the good is because we do not know what we are seeking. Like Ross, we understand Stevenson to be giving a description of what people in his time are doing. However, I believe it is an incomplete description.

Nevertheless, it is a helpful description because it highlights two problems for Modernity's form of empiricism: logical positivism cannot account for beliefs and instead must reduce them to emotions/attitudes/orientations/feelings; beliefs must be reduced to behavior, and the purpose of ethical attitudes is to change behavior. But this description is only as accurate as its assumptions grounded in logical positivism. The emptiness of this worldview as well as its inability to help solve the problems of the twentieth century was felt by existentialists.

EXISTENTIALISM

In an interesting way, existentialist philosophers fit into this discussion because they accept the claims of naturalism. Only the material world exists; humans are merely a collection of atoms. Their emphasis differs in that they see such a viewpoint producing a crisis of meaning. In the wake of the horrors of World War II, existentialists believe it is impossible to return to the beliefs of the past (theism of some kind). However, naturalism does not provide a basis for a meaningful human life. Therefore, the solution is found in some form of creating one's own meaning. Objectivity in morality is a chimera, but meaning can be determined by each individual. Although twentieth-century existentialists trace their lineage to Kierkegaard and Dostoyevsky, they rely more heavily on Nietzsche's metaphysical assumptions. Nietzsche is a kind of Raskolnikov (from Dostoyevky's *Crime and Punishment*) without any theistic hope of redemption or meaning. Ivan Karamazov (from *The Brothers Karamazov*) wrestles with similar problems, but Dostoyevsky portrays him as finding hope, whereas Nietzsche goes the way of Smerdyakov (also from *The Brothers Karamazov*). This is a firmly anti-intellectual position, or anti-Apollonarian in Nietzsche's terminology. Relying on Schopenhauer, Nietzsche elevates the will and reduces the intellect to a subordinate and illusionary place. In this sense he is firmly modern: Voluntarism and a focus on the will to survive has been the explanatory model from early Modernity. Similarly, his anti-metaphysical position is a firmly modern viewpoint. His rejection of theism can hardly be said to be new; he borrows much of it from Feuerbach. Additionally, it would be hard to find anything theistic in Hobbes, who was a materialist. In this sense Nietzsche is a "traditional" modern thinker.

And yet we must link him to the post–World War II existentialists as we transition from Modernity to Postmodernity. This link is found in the assertion that the whole pursuit of wisdom, the whole Apollonarian edifice, rests on mere dogma and cannot stand by its own principles. However, without some metaphysical basis, there is a real threat to the meaning of life. Rather than continue to hold dogmatically to truth and meaning, the authentic individual must abandon both. This is done in the name of autonomy, a strongly modern value.

Because of this reliance on the modern value of autonomy, we are again faced with the reality that Postmodernity is the outworking of modern assumptions. There is great continuity between the two. Perhaps it can be said that Postmodernity is Modernity gone to seed. It is facing the reality that what Modernity claimed to know is only dogma, no different from the dogma of the Medieval age, and definitely not the certainty Descartes was seeking.

Albert Camus viewed this as liberating. Whereas beliefs and worldview bind a person to consistency, absurdity provides freedom. Consciousness and revolt are rejections of renunciation to the status quo or the systems built by others to define away the individual. From the absurd we draw revolt, freedom, and passion. In many ways this is similar to the expressions of the Romantics. It revels in the continuing apparent tension between thought and feeling, between truth and beauty. Modernity emphasized freedom, but also causation, and because it defined freedom as "uncaused," it could not reconcile this tension. Therefore, those who wish to retain freedom are pressed to jump to the absurd. Modernity emphasized "truth" as defined by logical positivism; however, this cannot capture all of human reality, and so those who wish to retain meaning are pressed to reject truth and reason. These conflicts show us that Modernity did not provide us with the answers to questions wrestled with in previous ages, and the skepticism of Postmodernity is a witness to this.

By way of contrast with Camus but still within existentialism, Jean-Paul Sartre leaned toward an emphasis on responsibility. Being precedes essence. Once thrown into the world, man is responsible for everything he does. Man is nothing other than a series of undertakings, and he is the sum of the relationships that make up these undertakings. Relying on Heidegger, Marx, and Kant, Sartre's thinking is full of unproven assumptions about epistemology and metaphysics. Nevertheless, he gave a nominalist stamp to the post–World War II era in which individuals reject the idea of human nature and instead assert that they create themselves. A responsible individual is the one who sees this self-creation and acknowledges the responsibility for its consequences. The logical problems in being preceding essence, and in self-creation, go unaddressed, which is what we should expect in an age of radical skepticism and anti-intellectualism. And yet this anti-intellectualism is not completely unwarranted in that the modern intellectuals rejected medieval thinking as fideistic, and yet are guilty of the same kind of dogmatic assertion. Can knowledge be found?

Their emphasis on free will – or I should say a libertarian notion of free will – is important to their own philosophy, but it is also a mark of Modernity. The modern world emphasized autonomy in various ways. At one level it is the dictum to learn to think for oneself (rather than needing to be told). At another level it is the desire to escape all law. It is a form of antinomianism. That includes the law of causation, and the laws of thought. A free will in this case is believed to be a will that is entirely uncaused. William James argued that this is the only way to preserve moral responsibility, but of course it depends on what one means by responsibility. A being can be free, responsible, and follow laws. So although it is true that moral responsibility requires freedom, it is not true that moral responsibility requires uncaused events.

The need for a free will as an uncaused event adds to the existentialist's crisis. An uncaused will is hardly one's own. Nor can one be responsible for what is uncaused. And yet it is also true that the material causation that naturalists believe is all that exists is no foundation for moral responsibility. The solution of the existentialists is to determine good and evil for oneself. The absurdities of this if the basis for determination is uncaused and there is no self (only atoms) are evident. Another solution is to use these problems as reasons to reject naturalism and question its presuppositions about the nature of reality and the good.

KNOWING THE GOOD

To discuss flourishing, or the good life, might not appear to help with the problem of objectivity. What it is to flourish is thought to be a matter of opinion. Here I argue that there is a fundamental sense of flourishing that is more basic than any other. To flourish as a human is to have understanding and meaning. To understand the world is to find meaning in the world. Power, strength, beauty, money – all presuppose understanding. At the very least, without understanding, one will not realize that one has these other things, but more importantly, one will not know how to use them or how to live. To have understanding is to live as a human; to fail to have understanding is to deny one's humanity. To argue against understanding as the basic feature of human nature would be self-referentially absurd – it would be to try and make one's position understood by others.

From knowing that finding meaning through understanding is the good life does not necessarily follow that one will be motivated to do so. Here I must be specific about what exactly it is that must be understood to find meaning. To find meaning, a person seeks to make sense of the world. Minimally, this requires understanding what goals must be achieved to be happy. A more robust understanding that seeks to avoid temporary happiness, and seeks lasting happiness, requires knowing what is real in order to understand human nature and what is good for human nature. Failing to note the distinction between temporary happiness and lasting happiness is an error that will lead to acting in ways that are objectively wrong in that they are not furthering one's pursuing of what is good (but only what will make one happy at the time).

"Ought" statements are claims about what a person must do to achieve the good. If the good is finding meaning in the world and living accordingly, then an "ought" claim is about what must be done to find meaning and live accordingly. The following are initial examples that can be fleshed out further: one ought to know what is clear about reality – one ought not to be culpably ignorant; one ought to be consistent in what one believes and says; one ought to treat others with human dignity; one ought to seek justice through knowing the truth; one ought to avoid being discontent by knowing what is truly good. These are objective in that the reality of human nature and the good is not subject-dependent, although the extent to which a person understands the good and pursues it is dependent on that person's level of understanding.

Now we are able to respond to the intellectual tradition that has dominated the twentieth century, although it has roots in Hume's analysis of morality. We do not need to accept the assumption that morality is grounded in the individual's preferences, and we can reject the search for objectivity in some form of the idealized self as not sufficient. Hilary Putnam noted this narrowness in Hume and said, "The logical positivist fact/value dichotomy was defended on the basis of a narrowly scientistic picture of what a 'fact' might be, just as the Humean ancestor of that distinction was defended upon the basis of a narrow empiricist psychology of 'ideas' and 'impressions'."[50] Rather than concede to Hume or logical positivism, we can take a Socratic approach and understand moral statements to be claims about whether a person is living according to human nature.

50 Putnam, *The Collapse of the Factvalue Dichotomy: And Other Essays*, 190.

Consider the earlier example of children abusing a cat: arbitrarily inflicting pain on a living being, or finding personal pleasure in doing so, is contrary to the goal of human flourishing. This example is a trivial one, and most likely this kind of activity on the part of the persons involved fits within a larger lifestyle of finding enjoyment through reckless behavior. Rather than taking one such instance, the larger framework of how these persons live their lives should be considered. What do they view to be the good and how are they pursuing this? Is what they believe to be the good really the good?

Those who ground moral norms in the subject's attitudes/desires, like Gibbard or Hume, will respond that this is his point: All that needs to be known about a moral claim is what the person believes; it is subject-dependent. I argue, however, that it is subject-dependent in a way that scientific observation is also subject-dependent. In the example given by Gibbard, the scientist who sees a trail in the cloud chamber will only draw the correct conclusion (that a proton has passed through) if he has the correct understanding and set of beliefs about what is real. Similarly with moral claims: A person will only draw the correct conclusion about an action and its sufficiency in achieving the good if that person has the correct beliefs about what is real. A false belief about reality – say, an Aristotelian view of matter – will lead to a false conclusion about protons. A false belief about human nature will lead to a false conclusion about the good.

Moral claims and scientific claims are not different in kind. Discussions about whether or not moral claims are objective involve discussing their relation to the subject: Are they dependent on the subject's desires and tastes, or can they be shown to be real features of the world? I have argued that an appeal to an ideally rational self does not solve the problem of objectivity. However, I have also argued that the Socratic position can provide a solution by arguing that the good is based on human nature, which is a subject independent reality. The subjectivist defends his position by noting the diversity of moral theories but the apparent unity of scientific observation. It is true that there is great diversity about what is good and what ought to be done, but I argue that this is owing to the level of understanding about the good and the means to the good on the part of the person making moral claims. This is also true in science, where a misunderstanding on the part of a scientist will lead to a false conclusion. This does not mean that morality or science is subject-dependent. Rather, the extent to which an individual finds meaning in the world, whether in morality or science, is relative to the extent that the person has used reason to understand. Moral diversity should not be seen as the end of the pursuit of objectivity and unity, but as a challenge for greater efforts to be put forth in coming to a common understanding of the good.

CONCLUSION

Having traced this intellectual history and evaluated arguments given by twentieth-century thinkers about the nature of moral objectivity, a final question is: Why accept the Socratic view? Even if it does resolve the difficulties noted earlier in grounding morality in claims about the idealized self (etc.), it does not follow that we should accept it as the correct view. Furthermore, the ways that it was developed by Plato or Aristotle face significant problems of their own. What Socrates helps us do is keep in focus the central question of ethics, which is: What is the good? Furthermore, he helps us in answering the question by grounding the good in human nature: What is good for a thing is based on the nature of the thing. He thus calls us back to basic questions in philosophy, questions that can be lost in the compounded presuppositions of Modernity. To know the good, one must know what it is to be a human; human nature is objective and so the good is objective. Additionally, human nature is what is shared by all humans, so the good too is what is common to all humans. The good serves as a basis for unity and for further inquiry.

7

Contemporary Natural Law

Practical Rationality and Legal Opinions

Cas. *The fault, dear Brutus, is not in our stars,*
But in ourselves, that we are underlings.
Brutus and Caesar: what should be in that "Caesar"?
Why should that name be sounded more than yours?
Write them together, yours is as fair a name;
Sound them, it doth become the mouth as well;
Weigh them, it is as heavy; conjure with 'em,
Brutus will start a spirit as soon as Caesar.
Now, in the names of all the gods at once,
Upon what meat does this our Caesar feed
That he is grown so great? Age, thou art shamed!
Rome, thou hast lost the breed of noble bloods!
When went there by an age, since the great flood,
But it was famed with more than one man?
When could they say till now, that talk'd of Rome,
That her wide walls encompass'd but one man?
Now is it Rome indeed and room enough,
When there is in it but one only man.[1]

CRITICISMS OF NATURAL LAW'S METAPHYSICAL BAGGAGE

As part of a larger scene in which Cassius is trying to convince Brutus to kill Caesar, this selection illustrates practical rationality detached from the good. The values held by Cassius about how Rome is to be ruled permit a kind of practical thinking that endorses killing Caesar. On the other hand, Marc Antony holds a different view of Rome and consequently employs a different line of practical rationality. Cassius also represents "modern thinking"

1 William Shakespeare, *Julius Caesar*, Act 1 Scene II.

in his line about being masters of fate and not relying on the stars for explanation. If "the stars" were taken in a larger sense of "metaphysical thinking" with its medieval connotations, modern thinkers have sought to free the individual from such influences. "Freedom" is empty, however, unless we are free to pursue the good. If we do not know the good then we cannot be free to intentionally pursue the good. We will see how attempts to think of law only in terms of practical rationality and a multiplicity of common goods do not solve problems that face society today, nor would this have helped resolve the dispute between Cassius and Aeneas's promised ancestor Julius Caesar.[2]

Oliver Wendell Holmes voiced a common opinion of natural law when, in his 1918 *Harvard Law Review* article, he said, "The jurists who believe in natural law seem to me to be in that naïve state of mind that accepts what has been familiar and accepted by all men everywhere."[3] Holmes stated that it is simply another name for the return to tradition. Furthermore, natural law theorists confuse as an *a priori* duty what is actually just a conditional of practical rationality: If you want to live with others in this way then you must do the following .... Rather than being a deliverance of reason, natural law is determined by our "attitude" toward the cosmos, and we should not believe we can have final knowledge of the unimaginable whole. And so, twentieth-century American legal philosophy begins with skepticism about the ability for humans to successfully achieve knowledge in the area of metaphysics. By way of contrast, natural law, as an ethical and political theory, is associated with medieval scholastic metaphysics and Roman Catholic theology. These seem to indicate that natural law will not be a popular or viable theory in a contemporary setting.

However, since the 1970s, there has been a resurgence of natural law thinking that has attempted to discuss natural law theory without grounding it in any specific view of human nature or metaphysics. This is called the New Natural Law Theory. The increased popularity of the natural law theory raises the question as to how this should be assessed. This chapter defines what contemporary natural law theory is by looking at some of its main advocates, then contrasts it with alternative theories, and concludes

2 I say promised ancestor because of the lines in Virgil in which Julius Caesar is foretold as the one who will rule over an empire without end. There is reason to think that Virgil borrowed this idea from the book of Isaiah and fit it into his Roman national story. Virgil makes the messiah into a worldly king who rules over the city of man. He did not borrow from Isaiah the suffering servant of chapter 53, who becomes the vicarious atonement for his people. This marks a stark difference in how the city of man and the city of God understand the human condition.

3 Oliver Wendell Holmes, "Natural Law," *Harvard Law Review* (1918).

by arguing that although natural law provides a better framework for rationally justifying ethical and political actions in relation to the good, contemporary incarnations of natural law have not given a clear definition of the good as the end in itself. Contemporary natural law theory has not adequately addressed the concept of the good or grounded the good in the metaphysical absolute. If natural law theory fails to correctly define the good, its method will be unsuccessful and its return will not be permanent.

As far as secular moral philosophy is concerned, during most of the twentieth century, natural law ethics has been considered a lifeless medieval relic, preserved only in Roman Catholic schools of moral theology. It is still true that many of the chief proponents of natural law are of that particular religious persuasion, but they have recently begun to defend their position by arguments that make no explicit appeal to their religious or metaphysical beliefs. In an important way the claim that only natural law has metaphysical baggage is unfair. Even Holmes, for all of his claims to avoid metaphysics, clearly bases his legal philosophy on his own metaphysics: "If we believe that we come out of the universe, not it out of us, we must admit that we do not know what we are talking about when we speak of brute matter. We do know that a certain complex of energies can wag its tail and another can make syllogisms."[4] As a product of nineteenth-century naturalism, Holmes and his school are hardly free from metaphysical presuppositions. Indeed, this illustrates the point made in an earlier chapter that legal philosophy cannot avoid the relationship between the good, human nature, and the real, and rejection of natural law is really a rejection of "that natural law," not a rejection of this relationship.

Christopher Tollefsen helps define the New Natural Law Theory and distinguish it from its older counterpart. He says:

> The new natural law theory is grounded in a view about basic human goods and our apprehension of them. All action is understood on this theory to be action for the sake of some good or goods, but not all goods may be said to be basic. Some, such as money, or medicine, are clearly instrumental to the achievement of other goods. But the chain of explanation or justification for action cannot proceed to infinity: some goods must be pursued not for the sake of some other good, but for their own sake. The new theory identifies these goods, more or less, as life and health, personal integrity in its various aspects, and harmony with whatever source of transcendent meaning there

4 Ibid.

> may or may not be. Recently, the new theorists have identified marriage as a basic good different from the rest.[5]

What is especially helpful in Tollefsen's account is that he notices the role of epistemology in this theory. "Crucial, and controversial, to the new theory's account of these basic goods is the theory's moral epistemology. As basic, the fundamental goods are not inferred to be good from some other source of knowledge; but as good, and thus action guiding, they are not known by theoretical reason but by practical reason."[6] And so the theory is relying on the distinction between practical and theoretical rationality, and the distinction between what is immediately intuited and what is known by inference. I purposely use the terms "intuited" and "known," because what is intuited is not yet knowledge; to become knowledge the initial intuition must be given rational justification.

This has been one of the problems in identifying the good in the history we have considered here. Moral intuitions about what is good have been taken to be absolute without providing rational justification that this really is the good. When moral intuitions compete, the move is made to skepticism, or knowledge is impugned as insufficient even though the problem was with intuition, not knowledge. In this sense the New Natural Law Theory is not introducing anything new. It is continuing the Modernist tendency to focus on practical rationality aimed at the "goods" of this life, with some concession made for the transcendent without affirming that we can have clarity about what is transcendent (or as Tollefsen said, "what may or may not be" rather than "it is clear what is and is not transcendent").

The new natural law is also somewhat hesitant to put much emphasis on human nature. Again, Tollefsen is helpful in identifying the new approach:

> On any account of human nature as it is, there will be any number of tendencies, dispositions, and so on, of conflicting natures, even in one individual. Moreover, there are clearly tendencies and dispositions towards actions traditionally condemned by natural law theorists. ... But it is precisely by our theoretical study that we arrive at this problem: the problem is in human nature. It cannot, it seems, be simply by closer attention to that nature that the normative question gets resolved. Rather, one must reflect on the objects

5 Christopher Tollefsen, "Natural Law and Modern Meta-Ethics: A Guided Tour," in Mark J. Cherry, *Natural Law and the Possibility of a Global Ethics*, Vol. 11 (Dordrecht; Boston: Kluwer Academic Publishers, 2004), 200.

6 Christopher Tollefsen, "Natural Law and Modern Meta-Ethics: A Guided Tour," in Ibid.

> of the various dispositions and inclinations and ask oneself whether those objects are genuinely fulfilling or not.[7]

This quote shows us that the idea of a moral law based on human nature is being rejected, and also demonstrates once again the epistemology being used. Asking if an object is genuinely fulfilling is not much different than the ancient question of asking what it means to live well, or what is the happiest life. Thus in another sense this is not a new approach, and it will encounter some of the same tensions that were present between the Epicureans and the Stoics, which we considered earlier. The goods spoken of are no longer ends in themselves, but instead are the means to achieving fulfillment. The theory mistakenly identifies the good with fulfillment and then thinks about how to achieve fulfillment apart from knowing what is real. We can now consider some examples of natural law thinkers and determine if indeed this is how the new theory has progressed.

GERMAIN GRISEZ

To help explain what is new about the New Natural Law Theory, we can rely on Germain Grisez's book, written in collaboration with Russell Shaw, titled *Beyond the New Morality: The Responsibilities of Freedom.*[8] We find here that the theory is not characterized by a sharp split with metaphysics. Indeed, it posits that there is a human nature, and that humans stand in relation to God as creatures to the Creator. What the authors wish to communicate is that there are two traditions – the Judeo-Christian tradition with its belief in God the Creator, and the Greek tradition with its emphasis on human excellence – that together give us a picture of what it means to lead the good life.

The organizing value is "freedom." The authors discuss different levels of freedom, such as doing what one wants, political freedom, creative freedom, and the highest freedom, which they identify as self-determination. This self-determination was given to humans by God, and it was through the misuse of self-determination that evil entered the world. They argue that humans can use the freedom of self-determination to achieve human goods and lead a fulfilling life.

To help define what counts as a fulfilling life, the authors contrast it with the otherworldliness they find in St. Augustine.[9] The problem with

7 Christopher Tollefsen, "Natural Law and Modern Meta-Ethics: A Guided Tour," in Ibid.
8 Germain Grisez (b. 1929) is an American Catholic moral theologian.
9 Germain Gabriel Grisez and Russell B. Shaw, *Beyond the New Morality: The Responsibilities of Freedom*, 3rd ed. (Notre Dame: University of Notre Dame Press, 1988), 256.

the beatific vision and heaven as a goal is not simply that such a vision is not the good (as I have argued, contrasting a "vision" with what it means to actually know God); the problem is in thinking fulfillment lies in achieving goals. Much like Hobbes, these authors argue that once a goal is achieved, the person will no longer be satisfied. The mistake is in thinking that the good as a goal is the kind of thing that can be finally achieved and therefore exhausted, rather than as something that is grown in forever.

In a similar way the authors argue that Aristotle's view of human nature was too narrow in identifying human capacities with rationality. Rather, "[a] person is not a disembodied intellect; a person engages in other kinds of activity besides intellectual activity, and these other spheres of experience also make their special contributions to personhood."[10] This is an important argument because it helps illustrate how important "human nature" is to any theory about the good or law. For instance, I might change Aristotle's wording slightly to say that rationality is fundamental to the human person. In this way I would agree with these authors that human life consists of many activities and capacities, but that rationality as the means for understanding is fundamental to anything humans do (play, work, love – all require understanding, and our lives are enriched as we understand more). Even those who argue against this viewpoint are asking us to understand, making their argument self-refuting.

Grisez and Shaw identify eight categories of human goods. These are, roughly, those related to physical life, speculative knowledge, aesthetic experience, play, integrity, practical reasonableness, friendship, and religion. The first four are thought to be independent of human action, whereas the last four are aspects of practical rationality. The authors claim that this is an exhaustive list of the goods that can be sought as ends in themselves.

There is a hint that perhaps the highest good can be found. If so, it would be in the category "religion." First, the authors continue their critique of otherworldliness. "Any interpretation of Christian teaching which reduces life in this world to a second-level act, with heaven as its goal, deserves such criticism, and has no satisfactory answer."[11] By way of contrast, the authors suggest that there are interpretations of Christianity that understand the kingdom of God as "already present, though hidden, in this

[10] Ibid., 44.
[11] Ibid., 219.

life and this world."[12] This gives meaning to morally good acts that overcome social injustice in this life. Of course, this raises a question about how we are to understand the relationship between our actions and achieving the good. The "heaven" view says that our actions here might not produce much good, but we will be rewarded in the next life. Like Kant, these authors fall back on an appeal to God's faithfulness in protecting the relationship between doing what is right and human well-being. Another possible solution is to argue that what is right depends on what is good, so that by definition, doing what is right leads to what is good. This solution is only counterintuitive if the good is misidentified as happiness.

Another important contribution is that these authors believe hope in God translates into the belief that good will overcome evil. This is not explained beyond noting that the conclusion follows from the premises about the nature of God. Obviously this presupposes that there is a God, and it is here that the authors concede that any ethical theories rely on a worldview. Equally important is their claim that:

> People who wish to live good lives should seek the truth about the religious question. The task is not merely to sort out the claims of various religions and worldviews according to how congenial or uncongenial they might be to oneself, but to determine which gives a credible account of the source or sources of meaning and value, offers a reasonable plan for living in harmony with that more-than-human reality, and thus *deserves* to be accepted. If one finds a worldview which one has good reason to believe is true, one should accept it and make the commitment to shape one's life in accord with it, for this means living in accord with one's best understanding of reality.[13]

Although these authors do not make the point, it could be argued that knowing this truth is the highest good to which the other goods they identified are subordinate. Indeed, how exactly the eight categories of goods are shaped and understood will depend on which worldview is true. Furthermore, all of those categories of goods seem to be ways of saying we should understand reality and act consistently with this understanding.

Even so, one important problem seems untouched. The description of how to determine which worldview is true leaves the sense that perhaps the world is ambiguous at some level. What does it mean to have a "credible account" and a "reasonable plan"? Will people disagree about what these are and which worldview they qualify? Will this disagreement be rational,

[12] Ibid., 219.
[13] Ibid., 231.

so that rational people find competing worldviews to be "credible" within any failure in their use of reason? If so, it appears impossible to claim that humans are responsible for knowing which worldview is true, and therefore cannot be responsible for knowing any of the goods that depend on knowing the correct worldview. To affirm responsibility, it must also be affirmed that it is clear that God exists, so the alternative belief is without excuse.

NATURAL LAW WITHOUT METAPHYSICS

Having considered how Grisez framed the New Natural Law Theory, we can now consider a few other thinkers, although this is certainly not intended to be an exhaustive list. As noted in the preceding chapter, it is impossible to disconnect legal theory from beliefs about what is real. In this sense, all legal theories are "natural law" in that they all claim to best accord with human nature and reality. To move beyond a formal sense of what modern natural law looks like, it is necessary to examine some of those who are calling for a return of this approach. This will bring to the surface three common features of contemporary natural law: (1) the belief in universal laws based on human goods and human flourishing; (2) a focus on practical rationality directed toward the goods of human flourishing; and (3) an empirical method of discovering what it means for humans to flourish. Some of the thinkers considered will emphasize one or more of these, to different extents, but these points help distinguish contemporary natural law from its medieval form. The modern approach is empirical rather than rationalist and focuses on human flourishing as a knowable and universal empirical finding – and all of this without any necessary connection to theism.[14]

An example can be seen in Martha Nussbaum[15] and her book, *Women and Human Development: The Capabilities Approach*, which focuses on what can be called natural law with respect to women's rights. She summarizes her project by saying:

> The aim of the project as a whole is to provide the philosophical underpinning for an account of basic constitutional principles that should be respected and implemented by the governments of all nations, as a bare

[14] Parts of this chapter are based on my research which appeared in "Contemporary Natural Law Theory." *New Blackfriars*. Vol. 86. No. 1005 (2005): 478–492.

[15] Martha Nussbaum (b. 1947) is an American philosopher who studies ancient Greek philosophy and contemporary political and ethical subjects.

> minimum of what respect for human dignity requires ... the best approach to this idea of a basic social minimum is provided by an approach that focuses on human capabilities, that is, what people are actually able to do and to be – in a way informed by an intuitive idea of a life that is worthy of the dignity of the human being.[16]

Although Nussbaum applies this specifically to women, it is an example of how the three principles mentioned earlier are applied by a contemporary thinker. The focus is on what people are actually able to do and be, and then this is applied through practical rationality to ensure human flourishing. This does not resemble the critique of Holmes when he says that natural law tries to teach humans what they should want to want, indicating that this criticism is a straw man.[17]

Perhaps the name most associated with the return of natural law is John Finnis. His book, *Natural Law and Natural Rights*, is seen by many as the initiator of contemporary interest in natural law theory.[18] In it he defines the modern approach to natural law. Central to his project is practical rationality aimed at human well-being:

> The sense that the phrase 'natural law' has in this book can be indicated in the following rather bald assertions. ... There is (i) a set of basic practical principles which indicate the basic forms of human flourishing as goods to be pursued and realized, and which are in one way or another used by everyone who considers what to do, however unsound his conclusions; and (ii) a set of basic methodological requirements of practical reasonableness (itself one of the basic forms of human flourishing) which distinguish sound from unsound practical thinking and which, when all brought to bear, provide the criteria for distinguishing between acts that (always or in particular circumstances) are reasonable all things considered, i.e. between ways of acting that are morally right or morally wrong – thus enabling one to formulate (iii) a set of general moral standards.[19]

This approach is present in the other thinkers that are considered here, with only a slight variation. Their differences arise with respect to the content of natural law. What is relevant here is to see how these thinkers define

16 Martha Craven Nussbaum, *Women and Human Development: The Capabilities Approach* (Cambridge; New York: Cambridge University Press, 2000), 5.

17 Holmes, "Natural Law."

18 John Finnis (b. 1940) is an Australian philosopher who has taught at Oxford and Notre Dame, and is known for his work on natural law.

19 John Finnis, *Natural Law and Natural Rights* (Oxford: Oxford University Press, 1980), 23.

natural law and in doing this give a sense of how they try to avoid metaphysics. Finnis summarizes natural law in the following manner: "A theory of natural law claims to be able to identify conditions and principles of practical right mindedness, of good and proper order among men and in individual conduct."[20] Or consider how David Braybrooke summarizes his approach to natural law:

> I mean to present and stand by the basic view of moral rules found in St Thomas Aquinas's medieval natural law theory, a theory that makes three chief claims: first, there is a set of universally applicable moral rules, with principled allowances for variations in circumstances; second (another empirical thesis), people will thrive and their societies will thrive only if these rules prevail; and third (a further empirical thesis), human beings by and large are inclined to heed the rules.[21]

Two questions naturally arise in response to the empirical aspect of this theory. First, to what extent is natural law dependent on generalizing from a descriptive approach to humans (the fallacy of induction), and second, how can an *ought* be derived from a descriptive claim about human nature? Finnis does argue that sociological investigation can play a part in furthering natural law theory: "Descriptive knowledge thus can occasion a modification of the judgments of importance and significance with which the theorist first approached his data, and can suggest a reconceptualization. But the knowledge will not have been attained without a preliminary conceptualization and thus a preliminary set of principles of selection and relevance drawn from some practical viewpoint."[22] But this does not mean that natural law is a set of matter-of-fact claims about what humans do. Rather, Finnis introduces an important facet of contemporary theory by stating that it is based on self-evident principles about the good and not on descriptions of human nature:

> It is simply not true that "any form of a natural law theory of morals entails the belief that propositions about man's duties and obligations can be inferred from propositions about his nature" ... the basic forms of good and evil and which can be adequately grasped by anyone of the age of reason (and not just by metaphysicians), are *per se nota* (self evident) and indemonstrable.[23]

20 Ibid., 18.

21 David Braybrooke, *Natural Law Modernized* (Toronto; Buffalo: University of Toronto Press, 2001), 23.

22 Finnis, *Natural Law and Natural Rights*, 17.

23 Ibid., 33.

The skeptic will ask how these self-evident principles are known. If they are indemonstrable, and not inferred from sense data, then how can they be known? The short answer is that "by a simple act of non inferential understanding one grasps that the object of the inclination which one experiences is an instance of a general form of good, for oneself (and others like one)."[24] The skeptic will most likely see this as "spooky" ethics without any way to analyze the so-called results that follow from such an approach. Mortimer Adler,[25] who could be considered a forerunner of the contemporary revival of natural law, even though he is a committed Thomist, provided a better description of how these self-evident principles are known:

> It is by reference to our common human needs that we claim to know what is really good for all human beings. Knowing this, we are also justified in claiming that we can determine the truth or falsity of prescriptions or injunctions.... No one, I think, would question man's need for knowledge or the truth of the prescription that everyone ought to want and seek knowledge. That truth comes to us as the conclusion of reasoning that rests on two premises. The first is a categorical prescription or injunction: We ought to desire (seek and acquire) that which is really good for us. The second is a statement of fact about human nature: Man has a potentiality or capacity for knowing that tends toward or seeks fulfillment through the acquirement of knowledge.[26]

Here Adler not only provides an answer to how self-evident truths are known, but addresses another form of this same question, which asks how the practical rationality of natural law can operate without categorical truths:

> The truth of the categorical prescription that underlies every piece of reasoning that leads to a true prescriptive conclusion is a self evident truth. Anyone can test this for himself by trying to think the opposite and finding it impossible. We simply cannot think that we ought to desire that which is really bad for us or that we ought not to desire that which is really good for us. Without knowing in advance which things are in fact really good or bad for us, we do know at once that "ought to desire" is inseparable in its meaning from the meaning of "really good."[27]

24 Ibid., 34.

25 Mortimer Jerome Adler (1902–2001) was an American philosopher and educator. He was known for his advocacy of adult education through discussion of the great books.

26 Mortimer Jerome Adler, *Six Great Ideas: Truth, Goodness, Beauty, Liberty, Equality, Justice : Ideas We Judge by, Ideas We Act on* (New York: Macmillan), 79.

27 Ibid., 80.

Once categorical truths about the good have been established, hypothetical imperatives can be deduced to provide the content of the natural law. Robert George[28] states that knowledge of universal practical truths is knowable precisely because we can grasp basic underived practical principles.[29]

The second question that must be addressed is the is/ought problem that many accuse natural law theory of having violated. Finnis builds on his view of self-evident truths to answer this problem:

> They are not inferred from speculative principles. They are not inferred from facts. They are not inferred from metaphysical propositions about human nature, or about the nature of good and evil, or about 'the function of a human being', nor are they inferred from a teleological conception of nature or any other conception of nature. They are not inferred or derived from anything. They are underived (though not innate).[30]

The reason that there is no is/ought problem is that the moral imperatives of the natural law theory are not derived from facts, but from self-evident "oughts" about the good. Adler voiced similar thoughts in the earlier quotes. This is one way to interpret the Socratic viewpoint from works like the *Meno* and *Gorgias*. Contemporary natural law theorists seem generally to agree that the theory can begin with something like these self-evident goods that then provide the framework for practical rationality.

THE CONTENT OF CONTEMPORARY NATURAL LAW

Once the method employed by natural law is defined, how can it be filled in with content? There are some important differences between the thinkers presented here as to the specific content, but how that content is arrived at is very similar. Finnis says:

> As I understand the natural law, it consists of three sets of principles: first, and most fundamentally, a set of principles directing human choice and action toward intelligible purposes, i.e., basic human goods which, as intrinsic aspects of human well being and fulfillment, constitute reasons for actions whose intelligibility as reasons does not depend on any more fundamental reasons (or on sub rational motives such as the desire for emotional satisfactions) to which they are mere means; second, a set of 'intermediate' moral

[28] Robert George (b. 1955) is an American philosopher of law who currently teaches at Princeton.

[29] Robert P. George, *In Defense of Natural Law* (Oxford: Clarendon Press, 1999), 3.

[30] Finnis, *Natural Law and Natural Rights*, 33.

> principles which specify the most basic principle of morality by directing choice and action toward possibilities that may be chosen consistently with a will toward integral human fulfillment and away from possibilities the choosing of which is inconsistent with such a will; and third, fully specific moral norms which require or forbid (sometimes without exceptions) certain specific possible choices.[31]

Or consider a comparable passage from David Braybrooke:

> There are three main lines of thought on which the empirical grounds can be seen to be operating: (1) observations about one or another aspect of human nature, which can be pieced together to establish an empirical perspective; (2) the attention given to the need to adapt the laws to different circumstances, which implies that circumstances must be taken into account both before and after any specific adaptation; and (3) reasoning from the essence of the human species.[32]

The content is filled in through the use of hypothetical imperatives, or practical rationality, building on the self-evident truths of human well-being. The skeptic was right to raise an eyebrow at the idea of self-evident truths concerning human flourishing. It seems that once these are conceded, practical rationality takes over and provides moral content. The main issue will therefore be "What are these goods of human flourishing?" Whereas Finnis and Braybrooke differ as to their view of sexual morality, they first differ about what the self-evident truths are that should be employed to settle such disputes.

One final note of importance is that these contemporary natural law thinkers approach their theory without relying on theistic metaphysics. Some of them are more explicit in this than others, and some more consistent in this than others. Finnis and George see religion as a basic human good, and Finnis even speculates that friendship with God might be the highest good. But Braybrooke does not believe that mention of God is necessary in natural law. "The core theory does not invoke the will of God to establish the content of the moral rules that it upholds or to confer upon them their standing as natural laws."[33] Generally this is not seen as a hindrance to this form of natural law being accepted, because if one wants to include God, then Finnis and George are ready to offer

31 Ibid., 102.
32 Braybrooke, *Natural Law Modernized*, 37.
33 Ibid., 9.

their approach, and if one wants a purely secular version, Braybrooke is ready at hand.

ARE THERE ANY ALTERNATIVES TO NATURAL LAW THINKING?

Having seen how contemporary thinkers define natural law theory, it will be helpful to consider alternatives to this theory in order to understand if it is really different. We have already studied the emergence of these theories in Modernity and their attempt to formulate moral laws apart from metaphysics. Can natural law follow this example? Four major systems stand out as alternatives and opponents to natural law theory in Modernity: ethical relativism, positivism, deontology, and consequentialism. Each of these, in one form or another, has been put forward as a theory in the last two centuries while natural law has largely been out of favor. Nevertheless, as Alasdair MacIntyre has noted,[34] each relies on differing conceptions of justice and what counts as being morally rational. In this sense, each of these relies on beliefs about the nature of things.

That we can ask if the return of natural law theory is beneficial implies that natural law theory has been absent, and that other theories have been dominating the scene. Yet, in his preface to Heinrich Rommen's *The Natural Law*, Russell Hittinger comments that "every generation, it is said, finds a new reason for the study of natural law. For Rommen and many others of his generation, totalitarianism provided that occasion."[35] Indeed, this is what we will discover here: Supposed competing theories are simply alternative formulations of the good, human nature, and the real. When these come to rest on skepticism about the possibility of knowledge (and this is coupled with horrors such as World War II), motivation is rediscovered to articulate more clearly the good and the moral law.

ETHICAL RELATIVISM

One competing theory is ethical relativism. This theory argues that the central concept in ethics, "the good," is not the same for all persons, or it cannot be known what is good, and therefore each individual person's

34 Alasdair C. MacIntyre, *Whose Justice? Which Rationality?* (Notre Dame: University of Notre Dame Press), 410.

35 Hittinger, "Preface." In Rommen and Hanley, eds., *The Natural Law: A Study in Legal and Social History and Philosophy*, 290.

belief about what is good for themselves is equal to any other person's belief about the good. Perhaps the first philosopher to hold this position was the Greek sophist Protagoras, who claimed that man is the measure of all things. We saw in an earlier chapter that Modernity opened with this view as expressed by Hobbes. Contemporary thinkers holding versions of this view include Goodman, Putnam, and Rorty. A similar view that will be coupled with relativism in this chapter is ethical skepticism held by such thinkers as J. L. Mackie.

People can arrive at this position for a number of reasons. For instance, it could be the outcome of an epistemological method. If the method adopted is empiricism, and it is noticed that people make differing and often contradictory claims about what is good, then it might be concluded that, as a matter of fact, what is good is relative. Another approach that could lead to relativism is the assumption that what persons desire is what is good for them. This approach seems to believe that the satisfaction of desires is good, and because desires differ from person to person, so will the good. It could also be the result of metaphysical commitments. For instance, evolutionary theory may lead a person to believe that human nature is changing and therefore what is good at one point in time may not be good at another. Or, if persons believe that death is the end of their existence, they may also believe that they should do whatever will make them happy in this life, and that therefore the good is relative. Also, postmodernism asserts that the good is relative by noting that in the past, the concept of "the good" has been used by those in power to oppress others, and therefore this concept must be deconstructed to illuminate ways it has been used and to give greater freedom to individuals to determine what is good for themselves.

Whether a person is an ethical relativist for one of the aforementioned reasons, or for a reason that has not been considered here, this view is believed to be an alternative to natural law theory, and its proponents would resist a resurgence in natural thinking if it meant the decline of ethical relativism. Both ethical relativism and natural law theory cannot be true. This is because they make contradictory claims about human nature. Specifically, ethical relativism claims either that human nature cannot be known, or it is different for each individual, and therefore there is no such thing as "human nature" that is common to all. In contrast, natural law theory presupposes that there is something called "human nature" that is the same for all, is knowable at least in part, and therefore what is good for human nature can also be known at least in part.

In claiming that human nature is not knowable, ethical relativism is making epistemological and metaphysical claims. These are that human nature cannot be known and that there is no human nature – which of the two claims is logically basic is an interesting topic. There may be a number of reasons as to why these conclusions are reached, as noted earlier. In contrast, natural law theory makes metaphysical assertions about human nature and presupposes that human nature is in part knowable. One such claim about human nature is that it includes rationality broadly construed as the ability to think and draw inferences through the use of the laws of thought (identity, noncontradiction, excluded middle). Is it possible to consistently deny that humans have the property of rationality? Ethical relativism cannot claim *a priori* that humans are not rational without being self-contradictory, nor can it claim this is an *a posteriori* truth without the problem of induction. In contrast, natural law theory places as one of its foundations the realization that there is a common human nature central to which is the capacity for rationality. In this sense, a resurgence of natural law theory to replace ethical relativism should be welcomed.

Being called an ethical relativist is sometimes understood to be negative. Because of this it can be hard to find persons that gladly take the title. One is Richard Rorty, and he is discussed at a later point. Another is Bernard Williams, whom Hilary Putnam describes as a moderate relativist.[36] He is quoted by Putnam as saying:

> Precisely because we are not unencumbered intelligences selecting in principle among all possible outlooks, we can accept that this outlook is ours just because of the history that has made it ours; or, more precisely, has both made us, and made the outlook as something that is ours. We are no less contingently formed than the outlook is, and the formation is significantly the same. We and our outlook are not simply in the same place at the same time. If we really understand this, deeply understand it, we can be free of what is indeed another scientistic illusion, that it is our job as rational agents to search for, or at least move as best we can towards, a system of political and ethical ideas which would be the best from an absolute point of view, a point of view that was free of contingent historical perspective.[37]

36 Sir Bernard Williams (1929–2003) was an English philosopher known for his work in ethics and the history of philosophy.Hilary Putnam (b. 1926) is an American philosopher known for his contributions to metaphysics, the philosophy of mind, and the philosophy of logic. He argues in favor of a kind of internal pragmatism that he believes is different from relativism.

37 Hilary Putnam, *Ethics without Ontology* (Cambridge, MA; London: Harvard University Press, 2004), 160.

Putnam argues that Williams has accepted one side of a false dichotomy. Either values are merely contingent, or we need to find an absolute perspective. On this basis, Putnam believes that he (Putnam) is not a relativist, but instead offers an alternative. This he traces to Dewey and says:

> What is missing in this dichotomy is precisely the idea that characterizes my pragmatist "enlightenment": the idea that there is such a thing as the *situated* resolution of political and ethical problems and conflicts (of what Dewey calls "problematical situations"), and that claims concerning evaluations of – and proposals for the resolution of – problematical situations can be more and less *warranted* without being *absolute*. ... Dewey stressed that problematical situations are contingent and their resolutions are likewise contingent; but there is still a difference, an all-important difference, between *thinking* that a claim concerning the resolution is a warranted claim and its actually *being* warranted.[38]

What is missing, Putnam says, for a position like that taken by Williams, is pragmatism. It is his pragmatism that motivates Putnam to find a solution to the is/ought dichotomy.[39] Pragmatism accepts many of the problems that also excite postmodern thinkers, such as the claim that all is contingent and we cannot escape our historical situatedness. I include Putnam as a relativist because he rejects the idea of an absolute (either of knowledge or the good) and instead opts for fallibility.

Pragmatists, as relativists, are correct that "what works" is relative. It is relative to the good. Therefore, what a given person believes "works" is relative to what that person believes is the good. It does not follow from this that there is no human good that persists over time. To make such a claim is to have already accepted the belief that all is change and there is no "human nature."

In his book, *Persons, Moral Worth, and Embryos*, Francis Beckwith uses the phrase "human substance" to denote "human nature" and defines a substance as having (among other things) "the aptitude to exist in itself and not as a part of any other being."[40] This focuses his argument about why abortion is wrong, and also brings to the surface the nominalism of relativism. To say that all is contingent is to say that nothing persists as the same over time. Applied consistently, this undermines the possibility for knowledge. To resort to *fallibilism* does not stave off nihilism.

38 Ibid., 129.
39 Putnam, *The Collapse of the Factvalue Dichotomy: And Other Essays*, 190.
40 Francis Beckwith, *Persons, Moral Worth, and Embryos* (Leyden: Brill, 2011).

POSITIVISM

Another influential ethical and legal theory is positivism. This view claims that all human norms, whether legal or moral, are constructs of human society. It is not full-blown relativism in that the individual does not have the moral or legal ability to determine what is good; the good is determined by society at large in connection with its tradition and an externalist description of how law is produced. However, it is relativistic in that it disconnects law and ethics from human nature and must concede that different societies and traditions will have, and do have, different norms. It often disconnects the concepts of morality and law and focuses on the practical reality that law is determined by social facts. Contemporary thinkers that hold this position include Austin, Hart, and Kelsen.

A person often takes this position after realizing that there are diverse legal and ethical systems in the world, and this seems to contradict the idea that humans share a common nature that should give rise to common legal and moral systems. Thus this view also makes epistemological and metaphysical assertions. Consider, once again, Holmes in his article about natural law: "I used to say when I was young, that truth was the majority vote of that nation that could lick all others ... and I think that the statement was correct insofar as it implied that our test of truth is a reference to either a present or imagined future majority in favor of our view."[41] Like ethical relativism, to be consistent, it must deny that there is a human nature, or that human nature is a construct of the majority. If it is acknowledged that there is a common human nature, it follows that there is a common good for human nature: What is good for human nature in me will be good for human nature in you because it is the same thing.

There are two other aspects of positivism that are worth thinking about. The first is the form that claims the law, moral or legal, is given by tradition or divine command. This can be called heteronomy. Such positivism shares in common with its family theory the assertion that a law is a law by the will of a legislator or lawgiver. It is the legal theory following from the larger philosophy of voluntarism, which is itself a derivative of skepticism about the role and function of the intellect. This form of positivism looks to ground the law in an unchanging lawgiver but disconnects that source from human nature. Assuming that the claim of heteronomy is not that there is no human nature, but instead that the law is given apart from human nature, it can only make sense if the heteronomous

41 Holmes, "Natural Law."

law is still consistent with human nature. For instance, God, as the creator of human nature, would be the one who best knows what is according to human nature. If we take the meaning of the term "good" to be "that which is according to human nature" then for a law to be good it must be according to human nature. To say otherwise would be to assert that God commanded something that is not good and that is contrary to the human nature He created. This means that natural law theory can be consistent with divine command theory in maintaining that God commands that which is according to human nature. This avoids the problems of heteronomy and the disconnect it produces between law and human nature; in natural law theory the law cannot conflict with what is good (a law that does so is no law at all).

The second problem faced by heteronomous theories is that they separate the law from reason and rationality. Again, this is in keeping with voluntarism as an aspect of skepticism about the ability of reason. The law is known through tradition or command and is an act of the will rather than a deliverance of reason. This both denies a central aspect of human nature and raises questions about responsibility. If the law is knowable only through acquaintance with a given text or tradition, those without access cannot be held accountable. In contrast, natural law theory maintains that because human nature is knowable, and the law is based on human nature, responsibility applies to all. Because part of being human is the potential for the use of reason, all humans can use reason to know the law and know what they ought to do.

It is also worthwhile to ask if positivists really do escape the formal structure of natural law. Can they escape rooting their claims about law in the nature of reality? Hart's definition of legal positivism does not sufficiently distinguish it from what I call the natural moral law.[42] "Here we shall take Legal Positivism to mean the simple contention that it is in no sense a necessary truth that laws reproduce or satisfy certain demands of morality, though in fact they have often done so."[43] It becomes more distinct when he likens it to his understanding of what science does in discovering laws: "A scientific theory's claim to forward our understanding of nature is therefore, in the last resort, dependent on its power to predict what will occur."[44] He claims that natural law is part of an outdated

42 Herbert Lionel Adolphus Hart (1907–1992) was a legal philosopher who defended a form of legal positivism.

43 H. L. A. Hart, *The Concept of Law*, 2nd ed. (Oxford: Clarendon Press, 1994), 315.

44 Ibid., 184.

theory of nature that believed the natural world changes toward some goal or end.

Even so, Hart concedes that it is exceedingly difficult to avoid acting toward an end. Therefore, he accepts that there must be some general shared end to hold humans together, and posits that this end is survival. He believes this is a contingent truth, that it could be otherwise, but that in fact most humans desire to survive. Furthermore, it is this desire to survive that is presupposed by the need for justice and equity. He calls this an "attenuated version of Natural Law" and contrasts it with Aristotle and Aquinas who argued for "higher ends" but did not show that these are knowable.

Therefore, relying on Hume, Hart argues that humans cannot survive without each other, and communal survival requires laws that presuppose some sense of equity and justice. "We are committed to it as something presupposed by the terms of our discussion; for our concern is with social arrangements for continued existence, not with those of a suicide club."[45] Thus he claims to give a minimal natural law based on five truisms about human nature. All of these are related to the physical condition of humanity. Nevertheless, formally speaking, he is doing the same thing that the New Natural Law Theory is doing: giving his view of human nature and then positing goods necessary for that nature to be fulfilled. Once again we are forced to wrestle with the questions about what is real in order to answer questions about what is good.

DEONTOLOGY

A third alternative to natural law is deontology. Deontology's best-known representative is Immanuel Kant, and his influence continues to be felt in the emphasis on obligation in thinkers like Hart. Unlike the views just considered, deontology places rationality at the center of its theory and emphasizes the use of reason to direct the will. In this sense, it is often very similar to natural law theory. The difference we focused on here is that deontology emphasizes the concept of duty as the moral absolute (that by which an action is determined to be morally right or wrong), whereas natural law theory focuses on the concept of the good as the moral absolute. Unless this difference is explicitly brought out, it could go unnoticed, and a person might be tempted to think these

45 Ibid., 188.

theories are similar. Duty (as the means to the good) and the good (as the end in itself) are different and not to be confused. Kant famously said that the only thing that can be called good without qualification is a good will.

Deontology is an attractive position because it emphasizes the rational aspect of human nature, and looks to establish a universal moral law in contrast to ethical relativism and positivism. Its focus on the universal was important for war-torn Europe that had witnessed years upon years of rivalry and bloodshed based on tradition and national conflicts. In contrast, deontology argues that all humans should obey a universal categorical imperative and should do so regardless of how they feel about the matter. In fact, it calls a person to act only based on the rational will and not based on other considerations. However, it finds its universality by focusing on duty and in doing so disconnects the moral law from the good. Natural law theory does not do this and keeps the good at the center of its theory. By doing so, it can also properly define duty and provide categorical imperatives that are aimed at the good.

Deontology, for all of its discussion about, and affirmation of, reason focuses on the will – on duty and obligation in the face of severe limits on pure rationality. It advocates that one should base one's action on what can be universalized, or, more specifically, on what one does not want universalized. For instance, no person would want harming others to be universalized, and so each individual person should abstain from harming others. This norm, applied to all the various areas of life, will produce a person who is virtuous, whose actions are in accord with the categorical imperative. What it has not addressed is how a person knows which actions to desire as universal and which should not be universal. It is often presented as if a person has this knowledge intuitively, and this might be satisfactory within one social group. But once we look outside a relatively small group, we soon find vast differences about what is intuitively desirable. We might find a group that prides itself on how many persons from a neighboring community they have harmed. Intuitively they might say this should be universalized. The result will be that deontology is based on intuitions and cannot provide a universal system of moral laws in the face of competing intuitions. This becomes a *reductio ad absurdum* argument against deontology. The categorical imperative becomes the following: will only that which you would will.

The term "moral law" was used by Kant to describe this system, and it is of no small significance that Hobbes also opened Modernity with not only a discussion of the moral law, but also the same initial moral law that Kant later championed. Nevertheless, for both thinkers, this law is deeply embedded within their epistemological and metaphysical framework. It either becomes so specific that one must be a Kantian to properly follow it, or so general that it has no meaning (the Hobbesian materialist and the Vedantist both affirm it but give it different meanings).

Has deontology successfully avoided metaphysics and produced a theory of the good that is free from baggage? Natural law's honest affirmation of the relationship between the good, human nature, and the real can solve the problems indicated earlier with deontology. It asks people to universalize, based not on what duties they would want others to exhibit, but rather on the equality of human nature. Duty, defined as the means to the good, can only be properly defined after the good has been defined. What is virtuous or obligatory is that which will get one the good, and therefore virtue separated from the good is empty. There are different types of virtues, such as moral (perhaps what we think of first when hearing this term), natural (talent of various kinds), and material (money, a car, etc.). Whether something is a virtue or a vice depends on whether it is used toward the good (money is an easy example). Deontology asks humans to live the dutiful life, to choose action based on what is obligatory, but does not give a means for defining duty in a noncircular way (duty as what you will, and you should will your duty). Natural law theory provides a solution to the problem by giving humans a way to define duty. Minimally we can say it is our duty to seek the good. Natural law theory preserves the distinction between the good and duty, and offers the ability to define duty appropriately by placing it in relationship to the good. It is therefore to be preferred over deontology.

A contemporary proponent of deontology, Ronald Dworkin, has given an impressive statement of the position in his recent *Justice for Hedgehogs*.[46] In this book, he works to clear the way for the independence of values from metaphysics and metaethics. To do so, he relies on appeals to common sense, or the ordinary viewpoint:

> You would be puzzled if someone told you that when you express a moral opinion you are not really saying anything. That you are only venting your spleen, or projecting some attitude, or declaring how you propose to live,

[46] Richard Dworkin (b. 1931) is an American philosopher who studies constitutional law. He emphasizes law as consistency and the role of interpretation. The ideal judge would interpret the law correctly, and we aspire to that interpretation.

> so that it would be a mistake to think that what you said is even a candidate for being true. … The ordinary view is committed to taking judgment at face value.[47]

Dworkin rejects the claim that knowing the truth about value requires knowing the truth about metaphysics. "We have established, I think, that the ordinary view makes sense and that external critics of that view do not. … We are always guilty of a kind of circularity. There is no way I can test the accuracy of my moral convictions except by deploying further moral convictions."[48] Like Hart, but in a different way, he relies on Hume. He is defending Hume's claim that any argument that supports a moral claim must itself presuppose further moral claims. The way to determine the truth of the matter in questions of morality is to consider responsibility. In explaining responsibility he connects to Kant's work:

> His [Kant's] various formulations of the categorical imperative were in the spirit of the responsibility project I described. Being able to universalize the maxim of our conduct is hardly a test of truth; different agents will produce different schemes responding to that requirement. But it is a test of responsibility, or at least an important part of such a test, because it provides the coherence that responsibility asks. It also tests the authenticity that responsibility demands.[49]

Because Dworkin is not concerned with arguing in a circle, it does not matter that this view of responsibility presupposes the truth of deontology. He is arguing that we should accept the moral claim that we ought to be responsible, because it best explains his view of values. We could understand responsibility differently, in the sense that we are responsible to live according to human nature. This is a teleological understanding of responsibility and it requires we know what is real about human nature in order to know what we ought to do. The idea of responsibility plays the central role for Dworkin in defending his claims about how we determine which moral assertions are best, so the ambiguity of the term is a real problem.

Ultimately, Dworkin does not define "the good." In his epilogue, he distinguishes between living well and the good life: "Someone lives well when

47 Ronald Dworkin, *Justice for Hedgehogs* (Cambridge, MA: Belknap Press of Harvard University Press, 2011), [xiii], 506.
48 Ibid., 100.
49 Ibid., 110.

he senses and pursues a good life for himself and does so with dignity."[50] Like Aristotle, he claims that we can live well without living a good life as a result of bad luck. He recognizes that a good life cannot be a trivial life, and that a good life must connect with what is of highest value. However, he is not able to identify for us what this is:

> It is difficult to say what gives weight as well as dignity to a life: what else it needs to make it good. Some people's lives are made good by great and durable achievement, but as we noticed this can be true for only very few people. Most good lives are good for much more transitory effect: for skill in some challenging craft or raising a family or making the lives of other people better. There are a thousand ways in which a life can be good.[51]

As we saw earlier with Hart, there are formal similarities here with the New Natural Law Theory: a list of human goods or excellences without any unifying *summum bonum*. Problematically, Dworkin rejects the need to establish a metaphysical foundation, and yet his viewpoint presupposes commonsense realism (a metaphysical position). Once again we find that any theory about human nature or the good will presuppose beliefs about what is real.

CONSEQUENTIALISM

The final alternative to be considered here is consequentialism. Whereas deontology focuses on duty as the moral absolute, consequentialism focuses on happiness. It asserts that the action whose consequence is the greatest amount of happiness for the greatest number, all things considered, is the correct action. There are important nuances to how one is to determine which action will have the greatest happiness for the greatest number, and these nuances determine different versions of consequentialist thinking. The important point here, however, is that this approach treats happiness as the moral absolute rather than the good. Classical teleology is not the same as consequentialism in that teleology made its focus the good, which has happiness as its effect, whereas consequentiaism makes its focus happiness itself. Consequentialism is found in Hobbes, Spinoza, Mill, Bentham, Moore, and Sidgwick.

A person may become a consequentialist for a number of reasons, including hedonistic considerations as well as altruistic considerations. A

50 Ibid.

51 Ibid., 421.

person might think that his or her own happiness is the goal of life, and that the best way to achieve personal happiness is by there being a general happiness in society. Or a person might believe that the best life is the life of service, and that by giving themselves to the community to bring out a general happiness will in turn provide a rich and abundant life of self-sacrifice. For whatever reason a person is a consequentialist, happiness stands as the absolute value and determines which actions are correct and which incorrect.

There is an intuitive sense in which consequentialism is appealing. It does appear that the person who works for the happiness of others is a good person. But where consequentialism fails is in its analysis of the relationship between happiness and the good. As noted earlier in the discussion on deontology, the good must be defined prior to virtue being defined. This is because virtue is properly understood as the means to the good. Similarly, happiness is properly understood as the effect of possessing what one believes to be good. That is, persons are happy when they possess what they believe to be good and unhappy when they do not or cannot possess what they believe to be good. Further, what actually is good would provide lasting happiness, whereas a mistaken good would only provide temporary happiness. Everyone is aware of having believed something to be good, attained that thing, and then eventually tired of it and looked elsewhere for contentment. People often report having wanted something that they later realized they should not have wanted, or having been happy from possessing something that they later realized caused them harm. In these cases, happiness was present, but it was not the good. If a consequentialist were to argue that only some kinds of happiness are the good, then this concedes the point that some other element must be present, and not just happiness, for a person to achieve the good. If persons have the good, they will be happy, and where persons are not happy, they do not have the good.

In contrast to consequentialism, natural law theory first defines what is good based on human nature. The good is that which provides persons with lasting happiness. It is true that insofar as they do not believe what actually is good to be good, they will not find themselves happy in possessing it, but it is questionable whether a person could have the good and not know it. This means that there is necessarily a cognitive aspect to the good. But this consideration does not override the fact that until they possess what is actually good, they will not be lastingly happy, and that while they continue to pursue happiness itself apart from coming to know what is actually good, they will never achieve lasting happiness.

Happiness, as an effect of possessing what one believes to be good, cannot be achieved directly. It is always achieved indirectly by coming to have what is good. Natural law theory avoids the mistake of making happiness the moral absolute and instead makes the good the moral absolute. All other moral judgments, about virtue or happiness, are relative to the good.

For a contemporary example of consequentialism we can consider Robert Nozick.[52] Although he argued against simple utilitarianism, he also advocated a view that is in many ways consequentialist. In his book, *The Nature of Rationality*, he studied the role rationality plays in decision making. Rationality has to do with living according to principles that guarantee the best outcome. To justify a principle, you specify its function and demonstrate that it performs that function.[53] Thus, if we have the goal of living together without conflict that tears us apart, this goal can be used to determine which principles we should live by to guarantee the desired outcome. Both Hart and Dworkin also justified their theories by arguing from shared life to rules or values, and so we begin to see a pattern in how these problems are approached. I agree with Nozik that goals determine the rules or duties, and also agree with his arguments showing how other ethical thinkers are, upon analysis, reasoning in this way. Yet, like other consequentilaists, the problem arises for Nozik in assuming that the ultimate goal is happiness.

He distinguished himself from the Kantian position and its use of principles:

> The Kantian tradition tends to hold that principles function to guide the deliberation and action of self-conscious, reflective creatures; hence, principles have a theoretical and a practical function. We are creatures who do not act automatically, without any guidance. ... Doesn't this show that the purpose of principles is to guide us to something, whatever it is, that we could not reach by acting at random?[54]

However, in explaining why rationality is valuable, he struggled to avoid circularity: "Ethical action can symbolize (and express) being a rational creature that gives itself laws. ... Being ethical is among our most effective ways of symbolizing (a connection to) what we value most highly, and that

52 Robert Nozick (1938–2002) was an American philosopher. He is known for his libertarianism and for work in epistemology.

53 Robert Nozick, *The Nature of Rationality* (Princeton: Princeton University Press, 1993), 226.

54 Ibid., 40.

is something a *rational* person would not wish to forgo."[55] By being ethical, we are symbolizing our rationality, and we value this because we are rational. Our analysis of Dworkin tells us that he would respond by saying Nozik has not shown that value must rely on some non-value-laden rationality, that such circularity is inescapable.

In some ways, Nozik represents a kind of Postmodernity within the analytic school of philosophy. He reduces rationality to an evolved characteristic, "as an adaptation against a background of stable facts that it was selected to work in tandem with."[56] Such "rationality" is historically situated and cannot make pretentious claims about having arrived at "the truth" of matters. It continues to adapt in relation to historical changes. Change and particularity are themes of Postmodernity. "Because our linguistic ability evolved in tandem with those of others, all of whom were born in an environment of adult speakers – we can leave aside speculations about the origins of language – it would be surprising if the phenomena of language and meaning were independent of such social surroundings."[57] The problems in this view of rationality and truth have been addressed by Alvin Plantinga in his "evolutionary argument against naturalism."

Formally speaking, however, Nozik follows the pattern we have seen from the beginning of this study. Taking a metaphysical viewpoint as foundational (naturalism/evolution), he then builds a theory of value and the good.

REMAINING POSSIBLE OBJECTIONS

Hopefully this has shown that alternative legal and moral theories are not in the strong position Holmes and other critics of natural law believe them to be. Before concluding, it is worthwhile to consider three possible objections to natural law theory and the approach taken in this chapter. The first is that the discussion of alternatives offered here has been too brief and has not fairly represented the strength of these alternatives or the weaknesses of natural law theory. In one sense this is a fair assessment, but in another it unfounded. It is fair in that this study has not claimed to deal with all possible variations of these alternatives, or to offer a definitive account of how they approach ethical and political issues. However, it is the assertion here

55 Ibid., 63.
56 Ibid., 178.
57 Ibid., 179.

that such a study would only further support what has been said earlier. At the same time, this objection is unfounded if the basic beliefs of each theory have been fairly presented. If this has been done correctly, then comparison can be made to natural law theory to determine which best solves the ethical questions without having to deal with all aspects of a theory. This objection is a form of skepticism that assumes that viewpoints are obscure and hard or impossible to know.

A second objection is that natural law theory is too broad and never actually provides any solutions that can be universally accepted. If true, this objection would be devastating because what natural law purports to provide is a universal law that seeks the good for all. And yet natural law has been used as support for conservative and liberal agendas, for revolutionary and reactionary regimes. Indeed, it is often associated simply with the fallacy: "It ought to be this way because it is this way." Although the initial answer might be that natural law provides different answers in different circumstances and is therefore responsive to human need, this does not satisfactorily answer the problem because it is also used to justify both sides of a dispute at the same time and in the same situation. The response here is twofold. The less convincing answer is that we do not abandon an approach because its adherents have made mistakes; science has been used to justify both sides of disputes, and we do not consider abandoning the scientific enterprise. More convincing is that there does need to be a corrective mechanism in natural law theory as there is in science. Where science can hypothesize and falsify and thus correct itself, natural law needs a similar tool. Specifically, the different positions that natural law is used to support ultimately differ in their hypothetical imperatives because they differ as to what it means for humans to flourish. As previously noted, it was this kind of difference that led to a disagreement between Finnis and Braybrooke over sexual morality. Therefore, whereas two sides of a dispute may be using natural law in the sense of applying hypothetical imperatives to achieve certain goods, when they disagree about what these goods are, one or both of them is not truly using "natural law," just as phrenology is not truly empirical science. The central issue is "what is the good," and the answer to this can be the corrective tool used by natural law to repair mistaken applications of this theory.

This leaves the third and strongest objection: Contemporary natural-law theory has not given a satisfactory definition of the good and therefore will fail in its attempts to provide hypothetical imperatives. Granting the answers given earlier to the skeptic and the relativist, and granting that the is/ought problem has been solved, this objection threatens the very framework of natural law. Natural law proceeds by defining the good and then offering hypothetical imperatives – practical rationality – directed at the good. But what is the good? Finnis offers a plurality of goods, as do most other contemporary thinkers. This raises another problem: If there is more than one good, and therefore more than one hypothetical imperative that governs a given situation, then practical rationality cannot help us decide which action to pursue. As far as practical rationality goes, we would be frozen in action. This objection can thus undermine the self-evident goods of human flourishing and the reliance on hypothetical imperatives.

THE GOOD OR MANY GOODS?

Because the contemporary natural law thinkers discussed earlier have rested with a pluralistic view of the good based on intuition, direct answers to this objection are not forthcoming. Additionally, their "goods" are not actually ends in themselves and therefore do not help in defining "the good," but instead are, at best, a means to the good. Taking the liberty to speculate about how natural law theorists might respond, we can see that this objection is not insurmountable. Specifically, the good must be given a formal definition that grounds the good in human nature and unifies the good in the face of pluralistic accounts. For instance, the good is the moral absolute (as opposed to virtue or happiness), and therefore many of the "goods" named by Finnis turn out to be either means to the good or the effect of possessing the good ("life" is a means to the good, practical rationality is a means to the good, "play" is a means to the good, friendship is a means to the good, etc.).

This answers the pluralist problem and the possibility of being rationally frozen between choices. It also creates problems for those natural law thinkers that have been operating with numerous goods and deducing their hypothetical imperatives from these. Different sets of goods with different emphases placed on different parts would result in natural law theory being used to justify contradictory positions. But can natural law actually define the good and not fall into calling either virtue or happiness the good? If it cannot, then it will most likely fail again and become a lifeless relic alongside its medieval cousin. We already have deontology and consequentialism; what recommended natural law was that it placed the good (and not virtue or happiness) as the moral absolute. However, if natural law theory can actually define the good, then it will be a powerful force in ethical and political theory and make significant contributions to humanity's knowledge in these areas. This would be a significant step forward from the failures of Modernity and provide a basis for a lasting foundation in the Postmodern age.

CONCLUSION

This chapter has looked at contemporary natural law theory with the goal of deciding if its return should be welcomed. By looking first at a general definition of the theory, and then at specific thinkers in this recent project, natural law theory was seen to be: (1) the belief in universal laws based on human goods and human flourishing; (2) a focus on practical rationality directed toward the goods of human flourishing; and (3) an empirical method of discovering what it is for humans to flourish. This was then contrasted with four alternative approaches. These were found to be less attractive than natural law theory because they denied that human nature is knowable, that the moral law is connected to human nature, or that the good is the moral absolute. Because natural law theory avoids these problems, it is much better than these other views that often actually utilize natural law principles inconsistently. After this, three objections were considered. Answers are readily available for the first two, but the third one remained open. Will natural law theory be able to correctly define the good? Or will it continue to offer a plurality of goods (most of which are means or effects and not actually ends in themselves) and thus undermine its method of practical rationality?

Whether one classifies Modernity as having ended and a new age, Postmodenrity, as underway, or that Modernity has transitioned into a new form called Liquid Modernity, the lesson is the same. Modernity's failure to identify the good and the means to the good has resulted in a failure to provide a basis for a common human law. Such a foundation is necessary if the global age is going to avoid repeating the horrible mistakes of the past and instead learn how to cooperate in pursuing and achieving the good. We can now turn to studying how this might be accomplished.

8

Natural Law as a Theory with Metaphysical Baggage

Postmodern Law

Go, gentleman, every man unto his charge
Let not our babbling dreams affright our souls:
Conscience is but a word that cowards use,
Devised at first to keep the strong in awe:
Our strong arms be our conscience, swords our law.
March on, join bravely, let us to't pell-mell
If not to heaven, then hand in hand to hell.[1]

INTRODUCTION: POSTMODERNITY AS A CHALLENGE TO KNOWLEDGE CLAIMS

Although Richard III was greatly troubled by a dream during the night before the battle of Bosewell Field, in which the ghosts of those he had murdered appeared to him and said he would soon be joining them, he quickly dismissed this as cowardly conscience and continued with his plans. Rather than relying on conscience, Richard turns to the use of force and power as the source of law. In a similar way, postmodern thinkers argue that appeals to conscience or tradition are coverings that hide power used to get what one wants. This gets applied by postmodern thinkers even to knowledge and reason itself. Power and the will are the basic units of study to which all else in human life is reducible. This means that "systems" and consistency are not real but are also constructs, and one may just as well approach knowledge and understanding pell-mell.

We can approach the study of postmodern law by identifying Postmodernity as a thoroughgoing antinomianism. This rejection of law is framed within a rejection of knowledge, what can be called an extreme

1 William Shakespeare, *Richard III*, Act V Scene III.

skepticism. This skepticism is not simply the rejection of some knowledge claims; it is also the neglect and avoidance of basic questions. Postmodernity begins after the terrible events of World War II, and so therefore it is also self-consciously framed as dealing with the problem of evil. The combination of enlightened progress and the horrors of World War II are said to prove that human claims to progress and knowledge are hubris. If Postmodernity were simply a critique of failures in modern philosophy, then it would be helpful. However, it is itself an attempt to refocus which questions must be answered and to give answers without having knowledge become susceptible to the same acid of skepticism applied to the previous history of philosophy.

Postmodernity represents the end of Modernity. More specifically, it is the supposed end of the Enlightenment's search for universal knowledge from general revelation. It is not sufficient to return to a chastened Enlightenment vision, or a chastened Modernity. Postmodernity calls into question the very essence of these pursuits, so whether they appear in bold or chastened form, they are undermined. Although Postmodernity may make its presence known concretely in the arts, or architecture, or politics, I argue that it begins in philosophy, and more particularly that it begins as an epistemology, or perhaps a rejection of all epistemology. It is a conscious shift of focus from questions that occupied the Enlightenment, but it is also largely a movement unconscious of its assumptions. Its basis of law is the absolutizing of the individual and particular will in the name of equality and liberty. My assertion in this chapter is that for all of its efforts to avoid the universal and claims to knowledge, postmodern law must make metaphysical assertions. Furthermore, these are often making their influence not through their prominence and upfront role, but as necessary assumptions to what is said. As such, they are unspoken and unnoticed, but ever present. Postmodernity critiques the failures of Modernity, but at the same time has its own assumptions that risk the same errors if a basis for knowledge is not found.

I am dating the beginning of Postmodernity to the end of World War II. It does draw insights from philosophers before this point. Nietzsche is relied on heavily, as is Heidegger.[2] Its pragmatism represents James and

[2] Friedrich Wilhelm Nietzsche (1844–1900) was a German philosopher who, among other things, argued that the will is primary over the intellect. This translated into an emphasis on the will to power, the rejection of all previous metaphysical viewpoints. He is known for having written that God is dead, which can be taken to mean that the idea of God is no longer required for contemporary society.

Martin Heideger (1889–1976) was a German philosopher known for his study of being. He restricted the concept of being to temporal, finite, and changing being. This has been applied to say that all perspectives and beliefs are historically situated.

Dewey, and its works to cast aside all that came before as error is found in Whitehead.[3] While this philosophical foundation is being laid, world wars bring an end to the modern vision of secular unity. Even as Europeans boast of having moved beyond war as a means of resolving differences, the Great War erupts and brings devastation, followed by a short hiatus, and then World War II. These wars have theaters of action in various parts of the world, and draw from global resources. Just like the modern world emerged from the Wars of Religion, so the postmodern world emerged from world wars. Postmodernity is the attempt to explain this collapse and is the search for a point on which to rebuild. I speak about philosophical movements like Postmodernity and deconstruction as if they have some unity because I believe there is an essence to each, which we can identify while also noticing relevant differences in consistency between schools. For this reason I speak about Postmodernity as if it is a viewpoint that makes identifiable criticisms of the modern world.

It must be asked how Postmodernity is actually different from Modernity when it relies heavily on modern philosophers. For this reason it has been given names like "Liquid Modernity" and explained as another phase of the modern world. Yet I am arguing that it represents the end of Modernity. I do not believe there is any problem with this claim, for two reasons. One is that it may very well be the case that modern philosophers like Rousseau planted the seeds of skepticism, the fruit of which is Postmodernity. For all of his grandiose claims to knowledge, it is plausible that Rousseau came up short, and Postmodernity is pointing this out. Second, it is exposing the extent to which a person is conscious and consistent, and the extent to which postmodern philosophers themselves are conscious and consistent. Such philosophers often make assertions that contain many assumptions, all of which must be examined but none of which are. Yet postmodern philosophers themselves have assumptions that are often hidden or lightly passed over.

PROGRESS IN PHILOSOPHY

For us, this demonstrates how philosophy makes progress. Philosophy is often critiqued, compared to science, for its dismal history. In a few short centuries, science has provided technological marvels, whereas more than

[3] Alfred North Whitehead (1861–1947) was an English mathematician and philosopher. He is known for his work with Bertrand Russell on logic, and for his pantheism and claim that there is nothing transcendent.

two and half millenia of philosophy are said to have resulted in nothing but ongoing disputes. I do not doubt that philosophy can and should make greater progress toward unity, but I believe there is a definite "negative" progress that has occurred. That is, many philosophers, beginning with the Greek materialists, have given answers to basic questions, and have been critiqued by later philosophers who demonstrated that those answers are insufficient. This is what is happening between Modernity and Postmodernity. We can make the "negative" progress of affirming "that is not the answer," while continuing to keep the basic questions in focus as we pursue an answer.

A large part of turning away from the prior history of philosophy as an error is the affirmation that philosophers up until Postmodernity have been asking the wrong questions. The result is not new answers to these questions, but setting these questions aside as unanswerable, or not in need of answering, and turning instead to what is believed to be more important. This especially rests on the idea that philosophy has been an elitist program, asking questions not of relevance to the masses, which are then used to control others. By shifting focus to the will, postmoderns believe they can better achieve the goals of equality and freedom. These are believed to be primordial values that Modernity has failed to achieve. Obviously, such an assertion involves assumptions about human nature and its origins, but an attempt to focus the discussion on those points is avoided and resisted by postmodern thinkers as irrelevant.

Even though Modernity sought to distance itself from theology and the requirements of metaphysics, and instead to produce a secular law that governed this life, it nevertheless did make assumptions about this life and the world in which we live that, for all intents and purposes, bore the same metaphysical status as the theology it sought to avoid. Postmodernity exposes these assumptions and seeks to demonstrate how they shaped thinking about this world, and particularly how they shaped power structures.

Postmodern legal theory looks to the social theory of Montesquieu and democratic contractarianism of Rousseau while critiquing both.[4] Montesquieu is said to provide the insight that law is relative to a people. This becomes circular in that the law gives a form to a people, but the people give authority to the law. It is unclear which comes first. But the point being made is that while there are universal general laws, the particulars of

4 Anthony Carty, *Postmodern Law: Enlightenment, Revolution, and the Death of Man*, ed. Anthony Carty (Edinburgh: Edinburgh University Press, 1990).

the law are unique to a people group. Each group finds the other baffling and at times comical in what the other takes for granted. There is an incommensurability between peoples and their laws that we will need to explore.

Postmoderns appeal to Rousseau as having proven that all law is a social construct. Persons enter into the social contract to guarantee greater access to common goods that cannot be achieved in the state of nature. However, as thinkers like Paulo Freire point out, not every person willingly enters into the contract, and the contract itself is constructed in a way that causes oppression to many. In his view, this is justification for the many to reject the social contract and all that rests on it.

This view seems to be directly contrary to natural law. The latter says that there is a real nature, independent of human constructs, and that by studying the nature of things we can deduce laws that guide us to the good. The postmodern reading of Rousseau is that all law is a construct; there is no nature on which to base law in the sense meant by "natural law." This fits into a line of thinking from Kant through Bradley that ultimate reality is unknowable, and then through Nietzsche that the pursuit of this kind of knowledge is not of value and was a mistake from the beginning as an Apollonarian departure from the Dionysian.

KIERKEGAARD

Kierkegaard argued that theistic proofs are not needed both because they are unsound and more importantly because they are existentially unhelpful. Even so, within his rejection of theistic proofs is a reliance on a kind of transcendental argument to claim that we must assume God for meaning and coherence. This assertion involves Kierkegaard in making claims about human nature and what humans need to achieve eternal happiness. Eternal happiness cannot be achieved through practical rationality or through speculative rationality; indeed, it cannot be achieved through human effort – rather, it is the gift of grace.

Postmodern thinking derives important themes, directly and indirectly, from Kierkegaard, specifically the thread of antinomianism and downplaying of the role of reason and the intellect. Although Kierkegaard used these themes to defend his view of Christianity, postmodern thinkers have felt no compunction at taking them out of that context and using them for their own purposes. Here I trace some of these themes in Kierkegaard both because of how they are later found in postmodern thinkers and because even in those who believe they are defending more tradition views of natural law or Christianity, there is nevertheless often a hint of Kierkegaard's influence through fideism.

Given his understanding of *sola gratia*, Kierkegaard presents us with a challenge: If we can know God through the use of reason, then this relationship is meritorious and transactional, therefore not based on grace. However, if our relationship with God is based on grace, then it is not something we earn through "correct thinking" and instead is a gift. This theme comes out in works such as *Fear and Trembling*, *Philosophical Crumbs*, and *Concluding Unscientific Postscript*. Kierkegaard's understanding of the *sola gratia* doctrine is undoubtedly Lutheran and reflects comments made by Luther about reason. Furthermore, applied to his philosophical context, it is a rejection of Hegelian and rationalist rejections of the need for special revelation and justification by grace resting on the atoning work of Christ.

To some degree Kierkegaard is aware that this assertion about grace assumes a great deal about God and the world. This means that his assertions about reason and grace can quickly become table-pounding fideism in the face of challenges from other worldviews that reject his assumptions. In the following, I consider how he attempts to respond to this problem through positing risk and uncertainty as essential to the human condition, and also why God must be assumed as the background to existence. Although he provides insights about God's existence that are helpful in addressing some challenges, he nevertheless comes short in demonstrating why we should accept his conclusions as opposed to alternative conclusions.

This coming short is partly a feature of his approach. There is a noncognitive strain in his presentation, which seeks to produce an effect on his audience that is not subject to true/false analysis. There is a place for that kind of work. However, I am studying assertions he makes that are claims about the world and nature of reality. Such claims go beyond the noncognitive and are saying that something is, or that something is not, the case. Of particular interest are his beliefs about God's existence, God's relationship to humans, and what it means to have faith through risk and uncertainty while being upheld by grace. In a significant way the rest of his system, including his use of noncognitivism, relies on his beliefs in these areas. His claims about human meaning and existence, which have come to be influential in existentialist philosophy, are often said to transcend categories of true/false, but nevertheless rest on beliefs that are either true or false. If these presuppositions turn out to be incorrect, then the existentialism which rests on them, although having insights here or there, is as a whole misguided.

Kierkegaard speaks fondly of Socrates, and Socrates provides an insight about such persons in *The Republic*. These are persons who perhaps get things correct but only by accident, and are not able to give an account of why they were correct. The reason Socrates believes this happens is that they are not first able to give an account of eternal existence, and this inability then trickles into their thinking about the world of change and temporality.

Kierkegaard's existentialism also rests on his view of the eternal. This, combined with his epistemology, produce his theory of existence, meaning, faith, risk, and grace. As noted earlier, it is a system that fits well within Lutheran assumptions about soteriology, and is also a response to the rationalists of Kierkegaard's day. However, I argue here that it can be seen as a *redutio* pointing out why we should not accept this soteriology, and that there are other responses to the rationalists that more permanently put them to rest.

Kierkegaard and Knowledge

I believe the interpretive key that unlocks Kierkegaard is his epistemology, and not, as many have posited, his contrast of eternal happiness and human temporality. The latter is part of his response to critics like Lessing who argued that a historical event that occurred centuries ago can have nothing to do with our eternal happiness. How Kierkegaard understands this criticism is a revelation of his own epistemology. If I seek certitude then, as a human, I am seeking something beyond my temporality. He explains it this way:

> The existence-relation to the absolute good can only be defined negatively as the relation to an eternal happiness through suffering, just as the certitude of faith that relates to an eternal happiness is defined through lack of certitude. If I remove this lack in order to obtain a still greater certitude – then what I get is not a believer in his humility, in fear and trembling, but an aesthetic back-slapping show-off, a hell-of-a-fellow, who, figuratively speaking, wants to fraternize with God but, literally speaking, does not relate to God at all. The lack of certitude is the mark, and certitude without it is the mark of not relating to God.[5]

Here we are introduced to a number of his ideas. The absolute good, as eternal happiness, cannot be obtained directly by human effort, including the effort of the mind. If I attempt to get certitude, I am asking for something beyond my temporality and changeableness. Nevertheless, the idea of eternal happiness itself presents this problem. Faith is accepting this

5 Søren Kierkegaard, edited by Alastair Hannay, *Concluding Unscientific Postscript* (Cambridge: Cambridge University Press, 2009), 383.

apparent impossibility – what Kierkegaard calls a paradox – and embracing the uncertainty that comes with it.

The kind of thinking that seeks out certainty is practical rationality about worldly goals and the means to these goals. Within its sphere, it is appropriate. Once taken out of this sphere and applied to God, it becomes overextended, because God as wholly different cannot be understood the way that the goal of buying something at the store can be understood. The speculative thinker wants to relate to God directly, but Kierkegaard tells us that something existing (in history and therefore changeable) cannot relate directly to the eternal. He wants certitude that eternal happiness is in store for his future.

The key that I use to unlock his epistemology is that God is totally other and therefore cannot be known by humans, and that the need for knowledge and certainty is contrary to the act of faith. Because he is considering the existential human condition after the Fall, Kierkegaard is beginning with the reality of sin and the need for redemption. If a reader is not careful, he/she might be tempted to expand Kierkegaard's remarks about the knowledge of God as if they were comments *simpliciter* rather than comments taking into account the fallen human condition.

The Lutherans would agree with Augustine's articulation of the fourfold state of man. After the fall, humans are in the state of *non-posse non-pecare*, not possible to not sin. After regeneration, humans are *posse non-pecare*, possible to not sin. Much of what Kierkegaard says about the existential condition of humans applies to the fallen condition. In this condition, humans reverse the order of redemption and want proof or certainty or a sign in order to then accept regeneration. However, regeneration is a gift of God, not earned or "meritorious" as Kierkegaard says, and occurs before these other things can be understood.

And so the kind of person who wants to use practical rationality to make a decision about religion is like the "serious man" of whom Kierkegaard speaks:

> The serious man goes on: if he can obtain certainty respecting such a good in store, then he will stake everything on it, otherwise it would be madness. The serious man speaks almost like a joker; it is clear enough that he wants to make fools of us.... When it is proved, he will risk everything. But then what does it mean to take a risk? Risking is the correlate of uncertainty; once certainty is there, risking stops. If he acquires the certainty and definiteness that he seeks, he cannot possibly come to risk everything; for in that case, even if he gives everything up he risks nothing.[6]

6 Ibid., 356.

Given the distinction between the fallen and regenerate state, and that much of what Kierkegaard says applies to humans in the fallen condition with an unregenerate mind, I argue that although this idea of risk and uncertainty applies to many aspects of life, and perhaps particularly the Christian life, it does not apply to the level of what exists (God and the self). Furthermore, Kierkegaard sees this to some extent, as is evident from his analysis of proofs for God's existence.

Nevertheless, it is difficult to get a good sense of Kierkegaard's view of how God is known in the pre-lapsarian context. Granting that his concern is to speak to the condition of the church in his day, he seems to limit the knowledge of God in a way that hinders his call to repentance. When speaking of rationality itself, he divides it (as do so many Enlightenment thinkers) into practical and speculative (or theoretical) branches. Practical rationality is about means/end thinking concerning matters of this life and has little or no interest in the matters of faith and religion. Speculative thinking is more dangerous because it appears to want to prove the truth of Christianity: "The truth is not first given and its understanding what one then awaits; what is awaited is the completion of the speculative understanding as that which alone can bring about the truth. Speculative knowledge thus differs from knowledge in general, as something indifferent to what is known, so that the latter does not change by being known but stays the same."[7]

The fallen man gets himself into trouble with the method of first demanding knowledge and afterward being willing to give consent. Kierkegaard views this as a kind of works-righteousness against which Luther spoke so capably. Indeed, the Scriptures are filled with examples of humans needing to trust the will of God in their life circumstances, of contrasts between the limited understanding of humans and the infinite understanding of God in bringing all things to work together for the good of those who believe.

If this was all Kierkegaard meant to address, then perhaps there would not be much more to say. However, it would also be the case that Kierkegaard had done little to address the philosophical challenges of his day. Insofar as he is clear about his intention to do so, I take it that he is making broader claims about how humans know God, and that the knowledge of God is limited, in his mind, because of the aseity of God. This can be understood as a development of the Lutheran doctrine of the *deus absconditis*.

Let us consider some of the ways that Kierkegaard develops this theme. The first is his understanding of paradox. As he understands the doctrine of Christ, and *paradox*, the essence of Christianity is a paradox: "The

7 Ibid., 188.

proposition that God has come into being in human form, was born, grew up, etc., is surely the paradox *sensu strictissimo*, the absolute paradox."[8] He might look to Paul for support of this in the Apostle's claim that the Gospel is foolishness to the Greeks. Yet "foolishness" is not the same as a paradox, but rather involves a claim about the need for redemption that does not fit into the non-Christian Greek worldview.

He cannot look to Chalcedon for support of his claim in that this counsel took pains to show that the doctrine of Christ is not a paradox. As an ecumenical counsel, all three branches of Christianity look to it as resolving disputes about Christology (Eastern Orthodoxy, Roman Catholicism, and Protestants such as Lutherans). That Christ is one person with two natures seems to avoid the apparent paradox that Kierkegaard named earlier. It is not an infinite and a finite nature at the same time in the same respect – that would be a contradiction and does not require a counsel. So it is far from clear that this is indeed a paradox, or that Kierkegaard's understanding of Christology is orthodox and essential to the Christian message.

He explains paradoxes further: "Supposing the paradox to be the limit for the relation of someone *existing* to an eternal, essential truth, then neither can the paradox be explained by something else if the explanation is for someone existing."[9] We can use this to lead us up to his view on proving God's existence. Taking his beginning point in the assertion that God is the "unknown," what is the value or purpose of a proof?

> But what is this unknown thing against which the understanding, in its paradoxical passion, collides, and which, in addition, disturbs even a person's self-knowledge? It is the unknown.... So let us call this unknown *God*.... It can hardly occur to the understanding to want to prove that this unknown thing (God) exists. For if God does not exist, then it would be impossible to prove that he did. But if he does exist, then it is foolish to try and prove it, in that I have assumed this existence is not doubtful the instance the proof begins, since an assumption, to the extent that it is an assumption, cannot be doubtful, otherwise I could not get started, understanding, as I would, that the whole thing would be impossible if there were no God. If, on the other hand what I intend by the expression "prove God's existence" is to prove that the unknown, which exists, is God, then my expression is unfortunate, because then I would be proving nothing, least of all that something existed. I would merely be developing the content of a concept.[10]

8 Ibid., 182.
9 Ibid., 185.
10 Søren Kierkegaard, *Repetition and Philosophical Crumbs* (Oxford: Oxford University Press, 2009), 112.

It is here that Kierkegaard runs into problems. Whatever else he is trying to do with existentialism/noncognitivism, and with the fallen condition of man and unregenerate mind, in passages such as the immediately preceding one he is also making claims about the knowledge of God irrespective of the condition of man. He begins with a kind of ontological argument that says that if the idea of God is coherent (not doubtful), then we do not need to offer a proof as we would already be assuming God. We must assume God. Or, if what we mean by "prove" is what we otherwise call unknown is indeed the God of theism, then we are simply developing our concept of God more consistently. Either way, he is giving here a kind of proof – perhaps what has come to be called a transcendental proof. This can be seen in his discussion of how Socrates understood God's existence:

> The fool says in his heart that there is no God; but he who says in his heart, or to others: wait a minute and I will prove it – is he not a rare sage! If it is not, in the moment when we must begin the proof, undecided whether God exists, then he does not prove it; and if it is like this at the beginning, then he will never really be able to begin, partly out of fear that he might not succeed, because God may not exist, and partly because he has nothing with which to begin. ... [Socrates] assumed God existed and, operating on this assumption, endeavored to permeate existence with the idea of purpose.[11]

He goes on to indicate the absurdity in some kinds of proofs for God's existence. Many proofs proceed as if "God" is going to be picked out of a lineup of existing things, asking "is God one of the existing things?" Such an approach would never actually find God and would never end as the search is unlimited.

Furthermore, the aseity of God prevents any proof that attempts to show God exists from the order of things. "One cannot prove God's existence by the order of things. If I tried, I would never finish, but would have to live *in suspenso*, in case something so terrible should happen that my little proof would be ruined."[12] If God is wholly different from the creation, then any argument from the creation either assumes God or does not get us to God: "It would be strange if one of Napoleon's deeds were taken as a proof of his existence. His existence does indeed explain his deeds, but the deeds cannot prove *his* existence unless I have already assumed the word '*his*' in such a way that I have assumed he exists."[13]

11 Ibid., 116.
12 Ibid., 115.
13 Ibid., 114.

Thus, assuming that God exists while admitting that God's existence cannot be proven is the closest a human can get. There are no other paths: "And yet it cannot come any further even if it endeavors to get a result *via negationis* or *via eminentia*."[14] Kierkegaard expresses this as one of the existential crises the human faces:

> This individual is also God. How do I know this? I cannot know this, because then I would have to know God and the difference, but I do not know the difference because the understanding has made it like that with respect to which it was supposed to be different. Thus God becomes the most terrible deceiver, in that the understanding has deceived itself. The understanding has got God as close as possible, and yet He remains as far away as ever.[15]

This problem is a statement about what can be known irrespective of human nature in its fallen condition. Thus, we are presented with a dilemma between Kierkegaard's view of the knowledge of God and his Christianity: Either God cannot be known and consequently there is no sin for which atonement is necessary, or God can be known and it is the regenerate Christian above all who should be able to show this. The first part of the dilemma rests on the relationship between God, the good, and sin. If God the creator exists, then God is the determiner of good and evil. So, if God cannot be known, then neither can good and evil. If humans cannot know what is good, then they cannot be held accountable for failing to do what is good. If humans cannot be held accountable, then the idea of sin is empty and there can be no need for redemption or atonement.

On the other hand, if Kierkegaard takes Christianity for granted, he must assume that what is good can be known, and that this serves as a basis for holding humans accountable. Therefore, he must assert that God can be known. Excusing the fallen man is of no use, because being "fallen" is precisely to be in the state of not knowing what you *should* (and therefore *can*) know. And all the more, the regenerate Christian is the one in the place to show what can be known.

Unfortunately, Kierkegaard goes the exact opposite direction. Taking into account what has been quoted earlier, Kierkegaard goes further to insist that both pantheism and Christianity are consistent. "But if Christianity should perhaps be wrong, this much at least is certain: speculation is definitely wrong, for the only consistency outside Christianity is pantheism, the taking oneself out of existence back into the eternal way by way of

14 Ibid., 117.
15 Ibid., 118.

recollection, whereby all existence-decisions become a mere shadow-play against the background of what is eternally decided from behind."[16]

This cannot be taken merely as a statement from within the Christian's perspective where we assume that indeed Christianity is the case. The issue is whether Christianity is indeed the case. If pantheism is equally consistent, why not accept it? If pantheism is equally consistent, there can be no sense in which unbelief is a sin. There can be no need for atonement from this sin.

Furthermore, all of the existential crises and passion that Kierkegaard musters in favor of Christianity can equally be provided in favor of pantheism, dualism, or naturalism. The followers of each can get into a kind of "passion" match to showcase how each is more passionate and authentic than the other. Indeed, today it is common for my students to believe that if they passionately hold to a belief, then it is true in some sense ("true for me" perhaps). A similar attitude can be seen in the media and the political realm where persons argue passionately and fallaciously for their opinions. While passion may be important for some things, it is also the case that what we are passionate about is contingent on what we believe to be good and worthy of pursuit.

The outcome is that Kierkegaard has not shown that knowledge is not possible or that knowledge is not necessary for making the correct decision about God and the good. As a historical figure, however, he gives voice to what became a commonly held view of knowledge in postmodern thinking.

POSTMODERNITY, SKEPTICISM, AND THE DENIAL OF NATURES

The consequence is that postmodernism roots itself in a kind of skepticism about the human ability to know what is real. Indeed, it is not always clear if the skepticism is about knowledge or about reality itself. It follows empiricism to its consistent conclusion that humans only have access to the experience of particulars, and then relying on Kant to deny that this experience is of reality. The combination of these particulars in the constructs of human life can never rise above the status of the arbitrary. Against those who say that there are universal structures discernible in human language or society (relying on Kant's insights about how the human mind structures experience), Postmodernity "deconstructs" these to expose how they

16 Kierkegaard, *Concluding Unscientific Postscript*, 190.

are in fact merely assertions of the human will. Because these constructs marginalize some, and are therefore said to lead to oppression, the deconstructionists view their work as a fight against inequality.

The Enlightenment sought to secularize thought and modern (i.e., contemporary) man. The postmodern critique is that the Enlightenment failed on its own terms in that it incorporated religious and metaphysical assumptions into its content. Derrida called this "white mythology." For this reason, postmodernism is best understood as an awareness of the contradictory nature of the anthropology behind the Enlightenment. Thinkers like Montesquieu and Rousseau saw man as pulling himself up from change, anxiety, and darkness by a creative act of reason. The pre-Enlightenment was categorized as a time of superstition and ignorance, but through a self-willed act of reason, humanity has set all this aside and come to know what is true.

The work of Derrida and Foucault aims at, among other things, showing how modern humans are still controlled by mysterious and unknown forces. The confidence of Modernity in its realism and positivism is shaken when these are shown to have the same status as the superstitions of the premodern world. Providing the basis for this analysis were Marx and Freud, who argued that humanity is trapped in labor and struggle that ultimately is self-alienating.

Although the revolutionary era was self-styled as an escape from ignorance into autonomy, into man as self-determining, the law and state actually represent administrative forces of production and manipulation, which control and trap. Interestingly, this deconstructive work reintroduces ontology into law by demonstrating how Modernity, just as much as the Medieval, relies on metaphysics to justify its conceptions of law and society. The social contract as a theory is supposed to make humanity free from tradition and history, both of which lose their authority over social formation; instead, "founders" are given a mythic status and appealed to as the final authority of law and meaning. These founders speak for the people and construct the social contract, thus finding themselves in the ambiguous position of creating by elite fiat what is supposed to be based on the general will. The will of these founders then is said to be the foundation of society and is appealed to in order to settle disputes.

POSTMODERNITY AS ANTI-FOUNDATION

Postmodernity is anti-foundational. The claim is that the idea of a foundation contradicts itself: The people construct the law that is binding on the people. However, if the law has no greater power than the individual's will, then when the individual runs into conflict with the law, the will of the individual can change the law – or, more contradictory, it actually is the law. To abstract from the individual to the general will does not avoid this problem. How can "the people" ever run into conflict with the law when the law simply is the expression of their will? This means that while the people do what they will, they are following the law. Given that the people are always doing what they will, this seems to make law-breaking impossible.

What ends up happening is that law and society are made into binary opposites. The society is said to create the law, but it is the law that gives shape to the people as a society. It is this ontology that Postmodernity calls into questions, this status of the individual will as autonomous rather than as a composite of competing desires given form as a construct of society to serve social interest (say, as a consumer). Because the will is what grants authority to law, what constructs the social contract, it has the ultimate authority, and therefore Postmodernity affirms a total autonomy where the human is the determiner of good and evil.

By way of contrast with the Enlightenment, which seeks to create itself, postmodern thinkers like Heidegger bring to our attention that none of us are ever a blank slate, but we are always already in an interpretive mode with assumptions. This forms part of the rejection of foundations in that the foundation of law presides at its own institutions. The general will cannot be founded because it is always present.

We can take this as an insight relying on the method of historical studies outlined earlier. The Enlightenment thinkers cannot be abstracted from their own history and the challenges to which they were responding. The critical nature of Postmodernity serves to expose at least some of the presuppositions of the Enlightenment, although this critical eye is rarely turned on itself except in affirmation that even what it offers is a construct. Postmodernism is never critical of the human ability to be critical; rather, this function of reason is taken for granted as real and beneficial. We can take this to be an illustration of the self-attesting authority of reason – it cannot be questioned because it makes questioning possible.

Therefore, if a fundamental theme of Postmodernity is to deconstruct the idea of "people" as the basis for law in the Modern age, this is nevertheless a use of reason to question the meaning of the world and ideas about the world. In arguing that the sociological and political "we" does not resolve the dilemma of the authority and origin of law, the postmodernist is identifying circularity in thought and self-contradiction in legal theory, both of which are examples of not using reason. The postmodernist is holding the modern legal thinker up to the standards of rationality, and so we must make sense of how Postmodernity can also claim to deconstruct reason.

Part of the problem that is ready to be criticized in modern theories of law lies in the purpose given to law. When law is said to bring unity and structure to society – the law and order of Hobbes – this of course raises the question about which unity and structure. To avoid the need for a sovereign, Rousseau may speak about the general will, but within society it is impossible to find such a will; rather, there is difference. Law becomes the coercive instrument of those in power to attain their personal goals. Talk about rule for the benefit of the people becomes patronizing and abstracted from the actual will of the people.

FOUCAULT: KNOWLEDGE AND POWER

It is in light of this that Foucault speaks about how the social whole constructs knowledge to control individuals.[17] In this he relied on Durkheim's claim that objective knowledge is society thinking about itself. Thus, just as the people construct the social contract, so too what is "known" is part of this construct. Foucault identified the constructive function of reason, which builds a world and life view on basic beliefs that fill all areas of life. It is true that the worldview is constructed. Furthermore, Postmodernity uses reason critically to call into question the consistency of these constructed worldviews. And yet it seems to stop short in identifying the actual basic beliefs underlying worldviews and critically examining these. This is an important part of identifying the natural moral law, which is done in the next chapter.

Foucault is well known for calling into question what society deems to be other and outside of itself. This includes those labeled insane or illegal. If the law is a construct, if society is a contract, then so too insanity and the illegal are constructs. Once the social contract is written, what counts as insane or illegal is also determined. Because constructs are arbitrary, the terms that set people outside of society are also arbitrary. Therefore, Foucault concludes, such structures are merely the expression of a will and power. Although they masquerade as objective and caring, underneath

[17] Michel Foucault (1926–1984) was a French philosopher known for his study of the historical shift in definitions of madness and crime.

they represent a bare expression of what is desired by those with the power to construct the boundaries of society. Law is not simply a list of given rules; it is the whole system and its coercive force, and all those within that society are caught in it. The Enlightenment's belief of getting to the truth and escaping tradition is a failure that ends in the same trap.

Foucault believed this explained the colonial experience. The Enlightenment created the idea of civilization, a lofty level of achievement attained by some as they pulled themselves out of the state of nature. In this same move, the Enlightenment created the uncivilized, those who were not so inspired or adept to leave the state of nature and had to be helped along. In this act the Enlightenment created the entire colonial experience. The legal system that results from the social contract creates the other and defines them as contrary to society and so in need of confinement and reform. Thus it turns out that not only is society a construct out of the state of nature, but the story about the state of nature is itself a construct used to justify power relations.

In response to this, postmodern thinkers call for resistance to these power structures in ways that would expose them as arbitrary constructs. In an analogous way to how the Enlightenment questioned the authority of tradition and sought to replace it with the autonomous individual who, with others, builds society, so too Postmodernity calls into question the results of this Enlightenment project to expose them as without a foundation. The self-emancipating individual must express autonomy by resisting the structures imposed by the mythical social contract. This critique is especially powerful and troubling given that the Enlightenment project was to find the foundation, and many accept this as proof that there is no such thing.

In Foucault's analysis of the legal system, he claimed that civil law is rooted in investigation and inquisition. This is set in contrast to the trial by ordeal of the Dark Ages. By way of contrast, the "enlightened" jurist seeks to reactualize what happened, to recreate the event, and by way of doing this to apply pure justice to the accused. In the case of inquisition, truth is pulled from the prisoner for his own good, just as the modern scientist is said to compel nature to give up its truth. Foucault relied on Nietzsche, who idealized the trial by ordeal of the ancient German system and defined law as a struggle between two competing individuals. The Renaissance reached back into the theory of truth in the Appolonarian system, and this ends with panopticon and the disciplinary state.

Here I admit to feeling sorrow, because what Foucault identifies is the horror of a state based on power and the will apart from knowledge of the good. But Foucault cannot simply critique the state as having failed to achieve the good because he claims all knowledge is a construct. In emphasizing the constructive use of reason he neglects the ontological role of reason in applying to being as well as thought. Of course I need to take time to show that it indeed has such a role. But in so doing we can find a solution to the antinomy of intellectualism and voluntarism where the latter wishes to identify the absolutely free will of everything, including ideas and truth.

As always, there is a grain of truth in both sides of a false antinomy. The intellectualist notes that responsibility requires that humans can know, but the voluntarist notes that responsibility requires freedom. If ideas compel specific actions toward the good, then in what sense, asks the voluntarist, is the individual responsible? Modernity has been the victory of voluntarism and nominalism. These are related in that once we assume empiricism, that all knowledge is from sense data, we can never arrive at universals. The closest we can get is the direct perception of the eternal forms in escaping the cave where we are chained by the senses. But even this viewing is a perception of individuals, and it is too otherworldly for Modernity anyway.

The response to the failure of the Enlightenment is foundationlessness – an individual perspective with no Being. This lack of being can be taken in two ways, both of which we need to address. The first is the individual as having no being, no nature, only experiences (remember Hume's denial of the mind). The second is the supposed discovery that there is no God, no ultimate Being, and that humanity must make its way without God. I have been discussing Foucault as an arch-example of the post-structuralist thinker, and indeed as having given voice to an important strand within Postmodernity. His anti-humanism speaks to this first lack of being, to the lack of a human being. The last sentence of his *The Order of Things* says that the imaginary object of humanist discourse is like a drawing on the sand that will soon be washed away by the incoming waves. "Foucault's anti-humanist rhetoric goes along with his declared object of discovering a new discursive 'terrain', one that would enable him to take a stand outside and against the hegemonic truth-claims of reason."[18]

Foucault set himself in contrast to the Kantian picture of a rational, autonomous dispenser of moral laws. It is not surprising that Kant is taken to be the archetypical Enlightenment figure who set the standards for considering a rational moral law. We have seen earlier in this study that Kant must be contextualized within a history of challenges as giving a response to thinkers like Hobbes and Hume. Particularly in relation to Hobbes and the

18 Christopher Norris, *Derrida* (Cambridge, MA: Harvard University Press, 1987), 220.

idea of authority and morality being imposed from without (heteronomy), Kant argued for the rational individual and autonomy, rooting authority in the use of reason to universalize a moral law. Going beyond criticizing assumptions on which the Kantian project relies, Foucault argued that "these problems are henceforth regarded, not as crucial issues in the working-out of a coherent moral or political creed, but as symptoms of a merely local and transitory stage of discursive production. They are taken to belong to that episode of thought which produced 'man,' the transcendental subject, as a figment of his own unconscious linguistic devising."[19] This is to call into question Kant's noumenal realm, and instead insist that there is only the changing world of phenomenon.

Although Foucault believed this kind of insight is a new conclusion based on careful research, it follows consistently from his presuppositions. He is described by Christopher Norris as an "extreme epistemological skeptic who equates knowledge with power."[20] It is not that Foucault, after careful analysis of history, came to discover that knowledge is power. Rather, without describing how a person comes to hold a worldview, he approached the subject of history with this extreme skepticism and interpreted the data in light of his presupposition. Is the claim that knowledge is power the highest conclusion of contemporary scholarship, or is it a view that has been present in various ways from time to time, and to which there are important responses?

In Foucault's favor it should be emphasized that his anti-humanism was against the imaginary human invented by the modern mind. This is the common beneficial element in postmodern thought, its attempt to expose and critically examine the presuppositions of the modern world, which are hardly even noticed as people go about their lives. Such presuppositions are ever present as shaping the lives of individuals and the structures of community life. One way that Foucault helps us distinguish between the real and the imaginary can be found in his claim that man is the being who spends, wears out, and wastes his life avoiding death.[21] He brings our attention to a claim about the human condition. We might be tempted to quickly dismiss him as violating his skepticism by making a claim about human nature. I understand something different to be going on, which is illustrative of Postmodernity, and this is a focus on the finite, temporal, and changing feature of human existence. Postmodern thinkers often dismiss

[19] Ibid., 221.
[20] Ibid., 217.
[21] Michel Foucault, *The Order of Things* (New York: Vintage Books, 1973), 257.

all previous philosophy as the search for eternal ideas, and by way of contrast emphasize the situatedness of human thinking and being.

It would be difficult to defend the view that all of Western philosophy until the last century was a search for eternal ideas to the exclusion of the temporal and changing. But instead of citing postmodern thinkers with such a simple mistake, perhaps they can best be understood to be making the claim that only the temporal and changing exists – or perhaps more accurately, to be rejecting theories about existence altogether because these take one beyond experience, and instead to be limiting their theories to experience in as pure a form as possible. It is true that human experience is an experience of change, that nothing remains permanent in experience.

This is consistent with the pattern applied throughout our study. Any given thinker's context is set by epistemology. Relying on empiricism, perhaps more consistently than those before, postmoderns are nominalists who reject the idea of natures or universals, and therefore reject any claims to knowledge. Differing thinkers may represent different flavors of this commitment, although they share this basic feature. Such an analysis identifies an essence, or "nature," of Postmodernity, which such thinkers would reject. However, their rejection cannot be accepted as self-evidently true, and the problems of consistently holding to nominalism have been identified in the history of philosophy and can be further identified as we proceed.

Foucault, as a kind of extreme empiricist, rejected concepts and universals and followed this into extreme skepticism. He saw the entailment that knowledge is power, that "knowledge" is no longer cognitive. Metaphysically he only considered the world of change and experience. The combination of these requires that he rejects any form of natural law that ought to be followed, and his belief system cannot support the good. He does seem to take ethical positions, perhaps in the stream of increasing pleasure for all as the only good available to humans. Could any form of postmodern natural law find support in this system? Consistently, no.

MARX AND FREUD IN POSTMODERNITY

Although not themselves living in the postmodern era, postmodern thinkers rely heavily on both Marx and Freud for their assumptions about knowledge, reality, and ethics.[22] Epistemologically, both Marx and Freud

[22] Karl Marx (1818–1883) was a German philosopher and economist. He is known for his work explaining the historical development of communism, which relies on a materialist dialectic to explain change in history.

are materialists who employ an externalist description of human knowledge. What a person claims to know is reduced by these two thinkers to natural environment, background, or physical desires.

In contrast to postmoderns, Marx and Freud appear to be realists about the material world. Neither seems to have critically examined this assumption, but instead to simply have assumed the link between empiricism and naturalism. Once a person attempts to go beyond that link, they are in dangerous territory, and run the risk of being labeled "delusional," or at least under an illusion, by Freud. This metaphysical position takes on the status of common sense and goes unquestioned. Although to some extent the postmodern thinkers do question realism, and thus limit their discourse simply to experience, they nevertheless seem to do so for the same uncritically examined assumptions about empiricism and what is common sense.

Marx took from Hegel the description of change in history that relies on challenges and responses. However, just as with his epistemology, he naturalized this and ended up with what has been called the material dialectic. Again, postmodern thinkers have adopted this view of social change and social justice. It fits neatly into their epistemological and metaphysical assumptions. In this account, knowledge is reduced to power, and history is a story of power struggles. Defining "knowledge" is one way that a group attempts to retain power. Claiming that a given system fits into the "natural law" keeps people under control. As skeptics about the reality of knowledge, postmodern thinkers like Paulo Freire and Henry A. Giroux view themselves as exposing the roots of knowledge claims in the desire for power and control. In other words, there is no knowledge, and it is their job to disillusion those under the control of knowledge claims in order to free them.

It is this account of the confused individual to which Freud has contributed. Postmodern thinkers like Deleuze argue that the human is a confused bundle of desires.[23] Beliefs are attempts to rationalize these without fully understanding any of them. Deleuze "abandons the immanent critique of Kantian concepts and categories for a language that celebrates our emergence into an age when reason itself can at last be seen as nothing more than an agency of social repression. Like Foucault, Deleuze equates knowledge with power, and rejects any kind of philosophical critique that would theorize their relation from the standpoint of enlightened reason."[24]

23 Gilles Deleuze (1925–1995) was a French philosopher who relied on Kant, and called himself a transcendental empiricist.

24 Norris, *Derrida*, 222.

I believe we can incorporate insights from this analysis without adopting the epistemological and metaphysical framework of postmodernism. For instance, Freud seems to be struggling with the reality that people are most often in self-deception, and that accounts of their own actions amount to self-justification. Freud's own philosophical limitations – and perhaps he was in self-deception about these – kept him from questioning his presuppositions. Consequently, he reduces all knowledge claims to attempts to satisfy desires, and this turns into the viewpoint of knowledge as power struggles to satisfy desire.

If all this means is that humans are, to varying degrees, unconscious of their assumptions and how these shape their lives, and inconsistent in what they believe and do, then it is not a new insight. Explaining this inner struggle, and its manifestations in conflict between persons and groups, is part of the work of philosophy. What Freud does is gives a supposedly scientific authority to his epistemology and metaphysics, placing them beyond questioning by anyone who is not insane. The rejection of the possibility of knowledge and its reduction to power becomes an important part of the postmodern era.

And yet, there is a sense in which knowledge is power. When postmodern thinkers describe Rousseau and Montesquieu as portraying humans pulling themselves from darkness and chaos into light and order, they are employing metaphors that assume knowledge of reality allows us to achieve our ends, and ignorance always results in futility. However, they represent "Enlightenment knowledge" as purely a construct. In this sense it is not "knowledge," where this term means a true, justified belief. Instead, assertions about "how things are" become attempts to set up society in a way that makes it possible for some people to get what they want.

The troubling problem is, of course, that if we really do reduce away knowledge to desires and environment, then the claims of Marx and Freud are simply the results of their desires and environment. They are no more "scientific" than the system they sought to replace. This is not only a *reductio ad absurdum*, although it is certainly that; it is a reminder that basic questions persist to be answered and cannot be made to disappear because some thinkers, heralded as "notable," neglect and avoid them. To say that all knowledge claims are simply attempts to get what one wants is itself then just an attempt to get what one wants, no more worthy of acceptance than the views it is set up to oppose.

Instead, I believe we affirm that knowledge is power in the sense that knowledge is the attempt to understand the nature of things, and understanding the nature of things informs the choices we make. If what is good for a thing is based on the nature of a thing, then the good is achieved through choice based on knowledge. So knowledge is not power *simpliciter*, in an identity relation, but knowledge allows humans to have power.

Similarly, knowledge is the basis for authority. Much of the postmodern critique is about arbitrary authority structures that keep people, usually the masses, from getting what they want. But rather than make the assertion that all authority is arbitrary (which follows from the claim that all knowledge is a construct), can illegitimate authority be critiqued by exposing its failure to attain knowledge and the good? Marx and Freud have shed no more light on this than those they critique, and these problems are passed on to those that lean on such broken reeds.

The problems raised here bring our attention back to the persistence of basic beliefs. These begin with the epistemological question: How do I know? When Marx, Freud, or their disciples make assertions, it raises this question about how they know. If their answer is to reduce away knowledge, we are still left with the question "How do you know that's a correct account of knowledge?" The skeptic might retort that this proves the impossibility of answering such questions. My response is that if basic questions cannot be answered, and all other questions build on the answers to basic questions, then nothing can be known (the skeptic agrees). But if nothing can be known and one lives consistently with this, then the outcome is nihilism. However, the orientation toward social justice of post-Modernity is an indication that these thinkers are not ready to embrace nihilism, or even admit that if their view is true then social justice is simply one hobby they have chosen over others, not rationally justifiable over chess or golf.

So knowledge is power, and knowledge has authority, but we must show that knowledge is not merely a construct. This reduction is not limited to the post-structuralist continental thinkers considered thus far, but is also a key ingredient to Anglo-American Pragmatism. This view fits into the family of Postmodernity and shares in common the attempt to reduce knowledge to a noncognitive category.

RICHARD RORTY

Although writing within the context of analytic philosophy, Richard Rorty criticizes this tradition, and the history of philosophy, with the same sorts of tools employed by the postmodern thinkers discussed earlier.[25] Rorty is part of the critique of Enlightenment thought, which is really just a critique

25 Richard Rorty (1931–2007) was an American pragmatist.

of Kant and the problems attending his philosophy. "For Rorty, those problems are of interest only insofar as they figure in the unfolding narrative of Western philosophy to date."[26] Rorty appreciated Derrida for exposing the bankruptcy of all epistemology and "the need for philosophers to give up imagining that they might have special truths to impart."[27] In this he is continuing the theme of rejecting pretensions to eternal truths accessible by the human mind, and instead focusing on the present and changing conditions of human thought.

Whereas thinkers considered previously might fit more comfortably into the context of Marx, Nietzsche, or Freud, Rorty continues the American tradition of pragmatism. For legal theory, this is related to the positivism of Oliver Wendell Holmes, Jr. He fashions this in relation to what is called postmodern liberalism, which "conceives itself more on the American model, as a generalized consensus of ideas and interests that works to guarantee the flourishing and continuance of a certain communal self-image."[28]

This version of pragmatism puts answers to basic questions as beyond hope, and instead focuses on reaching consensus within a given community about how to meet the needs of the individuals and group. So once again, knowledge is set aside in favor of meeting immediate desires as they are then understood. The futility of achieving knowledge in the form of answers to basic questions rests on showing that it has not yet been done, and all attempts to do so have ended in futility. This is a standard critique of philosophy and needs to be addressed.

If we understand philosophy as the discipline that studies basic questions in the realms of epistemology, metaphysics, and ethics, and does so through the critical and constructive uses of reason, then in comparison to other disciples we may conclude that it has made little positive progress. These basic questions, which motivated Socratic inquiry, remain apparently unanswered almost 2,500 years later. Granting a lack of positive progress while also recognizing that such progress is desirable requires us to ask where the fault lies. It is possible that "the fault, dear Brutus, lies not in the stars but in ourselves." It could be that we are seeking diligently and yet the subject matter is beyond our comprehension. Given that these are basic questions, it seems more likely that we are in self-deception about the

26 Norris, *Derrida*, 151.
27 Ibid., 150.
28 Ibid., 153.

extent to which we are seeking to know. It may be that we think we seek, but we do not in fact seek, and therefore do not know.

A good example of this is pragmatism. "Thoroughgoing pragmatists like Rorty and Lyotard reject the principle of reason and argue that knowledge can only be assessed according to its practical or 'performative' effects. But this denial ends up in Rorty's case by producing a consensus view of truth which simply reaffirms the current self-image of 'North Atlantic bourgeois liberal' culture."[29] In other words, once again we have a partial rejection of reason, or reason in a limited sense, or reason as identified with a philosopher like Kant. However, this is not a full use of reason. Knowledge becomes culturally relative and not distinct from opinion.

For Rorty, his rejection of reason comes in the context of an affirmation of the situatedness of any human thinker. "Rorty's position is that of the sturdy, commonsense pragmatist, mistrusting all those grand theories (of knowledge, history, class consciousness or whatever) that claim to know more and see further than current beliefs would allow."[30] Marxism might be one of the intended targets, but so too is the preceding history of philosophy.

This criticism seems to contain an element of truth while overextending itself. It is true that at any given time a human thinker has both a past and a future; a past that informs what challenges must be met, and a future full of more growth. This is a helpful reminder against thinking one is done learning. It is a critique of those who say they have gone further than anyone else in the realms of difficult insights. But what about the most basic questions? These are repeatedly neglected. My question is about whether we can use reason to know what is most basic. If not, then this affects all other claims that Rorty makes. If he denies that we can answer the question "how do I know," he cannot then ask us to trust common sense. We should be expected to ask him, "How do I know you're right?" If he does not answer, then he has shown himself to be a fideist. If he does, he is attempting to answer a basic question and can no longer take refuge in skepticism.

The continued theme of Postmodernity as an age is criticizing the modern idea of an individual self that pursues knowledge independent of cultural or historical setting. We can trace this to Rorty's legal theory in that he says law need not assume that the individual is independent of a network of desires and beliefs. Once again, the claim is that humans

29 Ibid., 157.
30 Ibid., 153.

cannot escape their social context and know what is outside history and culture. But is this more than a rejection of Plato? Is it more than a nuancing of Descartes and the *cogito*? It may not even rise to that level, but is instead merely a setting-aside of doubt in some cases. Rorty says we inherit a tradition that says liberty is more valuable than perfection, and the best in politics is a good compromise. Implied is an ought, that we ought to work within our tradition. However, why not, with Descartes, doubt this? He says Neitzsche's desire for absolute personal fulfillment is not possible given liberal compromise. It is fair for us to ask "how do you know," and is this knowledge claim any different than an opinion?

Yet such claims are saturated with more than pragmatism can hope to support. If we are to take one of the beneficial insights contributed from early modern philosophy, and specifically from Descartes, it is inquiry into all areas of life with the question "how do I know," and especially tradition and culture. Where Postmodernity is simply continuing that critical inquiry it shares this method with Modernity. Here in Rorty, however, is a return to the premodern bracketing of tradition. Not only does the fact of tradition tell us nothing about what ought to be done; it is used, in this form of pragmatism, as a shutting-down of basic question as unanswerable and therefore unworthy of attention.

Rorty, and others like Habermas, are anti-foundationalist postmodernists who say common sense and social sciences are enough. In one sense, this is actually a continuation of an influential element in Western philosophy, the commonsense approach of Aristotle. He is known for his logic, but as one reads through works like the *Nicomachean Ethics*, his appeals to what is commonly acceptable, especially by tradition, are throughout and influential on how he draws conclusions. So, is Rorty offering anything new here? Is he simply applying one standard approach from the history of philosophy to his social context? The painting "The School of Athens" reminds us of Aristotle's focus on this world, in contrast to Plato's pointing to the other world of eternal ideas. This is to say that new insights are not being given in pragmatism, but instead represent another example of neglecting basic questions and avoiding critical inquiry about assumptions.

Other pragmatists, like Habermas and Searle, say universal pragmatism rests on universal conditions for all communication.[31] This implies a critique of natural law as rationalist metaphysics. Indeed, the entire idea of a term like "natural" before "law" must be rejected by such thinkers.

[31] Carty, *Postmodern Law: Enlightenment, Revolution, and the Death of Man.*

And yet there is a kind of meta-level law being applied here about "what works" as relating to satisfying desires. Some postmodern pragmatist philosophers reject the idea of such meta-level theory.

LYOTARD

In his work, *The Postmodern Condition: A Report on Knowledge*, Lyotard rejected foundations and meta-narratives.[32] One of his considerations includes the founding of the University of Berlin and its significant influence on the universities of other nations in the nineteenth and twentieth centuries.[33] This includes competing proposals for the focus of the university, which raise questions about what it means to study science for its own sake. Lyotard distinguishes two possible narratives for this discussion, one of which involves language games that take truth as their criterion, the other answering only to social, ethical, and political practice and so focusing on the just rather than the true.[34] A proposed synthesis is the pursuit of truth only within just ends. This is nothing new; it is a common theme, perhaps almost universal, in Western philosophy that there is a division between speculative and practical pursuits.

This division retains a Platonic flavor in that speculative knowledge is perhaps best described as "intuition," a direct or immediate knowing. Such knowledge is difficult to attain, perhaps impossible in this life. On the other hand, there is a practical knowledge that can be discovered in this life and that is unrelated to speculative knowledge. Lyotard says:

> But what is meant by the term knowledge is not only a set of denotative statements, far from it. It also includes notions of "knowhow," "knowing how to live," "how to listen" etc. Knowledge, then, is a question of competence that goes beyond the simple determination and application of the criterion of truth extending to the determination and application of criterion of efficiency (technical qualification), of justice and/or happiness (ethical wisdom), of the beauty of sound or color (auditory and visual sensibility), etc. Understood in this way, knowledge is what makes someone capable of forming "good" denotative utterances, but also 'good' prescriptive and 'good' evaluative utterances.... From this derives one of the principal features of knowledge: it coincides with an extensive array of competence-building

32 Jean-Francois Lyotard (1924–1998) was a French philosopher and central figure in shaping what is called postmodernism.

33 Carty, *Post-Modern Law: Enlightenment, Revolution, and the Death of Man*, 31.

34 Ibid., 32.

> measures and is the only form embodied in a subject constituted by the various areas of competence composing it.[35]

This is pragmatism. Part of the problem that we explore with pragmatism is that it assumes a definition of "what works," and this in turn assumes a definition of "what is real." For something to work in the sense of initially bringing satisfaction is simply a subjective statement about one's feelings. It does not tell us that lasting happiness has been discovered, or if there is any true good resulting. We can often be momentarily satisfied with something that turns out to be not good.

An important part of Lyotard's pragmatism is the rejection of metanarratives. He relies heavily on the idea of a narrative as communicating a kind of knowledge within a cultural context. He then speaks of knowledge as the opinions of one's peers, that narration is the quintessential form of customary knowledge. It is through the accepted narratives of a culture that one comes to know what is real and of value. These are sources to which an appeal to authority can be made. However, there is no way to appeal to one's own narrative in order to convince another person living within a competing narrative. The popular narrative is incommensurable with its counterparts in other cultures. Just as Wittgenstein described language games, so too Lyotard describes these narratives as games:

> There is, then, an incommensurability between popular narrative pragmatics, which provides immediate legitimation, and the language game known to the West as the question of legitimacy – or rather, legitimacy as a referent in the game of inquiry. Narratives, as we have seen, determine criteria of competence and/or illustrate how they are to be applied. They thus define what has the right to be said and done in the culture in question, and since they are themselves a part of that culture, they are legitimated by the simple fact that they do what they do.[36]

Indeed, Lyotard holds up Wittgenstein not only for his description of language games, but for having seen and turned away from positivism. Positivism, as the claim that knowledge is limited to the facts of experience, claims to have dispelled the myths of immature humanity. Through the systematic experience of the world, the positivist believes humans grow more and more mature in having more and more technical knowledge. Lyotard, as the archetype of a postmodern thinker, views positivism as the height of

35 Jean-Francois Lyotard, "The Postmodern Condition: A Report on Knowledge," http://www.marxists.org/reference/subject/philosophy/works/fr/lyotard.htm (accessed July 18 2007).

36 Ibid.

Modernity. Postmodernity is the coming of age when humanity sees that even the narrative of positivism and science is still just a narrative:

> Wittgenstein's strength is that he did not opt for the positivism that was being developed by the Vienna Circle, but outlined in his investigation of language games a kind of legitimation not based on performativity. That is what the postmodern world is all about. Most people have lost the nostalgia for the lost narrative. It in no way follows that they are reduced to barbarity. What saves them from it is their knowledge that legitimation can only spring from their own linguistic practice and communicational interaction. Science "smiling into its beard" at every other belief has taught them the harsh austerity of realism.[37]

And so he affirms that what is outdated is not the quest for truth or justice, but the belief that science has hit on a meta-narrative that explains reality, rather than realizing that the rules of science are immanent to it.[38] Lyotard claims that Godel gave the proof to show that all language systems are limited in what they can prove, and that there will always be rules within a system that cannot be proven by that system.[39] Indeed, it is this supposed discovery that put an end to the quest of analytic philosophers to find the perfect logical language. The early Wittgenstein was part of that work, but in his later work he incorporated Godel's conclusion to make the point that all languages are constructs and no languages are total. Lyotard uses this to argue against the possibility of a meta-narrative because all of these are merely constructs (not actually getting to reality) and include unprovable premises.

> Let us say at this point that the facts we have presented concerning the problem of legitimation of knowledge today are sufficient for our purposes. We no longer have recourse to the grand narratives – we can resort neither to the dialectic of Spirit nor even to the emancipation of humanity as a validation for postmodern scientific discourse. But as we have just seen, the little narrative [petit recit] remains the quintessential form of imaginative invention.[40]

The main historical reason why Lyotard believes we no longer have recourse to meta-narratives is what happened at places like Auschwitz. He uses this to argue against Hegeliansim and against the spirit of the revolutionary age. It shows that for all the supposed rationality of Modernity,

37 Ibid.
38 Ibid.
39 Ibid.
40 Carty, *Postmodern Law: Enlightenment, Revolution, and the Death of Man*, 60.

in the end it was lost in hopelessness and brutality, bringing greater harm that its predecessor. In reaction to Hegel's dialectic, Lyotard says nothing follows from anything else in a necessary way. No one is responsible, and the situation is neither good nor bad.

In arriving at this conclusion Lyotard is affirming both the need for consistency and the failure of the Enlightenment to provide an explanation of knowledge. In rejecting meta-narratives and confessing to the corrosive effects of positivism and its realism, he has nothing to put in its place. A nostalgic return to the past is impossible after the horrors of World War II. Living in narrative as if it actually got to reality is impossible. So consistency requires abandoning distinctions between good and evil as if they were parts of reality. This means that with regards to matters of good and evil, one must remain silent.

Must we accept that reason has been exhausted and has failed? Rather than accepting positivism as the height of rationality, perhaps the failure of Modernity was precisely in thinking empiricism could be a source of knowledge. But it would be a false dichotomy to believe these are our only options. Rather, if we use reason critically as a test for meaning to expose presuppositions, we can call into question the foundations of positivism. Rather than reject all foundations, we cannot be trapped into choosing between faulty foundationalism and postmodernism. However, before elaborating much more, there are other aspects of postmodernism to consider. Specifically, there is a social-justice perspective that calls on democracy and rejects "knowledge" as a construct that oppresses. "Natural law," according to this view, is simply one way to oppress others and impose on them a framework they did not invent and do not accept.

JACQUES DERRIDA

Like all of the thinkers considered here, there is a great deal to study about Derrida.[41] For the context of this study, however, it is his form of skepticism about the possibility of knowledge that is most relevant.

In many respects, his critical attacks on our ability to think or talk about God are not new, and rest on problems that philosophers and theologians have wrestled with in the past. However, his position in history is

41 Jacques Derrida (1930–2004) was a French philosopher who critiqued Western philosophy through the process called deconstruction. To deconstruct a text is to show that its meaning can be played with in any number of ways, and so to undermine the idea that there is only one meaning or interpretation. Deconstruction focuses on exposing power struggles and the way that texts are used to support those in power.

new. Like Levinas,[42] he was mistreated for being Jewish, and he was vitally aware of how the reality of Auschwitz brought into question all of the Enlightenment project. In this respect, his questions about the possibility of knowledge are historically situated in a way that gives them strength and must be addressed with more depth. Consider a passage in which Derrida, analyzing Levinas, wrestles with positive descriptions of God:

> Henceforth, if I cannot designate the (infinite) irreducible alterity of the Other except through the negation of (finite) spatial exteriority, perhaps the meaning of this alterity is finite, is not positively infinite. The infinitely other, the infinity of the other, is not the other as a positively infinite, as God, or as resemblance with God. The infinitely Other would not be what it is, other, if it was a positive infinity, and if it did not maintain within itself the negativity of the indefinite, of the apeiron. ... If one thinks, as Levinas does, that positive Infinity tolerates, or even requires, infinite alterity, then one must renounce all language, and first of all the words infinite and other. Infinity cannot be understood as Other except in the form of the in-finite. As soon as one attempts to think Infinity as a positive plenitude (one pole of Levinas's nonnegative transcendence), the other becomes unthinkable, impossible, ununterable. Perhaps Levinas calls us toward this unthinkable-impossible-unutterable beyond (tradition's) Being and Logos.[43]

In the last analysis, according to Levinas, nonviolent language would be a language that would do without the verb "to be" – that is, without predication.

> Predication is the first violence. Since the verb to be and the predicative act are implied in every other verb, and in every common noun, nonviolent language, in the last analysis, would be a language of pure invocation, pure adoration, proffering only proper nouns in order to call to the other from afar. ... The Greeks, who taught us what Logos meant, would never have accepted this. ... Thus, in its most elevated nonviolent urgency, denouncing the passage through Being and the moment of the concept, Levinas's thought would not only propose an ethics without law, as we said above, but also a language without phrase.[44]

Derrida quotes a passage from Nicholas of Cusa, which is a dialogue between *The Idiot and the Orator*. The Idiot is saying that in asking if

[42] Emmanuel Levinas (1906–1995) was a French philosopher who critiqued the role of ontology in Western philosophy.

[43] Jacques Derrida, *Writing and Difference* (Chicago: University of Chicago Press, 1978), 114.

[44] Ibid., 147.

God exists, one is presupposing God, and therefore has already found the answer. This, according to the Idiot, is how easy all the difficulties of theology really are.

Derrida has in common with Foucault the belief that there is no way for finite man to grasp the infinite and eternal.[45] This in part explains Derrida's return to the text.

> It is the authority of a no-longer-Holy Scripture, an exiled and wandering text, alienated from its own sense, the testament of an Absent Holy One. Derrida endorses the sentiment of Levinas, that it is better to remain with this text, as evidence of an absent God, than to face such a God directly. This is a revenge on Greek-Christian theology which has opposed the dead weight of the Law to the power of the Spirit (II Cor 3.6), the life of the Voice against the death of the text. Derrida is a Jewish mystic upholding the idea of tradition as a Revelation which constantly draws back.[46]

Perhaps best known for the method of "deconstruction," Christopher Norris quotes Derrida as distancing himself from that movement as it has been actualized, and instead defining deconstruction as asking about "meaningful frames, institutional structures, pedagogical or rhetorical norms, the possibilities of law, of authority, of representation in terms of its very market."[47] He does this by asking questions about the possibility of meaning and truth, and this method must be nuanced to understand how it avoids self-referential absurdity.

Derrida particularly takes aim at the philosophical tradition from Plato to Hegel, which sought to know the transcendent. There are two senses of truth: one is correspondence between a word and object, but the other, held as the more important of the two by Plato, is a kind of direct knowing of reality.[48] This kind of knowledge downplays the importance of the other, making it a secondary and less certain kind of knowledge. "What Derrida is out to resist as far as possible is the Platonizing drift that would restore interpretation to a quest for self-present meaning and truth."[49] This turns into a rejection of the transcendent. "There is no 'transcendental signified', no concept or meaning that would serve to arrest this chain of aboriginal supplements. ... Such is the effect of removing the 'transcendental privilege' that allows criticism to decide which terms shall be taken as the

45 Carty, *Postmodern Law: Enlightenment, Revolution, and the Death of Man*, 17.
46 Ibid., 31.
47 Norris, *Derrida*, 14.
48 Ibid., 54.
49 Ibid., 60.

key-words, the organizing themes or metaphors."[50] And so, "from Plato to Hegel, philosophy inherits this will to transcend the limitations of mortal experience in the quest for a knowledge ideally independent of mere sensory acquaintance."[51]

To distance himself from the caricature that he is simply another idealist metaphysician who denies a connection between language and reality, Derrida defines his work as "resisting the antinomies of classical reason that keep us from understanding the intricacies of the question of reference."[52] Nevertheless, Derrida is himself situated in a historical setting. Philosophically, this is a Kantian setting. "We won't understand what Derrida is doing unless we take stock of the problems created by Kant and his successors in the modern tradition of epistemological critique. That is to say, when we read some of Derrida's more 'outrageous' pronouncements – like his denial that perception, or anything like it, really exists – we will be missing the point if we think to refute such claims by a straightforward appeal to commonsense philosophy."[53] What he is doing is demanding a "reason for reasonableness itself."[54] It seems that what he means by reasonableness is classical, means-ends rationality. The line between knowledge and opinion blurs once we realize that there is no absolute "legitimizable competence for a phenomenon which is no longer strictly techno-scientific but techno-militaro-politico-diplomatic through and through."[55] Importantly, he is not simply dismissing all language and particularly philosophy as metaphors (as some of his literary critic disciples maintain), because "it is idle to maintain that philosophy comes down to a handful of disguised or occluded metaphors unless one makes this further concession: that metaphor itself is unthinkable outside a certain genealogy of philosophic concepts."[56]

This is illustrated in Derrida's debate with John Searle over the "correct" reading of J.L. Austin's literary theory. "Here, as in other works, it involves a reflection on writing (or textuality in general) as that which everywhere precedes and articulates the 'laws' of logical thought. His response to Searle may give the impression of totally rejecting reasoned argument in favour of elaborate verbal chicanery designed to head off serious debate.

50 Ibid., 62.
51 Ibid., 76.
52 Ibid., 144.
53 Ibid., 150.
54 Ibid., 160.
55 Ibid., 165.
56 Ibid., 170.

In fact, as I have argued, it should rather be seen as possessing a fugitive but nonetheless highly consequent logic of its own."[57] He wants us to read the whole history of philosophy, from Plato to Russell, as a circulating set of messages with no authoritative interpretation. The claim "I studied with Austin, so I know what he meant" can be shown to be mistaken on many levels. And yet, how does Derrida himself avoid the simple *tu quoque* that forces him to take seriously the implication of his own skepticism?[58]

This background helps us understand how his critique applies to any attempt to formulate a natural law. At a conference at the University of Virginia, Charlottesville, which commemorated the bicentenary of the American Declaration of Independence, Derrida delivered a paper that helps us in understanding how he critiques the idea of law. He especially asks who it was that put themselves forward as representatives and signatories for this document, who authorized them or gave them authority? Furthermore, how does a representative democracy get started given that at its beginning, the founders are not themselves elected representatives?[59] Derrida rejects commonsense solutions like that of Austin or Hart that think of such instances as speech acts that convention recognizes as binding. But Derrida wants us to see that there are multiple possible interpretations of the originating act, and that the Declaration itself appeals to a transcendent source for its authority (the Supreme Judge of the World). He believes this is a root contradiction in such democratic traditions, an appeal to authority that transcends the democracy and is lost in the past of origins.

Interestingly, Derrida also distances himself from Foucault, most prominently in his critique of *Madness and Civilization*. Foucault represents a radical antinomian position, one that seeks the end of the author as tyrant of meaning, and which denies that there is any human nature or "man." "Thus Foucault has a much-quoted passage in *The Order of Things*, describing 'man' – or the imaginary self-possessed subject of human discourse – as a figure drawn in sand at the ocean's edge, soon to be erased by the incoming tide."[60] Indeed, he has another oft-quoted passage from the preface of that book that helps illustrate his nominalism and antinomianism:

> This book first arose out of a passage in Borges, out of the laughter that shattered, as I read the passage, all the familiar landmarks of my thought – our

57 Ibid., 183.
58 Ibid., 194.
59 Ibid., 195.
60 Ibid., 218.

> thought, the thought that bears the stamp of our age and our geography – breaking up all the ordered surfaces and all the planes with which we are accustomed to tame the wild profusion of existing things, and continuing long afterwards to disturb and threaten with collapse our age-old distinction between the Same and Other. This passage quotes a "certain Chinese encyclopedia" in which it is written that 'animals are divided into: (a) belonging to the Emperor, (b) embalmed, (c) tame, (d) sucking pigs, (e) sirens, (f) fabulous, (g) stray dogs, (h) included in the present classification, (i) frenzied, (j) innumerable, (k) drawn with a very fine camelhair brush, (l) et cetera, (m) having just broken the water pitcher, (n) that from a long way off look like flies.[61]

This, Foucault believes, proves the impossibility of actual universals and shows us the limitations of our own system of thought as it encounters the "exotic charm" of another system. But Derrida goes a different way:

> Derrida's response is to show (via a reading of Foucault on Descartes) that thought is self-deluded if it tries to achieve a standpoint 'outside' or 'above' the very discourse of philosophic reason. ... Derrida's counter-argument once again comes down to a form of transcendental *tu quoque*. That is, he denies that it is possible for Foucault to advance a single proposition in support of his case without rejoining the discourse of reason by adopting its language and discursive strategies.[62]

This is consistent with Derrida's rejection of the transcendent. We are not able to transcend reason, thought, or language. This is his critique of common sense and traditional theories of law. Positivists like Hart give law meaning by an appeal to authority (in Hart's case secondary laws), and give this authority its authority by explaining its origin rooted in social norms. Furthermore, the passing from an is to an ought – something that Derrida notes occurs in the Declaration of Independence – but which also occurs in the movement from descriptions of law to commands that entail obligation, cannot be dismissed as a mere linguistic convention. Which ought follows from the is, and on what authority do we know? A mere return to analytic legal tradition and its process of looking for meaning in greater and greater refinement of words is misplaced hope.

There are more thinkers that come to mind, and a longer work would need to consider this. Two of these are John Rawls and Jürgen Habermas.[63]

61 Foucault, *The Order of Things*, xv.

62 Norris, *Derrida*, 215.

63 Jürgen Habermas (1929) is a German philosopher who is associated with the Frankfurt School and social critical theory. This view claims to critically analyze Western philosophy

These two thinkers bear the marks of living at the end of Modernity in that their theories attempt to address important challenges to modern liberalism. However, they both see something worth preserving from that tradition. Specifically, Rawls works to give us a basis for law founded on radical equality. All that can be made equal with respect to achieving goods of this life should be made equal. The focus is modern in that it is purely this-worldly, and assumes skepticism about the human ability to know what is not seen. Many criticisms of his work have focused merely on the political considerations; my point, however, is that his epistemological and metaphysical presuppositions are thoroughly modern. Like most modern thinkers, he wants to proceed as if he has no such presuppositions and is neutral, setting up a system where each individual can choose their own good. However, for Rawls this requires that in some sense individuals exist without any beliefs and are able to choose a system of equality. Furthermore, if the good is limited in this way, why should we choose? Is the highest good so limited, and if not, how do we understand other goods in relation to the highest good?

Habermas would also deserve more attention, but for our purposes here we can note that he argues in some places for a basic human rationality that governs all thinking and communication. He gives what I believe is a very important argument against the postmodern view that no knowledge is possible, or that there are no laws of thought, when he considers the possibility of denying all laws of thought:

> By refusing to argue, for instance, he cannot, even indirectly, deny that he moves in a shared sociocultural form of life, that he grew up in a web of communicative action, and that he reproduces his life in that web. In a word the skeptic may reject morality, but he cannot reject the ethical substance (*Sittlichkei*) of the life circumstances in which he spends his waking hours, not unless he is willing to take refuge in suicide or serious mental illness.[64]

This can be, and has been, taken to affirm a kind of cultural relativism. However, we can expand his observation that we are born into a shared social life, and note that we are born into a shared human life (something we have in common with other humans now and with other humans in the past). This forms a basis for discussing the reality of human nature. We

and religion for ways that power has been used unfairly. It relies on Marx and Nietzsche in forming its worldview. Habermas is known for his defense of a kind of democratic liberalism.

64 Jürgen Habermas, *Moral Consciousness and Communicative Action* (Cambridge, MA: MIT Press), 225.

do share something in common and we cannot deny this without denying the possibility of thought and communication. I believe we can take this insight in a direction that helps us know what is real and how this provides a foundation for the law.

THEMES IN POSTMODERNITY

There are at least two difficulties in presenting an overview of a philosophical age. One is that protecting against too great a length for keeping reader's interest means that there are inevitably other thinkers that could have been included. The other is that those thinkers who were considered above are importantly different in ways that could make a general connection of their ideas misleading.

Nevertheless, there are some unifying themes that I believe can be found in these thinkers and that can give us a picture of what any natural law theory will need to address after Modernity, most specifically skepticism about the possibility of knowledge, the rejection of any transcendent, the focus on particularity, and an emphasis on the will. What I want to consider in the remaining chapters is whether we must indeed conclude that there is nothing transcendent, that all is change and impermanence, and that therefore knowledge is not possible. What I hope to demonstrate through reason and argument is that we can know God, and that God is eternal and transcendent, the creator of the temporal world of change. I link the human good to knowing God and argue that it is the knowledge of God that is the highest good. This knowledge is given in general revelation through the act of creation, and deepened in special revelation as God reveals his justice and mercy to humankind in sin.

9

Natural Law as the Moral Law

Troilus and Hector are arguing about what to do with Cressida, and Troilus argues that Hector relies too much on reason and this crushes desire. The kinds of "reasons" given by Hector are reflections of practical rationality, not reason as the source of meaning about human nature and what is real. After Troilus rejects Hector's practical rationality, Hector replies:

HECT. Brother, she is not worth what she doth cost, the holding.
TRO. What is aught, but as 'tis valued?
HECT. But value dwells not in particular will;
It holds his estimate and dignity
As well wherein 'tis precious of itself
As in the prizer. 'Tis mad idolatry
To make the service greater than the god;
And the will dotes that is attributive
To what infectiously itself affects,
Without some image of the affected merit.[1]

Troilus responds with a comparison between what the Trojans have done to preserve Helen and what they now propose to do with Cressida. This is an important question about the integrity of Hector and others who are protecting Helen but are willing to give over Cressida, but it does not address Hector's point about the nature of the good and the relationship between duty and the good, or service and the god. We must first fix our attention on what is good, and then we can understand our duty and service.

INTRODUCTION

Natural law helps us understand that there is a reality, that things in reality have natures, and that what is good for a being is based on the

[1] William Shakespeare, *Troilus and Cressida*, Act I Scence II.

nature of that being. It argues that there are laws governing action in that once we know what is good for a being we can understand what actions will, and which will not, achieve that good. Nevertheless, I have identified problems that I believe are prominent in natural law theory whether found in Aristotle, Aquinas, Modernity, or Postmodernity. In essence, the problem with each is not having seen what is clear about reality, human nature, and the good. Or, to make a rhetorical point, it is not that natural law has engaged in too much metaphysics (a claim leveled especially at Aristotle and Aquinas), but that it has not done enough. Contemporary natural law theorist's desire to jettison such metaphysical work is understandable, but the idea that metaphysics can be avoided altogether is simply false.

After the historico-critical work presented earlier, we must now consider how progress can be made in our current context. I would not want to be blamed for having only given a critique of past failures but not attempted to provide any positive answers myself (a critique often leveled at Postmodernity). In contrast to other current natural law theories, I argue that the good must be one, and cannot be merely this-worldly or merely otherworldly, but must unite human existence and human nature into one chief end.

THE MORAL LAW AND THE GOOD

There is one good that unifies the moral law. The other possibility is that there is no good in the sense of a *summum bonum*, but only goods of human flourishing. In the contemporary literature, this comes to expression when human flourishing is limited to this life and disconnected from any transcendent meaning. This is what I have called mere this-worldliness. Such authors often do, on a personal level, believe in a transcendent meaning grounded in God, but continue to identify this with some kind of union with, or vision of, God in the next life and so disconnect it from this life. Therefore, they isolate "goods" that contribute to a "happy" life in this world, and include among them "religious ends" that help guarantee the beatific vision in the next life for those who are interested. However, this simply brings us back to the classical debate about what manner of living best guarantees happiness. To repeat an Aristotelian answer does not fill the gap between virtue (or flourishing, or achieving goods of this life) and happiness.

Although Aristotle affirmed that all things aim at the highest end, he did not adequately identify this, and the history of divisions between

Epicureans, Stoics, and Academics highlights this lack. Like that debate, the current discussion attempts to explain what life best secures happiness, and "new natural law theorists" say it is achieving various goods of human flourishing. These goods, then, take on the status of the virtues. Thus, the conversation continues as it did in the past by skipping the good and trying to link happiness and virtue directly. However, the idea of the good as the chief end persists, and we can identify some characteristics that attach to this idea in order to notice how objections can and have been answered.

For instance, Hobbes said that there can be no *summum bonum* because once attained, this would leave life empty. What he could have concluded is that the *summum bonum* is something that is attained and attainable in a continuing and unending way. Certainly knowledge is like this in that one can know some things, but also grow forever in knowledge. We can continue to grow in knowledge in this life as we mature, and presuming there is an afterlife, we can reply as Socrates did and say that we will continue to pursue knowledge there.

In considering objections to his own view of virtue and happiness, Aristotle considered the man of ill fortune, such as king Priam of Troy. What we can conclude from such instances is that virtue is not the good, and that whatever is good must be inalienable in the sense that life circumstances do not give it or take it away; instead, it is grounded in our nature. Certainly knowledge is like this, in that we can grow in knowledge in whatever circumstance. Job concludes, after his suffering, that he had heard of God but not known him as he should have (not seen him with his eyes).

To explain how to attain happiness and avoid discontentment, Stoics argued one should minimize desire. The more consistent outworking of this approach is Buddhism's Four Noble Truths, which takes denial to an epistemological and metaphysical level not considered by Western Stoics who largely confined themselves to the ethical and the political. In both instances, the response could have been to affirm that the good is comprehensive in that it can be and should be seen in all areas of human life (rather than minimized). Disappointment occurs not because of failure to attain desire but because of not understanding how a circumstance reveals the good. Certainly knowledge is something that can be attained in any circumstance of human existence, and what makes life interesting is the ability to know about all of human endeavors and expression and connect them to the highest reality. This pursuit is inexhaustible.

In relation to these characteristics, we can see that the good is achieved by humans together now and building through history, rather than being individually isolated to each person's life. This is because it is grounded in human nature, and human nature applies to all humans and what their lives reveal, not just to one person in the present. This highlights the need for taking account of what has come before, what contributions have been made, and what false starts must be avoided. Certainly knowledge builds in this manner, and certainly knowledge is shared in this manner, because as one shares it with others, it increases rather than is divided.

Nevertheless, none of these considerations are sufficient to show that knowledge is the good, the chief end. Indeed, knowledge in some generic sense cannot be the good. Few thinkers in natural law would deny that knowledge is a good, and many classical thinkers recognized it as the highest goal of humans as rational beings. Skeptics in every age, and postmodernists in ours, have called into question the possibility of knowledge and in doing so replaced it with desire or power. This has been made possible by dogmatic assertions of worldviews, which can be deconstructed and shown to be opinion not knowledge. For the good to be knowledge, it must connect with what is ultimate in order to be fulfilling. Mere opinion, or knowledge about what is not ultimate, will not be fulfilling and will not have the ability to transform a life from meaningless to meaningful.

THE GOOD AND KNOWING GOD

The good is knowledge of what is ultimate, or knowledge of the highest being. This knowledge is connected to human nature and this life, because the world as a creation of God reveals the nature of God. Thus, claims about knowing the unmoved mover who is unaware of anything else and is not the creator do not connect the good to human nature. Similarly, claims about the good as a direct vision of God in the next life disconnect the good from knowledge (knowledge is inferential, not direct) and disconnect the good from this life. Claims that the good is knowledge of a highest reality, which is an eternal process (such as the Stoic worldview or the Platonic system of eternal souls learning and forgetting forever), dissolve any rational distinction between good and evil, knowing and ignorance (all is one, both are eternal).

Thus, in contrast to Modernity's skepticism about knowing God and how that relates to this world, and Postmodernity's more radical skepticism about knowledge itself, I am arguing that the good is the knowledge of God, which is clearly seen in what has been created so that there is no excuse for failing to know God. As humans' chief end this unites all of human activities and all human life into one goal that can be grown in forever. It unites human existence rather than dividing it into this and the next life. It unites humans in the present as we seek a way to work and live together, and it unites humans over time as we build on the knowledge attained by those who went before and lay a more firm foundation for those that come after.

Objections to this view are reducible either to the modern and postmodern claim that we cannot have this kind of knowledge, or the medieval claim that knowledge of God is attained directly and immediately, not through inference and mediation of the works of God. The claim that God is known directly in the next life can be understood as saying that God is only known this way, or that God is known this way in addition to being known through the works of creation and providence. The minimal work done by those holding to the beatific vision in knowing God through the works of creation and providence and affirming the clarity of God's existence in this manner seems to witness to their holding that God is only really known directly in the next life. Although we can note a distinction between knowledge by acquaintance and knowledge by inference, and between knowing how and knowing that, there is a sense in which all that is knowledge (as true, justified belief versus opinion) is through inference and requires the ability to respond to objections. This means that knowledge is propositional rather than direct sensory input about which a person is unable to explain or answer objections. Furthermore, many people perceive the same thing and have different interpretations of what they are perceiving (consider those who were with Christ and how they variously understood him – Peter and Judas, the Apostles and Pharisees). In this sense, direct perception does not give knowledge, only appearance. The beatific vision promises a direct perception of an appearance, but not that persons will know the reality. There are many ways to interpret an appearance, and the appearance itself does not tell us which interpretation is correct. By way of contrast, the works of creation and providence reveal that there is an eternal creator by the very fact of their temporal existence.

The objection from Modernity and Postmodernity is best understood epistemologically. It is the claim that humans, for a variety of possible reasons, cannot know God, and so if there is a good then the knowledge of God is not it. This view need not rule out that there is a God, but that means shifting the discussion to metaphysics. Instead, it is a claim that whatever is good and the source of unity between persons must be knowable by all those involved, and God is not knowable.

This kind of skepticism about the inability for a person to know God results in a shift to an externalist description about human flourishing. Such accounts are third-person descriptions of what a good life would look like to a scientist or observer considering the human condition. The person who is the subject of such descriptions need not have knowledge of the good or human flourishing in order to be flourishing (knowledge of this kind is either not possible or not necessary).

I argue that the good life requires living the examined life, and one must know what is good in order to be good. Accidentally being good is not simply of no benefit; it is not possible for rational beings whose deepest need is the need for meaning. The standard externalist critique that such an internalist viewpoint leads to an infinite regress of justification (do you know that you know, etc.) is easily answered by noting there is the most basic level that stops all inquiry because it makes inquiry possible. That is, the laws of thought that make thinking possible cannot be further questioned without using them. I appeal to these laws as an example of something that is transcendental.

It is the question "is my life worth it?" that must be answered in order to find meaning and live the good life. That in fact one's life is worth it is not helpful to the person who believes everything is meaningless. The following questions are related: Is my life worth it? Can I even know if my life is worth it? What is there to be known, is there anything permanent or is all change? Externalist descriptions of human flourishing have begun by assuming answers to these questions; the answers of the New Natural Law Theory are entrenched in standard Western beliefs such as the reality of the material world, the permanence of the human person and the material world, and skepticism about anything outside of these. But why begin with these answers? If these answers are wrong, then the picture of human flourishing is also wrong. If all is suffering, and suffering can be overcome by denying the reality of the self (part of Buddhism's Four Noble Truths), then the new natural law theorists are mistaken about human flourishing.

HUMAN FLOURISHING AND PRESUPPOSITIONAL THINKING

Therefore, to understand human flourishing and the good, we must know what is real; we must study metaphysics. This does not mean that we must study metaphysics the way that Aristotle or the schoolmen studied the subject. It simply means we must know what is real in order to know what is good. And we must be able to know. Specifically, we must be able to know the most basic things if we are to be able to move on to what is not basic. Not simply that we must be able hypothetically to know them, but that if there is any responsibility for knowing anything, then the most basic things must be readily knowable.

So that it does not appear that we have departed from discussion of the law, we can refocus our attention on the moral law and another level of laws introduced earlier: the laws of thought. If we can distinguish thought from non-thought, then there are some laws governing this distinction the use of which is thought, and the failure to use these is not thinking. These have been understood to include the laws of identity, excluded middle, and noncontradiction. Although I am aware that questions have been raised about each, particularly in contemporary post-classical logic, I have not been impressed with these as much more than obfuscations that in themselves require these laws of thought to be meaningful (the problems are problems, and not non-problems, for instance).

Applying this, we can say that in choice we distinguish between what we believe to be more and less valuable to us at the moment, and the idea of value presupposes the distinction between the good and what is not the good. This is the application of the laws of thought to moral concepts, and the result is that it is clear what can be sought as an end in itself and what cannot. We can know this. The next step is to say that we can know what laws govern choices that lead us to the end in itself; this is the moral law.

From this internal perspective, a person can reason that knowledge of the highest reality is an end in itself. It is not practical knowledge; we do not come to know it in order to solve a particular problem in life. Rather, it is worth knowing because there is nothing higher to know about. By implication, any view that says there is no highest reality (for instance, all is one, all is change, all is impermanence, good and evil are dualities of the same reality, etc.) is also denying that there is the highest good. It is not surprising then to study the actual history of these views and discover that indeed they either explicitly deny a *summum bonum* or that there are multiple and irreconcilable views in each tradition (Epicureans, Stoics, Academics; Utilitarians, Deontologists). If humans cannot know the highest reality (we can consider this in its epistemological and metaphysical senses), then there can be no highest good as an end in itself, toward which all else aims.

On the other hand, if there is such a good, then the moral law that explains how to achieve the good provides unity to the individual and the group. All areas of human life, as manifestations of human nature, are knowable and reveal something about the origin of human nature. The many different virtues are united in the moral law as different means to the good. We do not identify the virtues first, but we understand them in relation to the good. Similarly, while many things make us happy for a time, only by knowing what is actually the good will we know what will bring lasting happiness in any circumstance. If humans can know God, this knowledge is revealed and deepened in any circumstance. Such a claim necessarily brings to mind the problem of evil, although I have alluded to a solution earlier in the life of Job who came to a deeper knowledge of God through suffering, and repented of his culpable failure to know.

All of these claims will appear airy-sounding but unsubstantiated if it cannot be shown that indeed it is clear what is good. In order for it to be clear what is good, it must be clear what is real. And this is where any moral law must begin. If we are to know anything else, we must begin with knowing what is most basic and presupposed by everything else. We must begin the moral law by affirming what is clear at the most basic level.

The alternative – that nothing is clear – is what Postmodernity sometimes seems to assert. However, if this claim is held with logical consistency, it leads to the denial of all meaning. If nothing is clear, then nothing we say or think is clear. If nothing we say or think is clear, then there is no meaning (including the claim that nothing is clear). Similarly, if we hold this with existential consistency, we cannot expect anything we say or think to be considered by others or even ourselves as meaningful. There is no meaning to thought, and yet we cannot stop thinking. These conclusions must force us to reject the claim that nothing is clear.[1]

While many might agree that some things are clear, the pattern has been to say that what is clear has to do with our intuitions or commonsense beliefs about the material world. Indeed, contemporary epistemology often titled such beliefs as our "basic beliefs." I use the phrase "basic beliefs" differently, however. I do not use "basic" to mean "immediate," which this literature seems to do, but rather as "logically basic," where we take into account what such beliefs presuppose about what is real.

To illustrate this point, we can consider how the Declaration of Independence grounds rights in the claim that all men are created equal. Or we remember the noncognitivists and their worldview assumptions about naturalism, or Darwin's assumptions about uniformitarianism, or Marx's assumptions about the material dialectic. Any moral claims proposed by such thinkers are founded on these metaphysical assumptions. If we are going to make progress in knowing the good, we must begin by making progress at this most basic level: What is real and what does this tell us about the good?

An objection worth considering before going much further is that this appears overly intellectual. Most people simply find themselves with moral

[1] Gangadean, *Philosophical Foundation: A Critical Analysis of Basic Beliefs*, Lanham, University Press of America.

beliefs, and the law is an attempt to negotiate and harmonize the many different individuals into a community. Descriptively this might be true (at least in part), but it involves a hidden judgment implying that such a condition is acceptable or that we should not expect more from people. I understand the situation differently and believe it can be stated in Socratic terms: Most people simply find themselves not living the examined life. They can, but are not. Failure to do so is the cause of all the other failures to make good choices.

We can take the force of this objection and affirm that the moral law begins with an attitude of living the examined life and asking the most basic questions that can be asked about the good and God. People do make choices out of their beliefs about the good. This is what is meant when Socrates affirms that we cannot knowingly do evil. Here the word "know" is reserved for those beliefs that we can give rational justification to support by arguing their opposite is false (thus giving certainty). It may often be the case that we act while having nagging doubts, but this proves the Socratic point that we do not have knowledge at that time and so are not knowingly doing evil.

It follows that our beliefs about what is good and evil are vital; they are a matter of whether we lead the good life, and we should not use those who are less thoughtful or aware of their assumptions as the example of how to live. Furthermore, if it is true that most, perhaps all, people do not live the examined life but rather act out of their received beliefs about what is good, then it cannot also be maintained that critical thinking has gotten us nowhere. People are in a condition of not critically thinking, and as a consequence they have disagreements and fights over what is good and how best to achieve the good. We can continue trying to negotiate these (but leaving them as givens) or we can question the assumptions on which they are based in an attempt to reason together about what is real.

Beliefs about the good are nested within a worldview, and worldviews are logically structured from most basic to least basic. This means that once basic beliefs are chosen, the rest of the worldview is shaped by implication. From these considerations let me make some moral assertions:

1. We ought to know (where "know" means being able to give a justification for your belief in showing it is true in contrast to its alternatives).
2. We ought to know what is most basic.
3. Disputes at less basic levels between worldviews ought to be resolved by working back to the most basic level of dispute.

4. We ought to know the metaphysical absolute.
5. We ought to know the moral absolute.

The first kind of objection to these will have to do with whether or not knowledge is possible. Interestingly, on this point Modernity and Postmodernity seem to agree. Modernity began by assuming God's existence – some philosophers offered overextended proofs for God's existence (design, therefore theism; first cause, therefore theism) – but naturalism replaced theism as Modernity matured and ended. Religious divisions continued unresolved, and increased as the religion of naturalism was added to the mix.

I believe these oughts transcend the practical/theoretical rationality distinction. They are a form of means/end reasoning, but they are also about what is necessary for any other reasoning. It would be self-referentially absurd to argue that we ought not know. Similarly, if we ought not know what is basic, we cannot know anything unless we know what is basic. If we give up on knowing what is basic and try to resolve disputes at less basic levels, we are really just denying moral assertions 1 and 2 from the preceding list. The same is true if we claim that we cannot know the metaphysical or moral absolutes; this is to say we cannot know what is basic.

The next kind of objection will be about what exactly is the metaphysic or moral absolute. That is, people will argue in favor of their views. This kind of objection assumes we can know, that we should give justification for our beliefs. This objection makes reason (as the laws of thought) – rather than personal opinion, intuition, common sense, a tradition or received teaching – the standard for growth together and in knowledge. In a previous chapter, I relied on Allan Guth to help us identify the most basic options:

1. Everything came from nothing (no being is eternal).
2. All being is from eternity.
3. Some being has existed from eternity, some being has not existed from eternity.

I argued earlier that the belief "none is eternal" and its implication that being came from non-being is meaningless in the strict sense (and so cannot be true). That is, any assortment of the claim that being came from non-being fails to understand these two concepts. The distinction of being and non-being is the most fundamental distinction, a distinction presupposed by all other talk about what is. To then assert that non-being can be something by way of having being come from it, be caused by it, be brought about after it, is a misunderstanding of non-being. Indeed, persons like Guth and Hawking, who make claims about everything coming from nothing, always end up calling "nothing" something, such as the law of gravity or quantum foam.

We are thus left with two options: either all has existed from eternity or only some has existed from eternity. Within each, there are various versions depending on how consistent a given person or group is in their thinking. But we can see that worldviews such as naturalism, Hinduism, Greek dualism (and its remaining forms), or Buddhism assert that while there may have been "beginnings" to world cycles, all that exists has always existed (there was no creation *ex nihilo*). By way of contrast, we can see that Judaism, Christianity, and Islam all agree that while God is eternal, God is the creator of everything else. Relying on a kind of ontological argument to show that something must be eternal, we can then use a kind of cosmological argument to show that what is eternal is God (theism) and a kind of teleological argument to understand the nature of God.

I believe we can make progress in knowing that while the material world exists (versus all forms of absolute idealism), it is not eternal (versus naturalism). And that we can make progress in knowing that while the human spirit exists and is not reducible to matter (versus naturalism), the human spirit is not eternal (versus Greek dualism and other forms of reincarnation). Furthermore, that we can know by implication that what is eternal is a spirit (not material but conscious), and is infinite, eternal, and unchanging (the incommunicable attributes of God, which logically come together) in power, knowledge, and goodness (attributes following from God being personal/spirit). Creation and providence as acts of God are a revelation of God, knowledge of which is the highest good.

This helps identify where the differences are, and I believe I have provided resources in my bibliography for further explanation that would take us beyond our current topic. Here we can note that the rejection of the knowledge of God as the good must either be an epistemological or metaphysical rejection (we cannot know or there is no God). Either way, some other view of the real and the good will be affirmed, and law will be shaped accordingly. Therefore, conflicts about what should or should not be law are more basically conflicts about what we can know and what is real.

Modernity did not begin with this insight. Modernity began assuming God exists, and that any good connected with God was in the afterlife. Moderns began their theories of natural law with survival and physical goods, as if humans live by bread alone. Modernity progressed to deny that there is a God and instead that only the material world exists. Old Natural Law Theory centered on the belief in the beatific vision of the afterlife, and New Natural Law Theory relies on common sense and practical rationality to give arguments concerning the goods of this life. Neither has made the argument that the good begins with knowing God, and that knowledge requires giving a justification for your belief that establishes it in contrast to its alternatives.

Postmodernity did not begin with this insight. It correctly argued that the naturalism of Modernity is not neutral, that theism has been asserted but not proven, but it did not go further to examine its own assumption that all is change and nothing is transcendent. It is a false antinomy reaction against the failures of the modern world.

My case has been that divisions about law are based on divisions about the good and what is real. Therefore, because we must resolve divisions about the law if we are to continue living and working together, we must also resolve divisions about what is good and what is real. These cannot be relegated to the area of public opinion. However, my position might be heard to argue that the government should somehow force us to know what is good (which is certainly not what I am claiming). Therefore, in the next and final chapter, I consider a contemporary debate about law in order to illustrate how it is full of unaddressed assumptions, and then conclude by identifying ways that humans avoid this discussion and the inherent consequences of such a process. My hope is to redirect the cultural debates about law to more basic beliefs presupposed in those debates but left unaddressed.

Conclusion

Natural Moral Law in a Postmodern World

> Come then, father mine,
> Mount thee upon my neck; these shoulders, see!
> Come what come may, one peril both shall share,
> Or one deliverance. Hand in hand with me
> Let walk the child, Iulus, and my wife
> Follow our footsteps from behind ...
> Father, do thou the sacred emblems take,
> Our country's household gods, within they hand:
> Fresh from the slaughter of so fierce a strife,
> For me 'twere sin to touch them, till I wash
> Me clean in running water.[1]

Before leaving Troy on the shoulders of his son, Anchises offered up a prayer to his gods. Aeneas tells Anchises to bring the household idols. There is a relevant lesson here. Although he is preserving his father from the flames of Troy, Aeneas is also preserving his idolatry. These idols will form the basis of the new system he builds, which becomes Rome. To avoid this, a new beginning requires self-examination to identify and eliminate the falsehoods that caused decay and collapse. If it is true that "we are in the midst of a natural law revival,"[2] can we be sure this is more than a mere return to what has already been tried but has failed?

CURRENT LEGAL DEBATES

Two examples of debates about law can help us bring some of the foregoing considerations into the present application. The first involves the

[1] Virgil, *Aeneid*, Book II.

[2] Robert P. George, *Natural Law, Liberalism, and Morality: Contemporary Essays* (Oxford: Clarendon Press, 1996), 311.

current Vice President of the United States Joseph Biden. During his time as the chairman of the Senate Judiciary Committee, Biden presided over the confirmation hearings of both Judge Robert Bork and Justice Clarence Thomas. Bork was criticized by Biden (and not confirmed as a Supreme Court Judge) for not taking the "background rights" of the people given by the Ninth Amendment seriously. Bork had compared this amendment to an ink blot. After this, all Supreme Court nominees are asked about these rights. In contrast, Justice Thomas was criticized for relying on natural law in his interpretation of the Constitution. Biden explained his criticisms in the following manner: "Remaining true to his stance during prior hearings, Senator Biden endorsed the priority of natural law but said, for him, the important question to be answered by the hearings was which version of natural law the nominee adopted."[3] The real debate is not about whether to do natural law, but which law and what is the nature of things.

A second example is a debate between legal scholars Joseph Raz and Christopher Wolfe. In their respective essays, "Liberty and Trust" and "A Response to Joseph Raz,"[4] these thinkers debate the role of a modern liberal government in the lives of its citizens, particularly with respect to homosexuality. Should the government get into the business of teaching its citizens which ways of living are and are not directed toward the good? Of course, to do this, the government would first need to have identified the good, and if it has made a mistake in this identification, then what it teaches is incorrect. If the "main purpose of government ... is to assist people, primarily its subjects, to lead successful and fulfilling lives, or, to put the same point in other terms, to protect and promote the well-being of people," is there any role for coercive moral paternalism?[5] The example used by both thinkers is the homosexual lifestyle. Professor Raz argues that:

> If I enjoy full citizenship the government can use coercive paternalism against me where this is justified by right reason. However, if it pursues coercive moral paternalism against me it will, by definition, be preventing me from following my way of life, and it denies, in a purposed exercise of its authority, the validity of propositions I hold true and which underpin my way of life. If it does so, however, it denies me full citizenship. It undercuts my trust that I and my interest are seriously being taken into account in deciding public action.[6]

3 Ibid., 152.
4 Ibid.
5 Ibid., 113.
6 Ibid., 127.

Raz's perspective is that it is the role of the government to teach its citizens that homosexuality is an acceptable way of life. He interprets any arguments to the contrary as simpe prejudice. Of course, claiming that an argument is prejudiced is not actually dealing with the content of the argument, but relying on an *ad hominem*. Questions about what the government can teach its citizens while staying within the limitations of its sphere presuppose that we have identified the human good. If a way of life is contrary to the good, this does not necessarily entail that the government should become involved, because doing so could take it beyond protecting against external harm. But it does mean that the government should not promote as acceptable what is in fact contrary to the good. Wolfe argues:

> The case against the unrepentant homosexual lifestyle can take various forms (which may overlap to some extent). One form would focus more on the well-being of individuals: the position that homosexual acts are seriously, morally wrong and therefore that society ought to prohibit them as a way of promoting, directly and indirectly, the good of those who might be tempted to engage in them. Another form would focus more on the well-being of society: the position that society depends on certain institutions, such as the family, that in turn depend on certain moral dispositions in the citizenry, which are incompatible with the acceptance of the case for the unrepentant homosexual lifestyle. Raz accepts the perfectionist principle that society ought to promote the well-being of its members. The unrepentant homosexual lifestyle is alleged by some to be incompatible with that well-being. If those allegations are true, then society has reasonable grounds to discourage that lifestyle. The validity of this argument turns, then, on the truth *vel non* of the allegations about the unrepentant homosexual lifestyle, i.e., on whether "homophobia" (in the sense of moral objections to homosexual conduct) "is an unfounded prejudice."[7]

These two debates help us focus our attention on the role of natural law. The value of this legal theory often rests on whether it can have direct bearing on shaping legal interpretations and drafting legal policies. Objections to the use of natural law for interpreting the Constitution rest on the claim that some notions will be artificially applied to the constitution and are really just the individual's pet priorities. I believe that then Senator (now Vice President) Biden was correct that the issue is not whether natural law will be applied, but which natural law. It is impossible to escape the formal features of natural law in thinking about human rights and dignity. Natural laws and human rights are based on human nature, which

7 Ibid., 143.

in turn is based on its creator (God, chance plus time, etc.). How a person understands these steps will in fact be how that person interprets law and the constitution.

These debates also show how quickly government comes into the picture, and the concern turns to what is legal and illegal. If instead we think first of our own pursuit of what is good, we can then put the institutions of human civilization into the context of how they promote and protect that good in relation to their unique functions. The state is only one of these institutions and should not be permitted to become total over the other institutions, nor should it be disconnected from the good in how it determines what is and is not legal.

PHILOSOPHICAL AMBIGUITY ABOUT THE GOOD

Furthermore, the debate about the purpose of government helps bring into focus the role of thinking about the good. Both participants hold to a perfectionist viewpoint, and yet come to different conclusions. How can this be explained except as an example of academic pedantry? I suggest it is illustrative of how our presuppositions (often uncritically held) shape our thinking. Both maintain that "[f]or most people in the developed world 'the good life is a successful autonomous life, that is life consisting in the successful pursuit of valuable activities and relationships largely chosen by the person involved'. Thus, a perfectionist government must 'be sensitive to the need for people to be free in the sense of being capable of leading a successful autonomous life'."[8] Yet, whereas Raz excludes any coercive moral paternalism, Wolfe does not entirely rule out its use in principle. Indeed, it may be that Raz too uses moral paternalism, although against those he disagrees with on such moral matters, by forcing them to accept as amoral what they find immoral.

The different rests on what it means to harm oneself and society. The difference is allowed to go unnoticed in the common definition of a good life because of how philosophically ambiguous that definition is. Terms like "successful" and "valuable" are too closely synonymous with "good" to be helpful. My case is that unless a clear definition of the good is given, differences about particular policies will continue, and these differences left unresolved will lead to decay. Similarly, as long as "which natural law" is unresolved, because there is no clear understanding of the good, divisions will persist and decay will be inevitable.

8 Ibid., 131.

Therefore, I want to conclude this book by asking if anyone can seriously believe that the good is clearly knowable after the vicissitudes of Modernity and the critique of Postmodernity. Is the attraction of natural law simply in the myth of more stable past times, or can a law about how to achieve the good actually be delineated?

As in these two examples, this debate often takes as its starting point the role of government and "hot button" legal topics. I believe we can resolve these questions. However, I do not believe starting with them is the correct order in which to proceed. Rather, we must begin with the individual leading the examined life in pursuit of knowing what is good. Why should we listen to a "professional" or "authority" who cannot show us, prove to us, what is good? Or, why should anyone listen to one of us about these kinds of subjects if we have no proof either?

Allowing the debate about law to be framed in the political has already accepted the assumption so prominent in Modernity and Postmodernity that the government gives humans the good or is the source of the good. By way of contrast, if we recognize that, at most, government can protect and promote what is good (but is not the determiner or source of the good), then the responsibility falls back on individuals to know the good. Any government authority who claims to be working for the good must be able to show us what is good and respond to objections if a standard mistaken view is given (such as the good is happiness or duty).

In the case of two standard high-profile disagreements – marriage and abortion – the question about what should be the law depends on what marriage and human life are. If marriage is an agreement between any two people about personal and private love, then the answer will come out one way. If marriage is a union between male and female instituted by God to reveal the relationship between God and humanity, then the answer will come out another way. Similarly, if human life is only present once personality traits can be recognized or once value is assigned by others, then the debate will come out one way. On the other hand, if human life begins with an individual who is different from both parents and valuable because revelatory of God apart from others or level of current development, then the debate comes out differently.

To believe that these differences can simply be harmonized by the state to promote smooth living together is a failure to understand the role of beliefs in human life. The debate about a perfectionist government or a liberal government has overlooked the problem. A perfectionist government assumes that those in the government know the good. A liberal government requires that those in government know the good so as to make minimal rules about living together without infringing on freedom. These are antinomies that have arisen because the good is not known and not pursued.

BELIEVING OR KNOWING THE GOOD

What I want to add to the discussion is:

1. Belief about the good is not the same as knowledge of the good.
2. In general, people do not *know* the good.
3. In general, people hold competing *beliefs* about the good.
4. This division results in what is called *akratic* action.
5. The division within a person about the good, and between people about the good, can be resolved by knowing the good.

Joseph Raz can help us in understanding the difference between belief and knowledge of the good, and the role beliefs play in choice. In his chapter titled "On the Guise of the Good," he considers some examples where it appears that a person did not act to achieve some perceived good, and argues that traditional formulations of the "guise of the good" are insufficient to explain these. However, he then offers his own formulation that he believes addresses the problems. For our purposes, here is what he says that is essential: "From its earliest origins, whatever version of the Guise of the Good was viewed with favor was the keystone keeping in place and bridging the theory of value, the theory of normativity and rationality and the understanding of intentional action."[9]

Insofar as a person made a choice, and had a reason for that choice, this thinking process can be examined. Raz also identifies the way that people can hold contradictory and confused beliefs:

> Perhaps, you will say, but does that not establish that he believes that there is some value in his action, given that he denies having the belief in its value. I think that his denial shows that he disapproves of his own action even while he is so acting. But that is typical of cases of *akrasia* ... his disapproval of his own action leads him to be less than completely honest with himself.[10]

I will call this condition "self-deception," and argue that this condition is even worse than Raz imagines. We are not simply in self-deception about

[9] Joseph Raz, "On the Guise of the Good," in *Desire, Practical Reason, and the Good*, ed. Sergio Tenenbaum (Oxford: Oxford University Press, 2010).
[10] Ibid., 133.

what we value, or about how divided we are in our beliefs. We are also in self-deception about the extent to which we seek to know the good. Most discussions seem to begin with the assumption that people know what is good but have a hard time doing what is good. However, a few Socratic questions will quickly reveal that persons do not know the good. Redefining "knowledge" so that people do know without being able to explain or show what they know is simply a form of skepticism. It is conceding that the kind of knowledge Socrates was looking for does not exist, and it is a further instance of self-deception about our condition in that it wants to say that most people do in fact know, so let us call what they have knowledge.

However, the distinction between knowledge and opinion is then lost. Like Socrates, I proceed with the assumption that these are different, and that the difference lies in being able to demonstrate what something is (what the good *is*) by showing that alternatives are incorrect. This is rational justification. The study of the moral law begins with asking for rational justification about the good. It is important to apply the law to issues such as marriage and abortion, but these application cannot be made if the good is not known.

Consider this dialogue between two murderers sent by Richard III to kill his brother Clarence. As they watch Clarence sleep, they discuss the morality of what they are commanded to do, and we get a picture of how quickly humans switch their beliefs about what is good and what ought to be done:

2ND MURD.	What, shall we stab him as he sleeps?
1ST MURD.	No; then he will say 'twas done cowardly, when he awakes.
2ND MURD.	When he wakes! Why, fool, he shall never wake til the judgment-day.
1ST MURD.	Why, then he will say we stabbed him sleeping.
2ND. MURD.	The urging of that word "judgment" hath bred a kind of remorse in me.
1ST MURD.	What, are thou afraid?
2ND MURD.	Not to kill him, having a warrant for it; but to be damned for killing him, from which no warrant can defend us.
1ST MURD.	I thought thou hadst been resolute.
2ND MURD.	So I am to let him live.
1ST MURD.	Back to the Duke of Gloucester, tell him so.
2ND MURD.	I pray thee, stay a while: I hope my holy humour will change; 'twas wont to hold me but while one would tell twenty.
1ST MURD.	How dost thou feel thyself now?

2ND MURD.	'Faith, some certain dregs of conscience are yet within me.
1ST MURD.	Remember our reward, when the deed is done.
2ND MURD.	'Zounds, he dies: I had forgot the reward.
1ST MURD.	Where is thy conscience now?
2ND MURD.	In the Duke of Gloucester's purse.

What a miserable human condition, to be so changeable in one's opinions within such a short period of time. While I hope none of us are contemplating murder, I see no reason why we cannot apply this condition to humanity in general with respect to the good. Rather than assuming that we all know what is good, and the problem is one of the will or application, it seems rather that we shift frequently in our beliefs about what is good and in no case do we know what is good.

Even so, the human condition is not one of simply needing instruction about what is good. The problem is not simply faulty means/end reasoning, or a mistake about the ordinary facts of daily life. The problem is one of critical thinking about the most basic questions. However, it is more than that as well. It is a matter of going from the condition of not seeking or using reason in this way, to seeking and through the use of reason coming to know the Good. Just as people in general would not be able to answer many questions about why they hold beliefs about the good, so too people's belief or non-belief in God is held uncritically. So what we find is that people hold competing beliefs about God and the good; this results in great changeability in what they want and do, and contemporary political and legal thought takes such a condition as a necessary given rather than as the problem.

THE HUMAN CONDITION OF NEGLECT

If the problem requires more than a lecture concerning the good, what does it require? I believe the answer helps solve a problem that Modernity sought to bypass and avoid. That is, whereas we can know the good from general revelation, we can also know the human failure to know what is clear about God and the good. This is not a problem of practical rationality, nor is it a result of some epistemic disability. A person who seeks to know God and the good will know. The problem is not in the human ability to know or the availability of knowledge about God and the good. The problem is in not seeking, and in self-deception about this condition.

The problem is that of not using reason to know what is clear. The solution cannot simply be to argue that we should use reason to see what is clear. A person who is not using reason will not accept the conclusion of a sound argument about needing to use reason. Rather, this is a matter of life and death insofar as reason is the light of nature the use of which brings understanding and the denial of which brings confusion and a darkened mind.

In the Introduction, I brought up the problem of evil and pointed out that Modernity has focused on the problem of pain and suffering as common ground on which to work tougher between incompatible worldviews. I also argued that the problem of evil is much larger than the problem of pain – that it is a problem about meaning. Modern liberalism has made the important contribution of noting that governments cannot coerce people into accepting a meaningful life. As a statement about what a government can and cannot do, I believe this is true. However, the modern world and political liberalism has also gone a step further and argued that we cannot know, and that many incompatible worldviews are reasonable (recall the quote from Rawls on this point in the Introduction).

If true, this raises a real problem for meaning. If it is not clear whether all or only some is eternal, then it cannot be clear what it is to be a human. If it is not clear what it is to be a human, then it cannot be clear what it means to be a good human. If these are not clear, then we have no obligation to listen to persons who make assertions about them. Furthermore, we have no basis for claiming to know what is meaningful for ourselves or to be leading a meaningful life.

The thread throughout this book has been the relationship between beliefs about what is real, human nature, the good, and law. In the largest instances of cases, the approach to law has been to isolate it from these other concepts, or at best to vaguely discuss the good or human nature, although in a way that is philosophically ambiguous. I believe this hints at something more problematic in human nature than simple ignorance.

Neglect of seeking to know is coupled with believing one already knows or that one does not need to know. If the medieval world ended in wars about how to be redeemed, perhaps part of the problem was that exactly what humans need redemption from was not clearly in focus. Similarly, if the modern world set aside these problems as irresolvable and instead concentrated on overcoming physical suffering, and consequently this solution naturalized suffering as "just a part of life," then it is not surprising that suffering appears meaningless and arbitrary. Suffering can be common ground in that humans can work together to understand it. That there has not always been physical suffering, and that it is related as a call back from the human condition of not seeking, understanding, or doing what is right, stands in contrast to the naturalization of suffering, which promotes taking it for granted and not considering its meaning.

This attitude can be illustrated by a passage from Hamlet in which Hamlet's uncle urges him to stop mourning the death of Hamlet's father:

Act 1 Scene 2

KING CLAUDIUS
'Tis sweet and commendable in your nature, Hamlet,
To give these mourning duties to your father:
But, you must know, your father lost a father;
That father lost, lost his, and the survivor bound
In filial obligation for some term
To do obsequious sorrow: but to persever
In obstinate condolement is a course
Of impious stubbornness; 'tis unmanly grief;
It shows a will most incorrect to heaven,
A heart unfortified, a mind impatient,
An understanding simple and unschool'd:
For what we know must be and is as common
As any the most vulgar thing to sense,
Why should we in our peevish opposition
Take it to heart? Fie! 'tis a fault to heaven,
A fault against the dead, a fault to nature,
To reason most absurd: whose common theme
Is death of fathers, and who still hath cried,
From the first corse till he that died to-day,
This must be so.
...

HAMLET
O, that this too too solid flesh would melt
Thaw and resolve itself into a dew!
Or that the Everlasting had not fix'd
His canon 'gainst self-slaughter! O God! God!
How weary, stale, flat and unprofitable,
Seem to me all the uses of this world!
Fie on't! ah fie! 'tis an unweeded garden,
That grows to seed; things rank and gross in nature
Possess it merely. That it should come to this!

While Hamlet's uncle wants to move on, and dismisses the problem of evil as just part of life that others have had to live with also, Hamlet is not able to get past the problem and how it empties life of meaning. Hamlet wonders how can others move on so quickly after the death of a loved one?

Although Hamlet is known for going back and forth on how to handle the situation, and although he does not come to a conclusion about why there is evil, he is more sensitive to the problem than most.

In this study we do not have the appropriate time needed to study the problem of evil in all of its nuances. However, we can note that at the beginning of Modernity, the Protestants who wrote and adopted the Westminster Confession of Faith (particularly influential among Christians in the American colonies and then in the United States) affirmed the following about the origin of moral evil:

> I. Our first parents, being seduced by the subtilty and temptations of Satan, sinned, in eating the forbidden fruit. This their sin, God was pleased, according to His wise and holy counsel, to permit, having purposed to order it to His own glory (chapter 6).

This thread in Modernity affirmed that God reveals Himself in his works of creation and providence, and this extends to the actions of humans, which become greater sources of the revelation of the justice and mercy of God. With respect to our study of the good, this affirms that the knowledge of God is the good, and that all things work together for this good. As modern thinkers moved away from the good as knowing God (replacing this with heaven or this-worldly pleasures), the problem of evil became important because suffering in this life has no meaning.

The implication is that we must address these questions as humans (individually and collectively). Furthermore, if basic beliefs about God and humans, good and evil, are clear to reason, then our failure to know is culpable. What progress has been made in some areas of practical rationality in the past few centuries does not mask this basic culpability, which is more at the heart of our humanity. If all humans ought to know, and knowledge begins with the basics, then failing to know the basics is a fundamental failure to do what we ought to do. I believe that on this foundation we can make sense both of the clarity of general revelation and the need for redemptive revelation.

CONCLUSION: THE END OF BABEL

> At the heart of liberty is the right to define one's own concept of existence, of meaning, of the universe, and of the mystery of human life. Beliefs about these matters could not define the attributes of personhood were they formed under compulsion of the State.[11]

[11] *Planned Parenthood of Southeastern PA v. Casey*, 505 U.S. 833 (1992).

Although this quote from Supreme Court Justice Souter affirms the division between church and individual beliefs, it highlights the emptiness of the term "right" when it can be extended to claim that humans have a right to "define" their own meaning, as opposed to discover what is good for humans. The modern solution to the Wars of Religion in which the state is kept from coercing citizens in matters of belief has been challenged by Postmodernity as a myth that never existed. There are always beliefs behind any government that the system seeks to support in order to defend the existing power structure. It may be true that the state should not and cannot force persons to believe against their will, but this does nothing to help us know what is actually meaningful, what actually should be believed. I have argued here that the way out of this is not to apply greater energy to refining the same failed solution, nor is it to abandon ourselves to skepticism or postmodern mysticism. It is rather to notice that we have been operating with unquestioned presuppositions, and that the full use of reason requires us to examine these. These are presuppositions about God (or confusion of God with the world) and the good (or failure to identify the good). To borrow from Francis Bacon and Friedrich Nietzsche, we can use the term "idols" and argue that progress forward requires removing idols about God and the good. But idols are rooted in our thinking that we know and the subsequent failure to seek. Overcoming this condition requires a greater level of repentance and self-examination.

There is a new global reality in which the skepticism of Postmodernity is permeating. This is a new level of contact between all people groups and nations made possible by technology such as the Internet and mobile phones. This new level of contact will require a common understanding of human nature and the good if significant divisions and conflicts are to be avoided. Just as Europe worked its way out of the Wars of Religion by a focus on the goods of this life, commerce plays a large role now in bringing people together in discussion. Nevertheless, the skepticism behind the modern solution, along with the antinomianism and nominalism of Postmodernity, cannot provide a basis for unity.

Joseph Boyle described globalism and the need for a global ethics in this way:

> Global ethics is not simply the sum of the ethical practices and beliefs of all the people and communities inhabiting the earth. Global ethics aspires to a kind of unity lacking in a complete listing of the forms of moral life now existing around the world. That unity arises from globalization – the

> fact that human beings around the world now communicate and interact economically and politically in ways impossible until fairly recently, even for those within the same community or region. The effect of this new level of international interaction is that institutions and systems of institutions can make decisions affecting many, if not all, of the morally differentiated groups of people around the world. Common standards to guide such decisions appear desirable.... Even more so does the possibility of actions undertaken on behalf of the entire human race, understood as acting together as a community for a unified common good. ... I turn now to the notion of natural law: its core idea, as a thesis about morality, law and other forms of social authority is that some action-guiding thoughts and statements, that is, some precepts or practical principles, are natural in the sense that they are not dependent for their validity on human decision, authority or convention ... this universal accessibility of moral knowledge is in turn closely connected to another characteristic of natural law, namely, the universality of its principles and some of its norms, that is, the universality of moral statements addressed to anyone at all facing a choice upon which principles and norms bear.[12]

This stresses the themes of a common humanity with a shared good that can be known by all and what I have called a natural moral law that teaches us how to achieve the good. I do not believe that a global unity will be reached if the good is identified with the "goods" of this life, or if the debate between duty and happiness continues. Rather, I believe that the *summum bonum*, the end in itself that is sought for its own sake, is the knowledge of God, and that this knowledge is attained by inference from the works of creation and providence, and this more clearly states the good than the thinkers we have considered.

It should not surprise us that the good has remained ambiguous or unknown given the amount of division and conflict in the world. But it is also not surprising that it has been identified and simply stated in the following manner: The chief end of humanity is to glorify God and enjoy Him forever. It should not surprise us that Plato, Aristotle, Augustine, Aquinas, and others identified the highest good with the knowledge of God. Nor should it surprise us that they had competing conceptions of God and of knowledge, and that therefore they handed down differing conceptions of the natural moral law. Otherworldliness and mere this-worldliness remain with us. Fideism and skepticism remain with us. Nevertheless, I conclude by claiming that it is clear what can and cannot be sought as an end in itself,

12 Joseph Boyle, "Natural Law and Global Ethics," in *Cherry, Natural Law and the Possibility of a Global Ethics*, 200.

and that the hope for meaning in human life individually and together is in identifying the good.

I have relied on the example of Socrates as one who questioned the meaning of what is assumed. This process exposed presuppositions. However, Socrates also had presuppositions that he did not commit to this level of scrutiny. His belief in the eternality of the soul is one such example. I do not think we should be surprised about this. The same thing can be exposed in Christianity. Perhaps Modernity challenged Christianity on its limited view of soteriology and its otherworldliness. Postmodernity has now challenged modern thinking about knowledge and what is neutral. At the end of the day, this process has not resulted in a sound argument against belief in God, but has rather exposed ways in which we have attributed eternality to something beside God, and have neglected thinking about the good in favor of the temporally satisfactory. If the basic things are clear, then we can make progress in the natural moral law, but not apart from recognizing our need to do so and our culpable failure to have done so.

> Someone will say: Yes, Socrates, but cannot you hold your tongue, and then you may go into a foreign city, and no one will interfere with you? Now I have great difficulty in making you understand my answer to this. For if I tell you that this would be a disobedience to a divine command, and therefore that I cannot hold my tongue, you will not believe that I am serious; and if I say again that the greatest good of man is daily to converse about virtue, and all that concerning which you hear me examining myself and others, and that the life which is unexamined is not worth living – that you are still less likely to believe.[13]

[13] *The Apology*.

Bibliography

Adler, Mortimer Jerome. *Six Great Ideas: Truth, Goodness, Beauty, Liberty, Equality, Justice: Ideas We Judge By, Ideas We Act On*. New York: Macmillan, 1997.

Anderson, Owen. "Charles Lyell, Uniformitarianism, and Interpretive Principles." In *(Re)Creating Science in 19th Century Britain*, edited by Amanda Caleb. Newcastle upon Tyne: Cambridge Scholars Press, 2007.

Aquinas, Thomas. *Summa Theologica*. Great Books, edited by Mortimer J. Adler. Vol. 19. Chicago: Encyclopaedia Britannica, Incorporated, 1955.

Aristotle. "Metaphysics." In *Aristotle: 1*. Translated by W. D. Ross. Vol. 86, 499. New York: Encyclopedia Britannica, 1952.

"Nicomachean Ethics." In *Aristotle II*. Translated by W. D. Ross. Vol. 21, 339. New York: Encyclopedia Britannica, 1952.

"Physics." In *Aristotle: 1*. Translated by R. P. Hardie and R. K. Gaye. Vol. 86, 259. New York: Encyclopedia Britannica, 1952.

Asimov, Isaac. *Isaac Asimov's Guide to Earth and Space*. New York: Random House, 1991.

Audi, Robert. *The Good in the Right: A Theory of Intuition and Intrinsic Value*. Princeton: Princeton University Press, 2004.

Augustine. "Confessions." In *Augustine*. Translated by Edward Bouverie Pusey, edited by Mortimer Adler. Vol. 18, 1. Chicago: Encyclopedia Britannica, 1952.

Bacon, Francis. "Novum Organum." In *Francis Bacon*. Vol. 30. Chicago: Encyclopedia Britannica, 1952.

Bacon, Francis Sir. "Advancement of Learning." In *Francis Bacon*. Vol. 30, 1009. New York: Encyclopedia Britannica, 1952.

Barbour, Ian. *Issues in Science and Religion*. New York: Harper & Row, 1971.

Beckwith, Francis. *Persons, Moral Worth, and Embryos*. Leyden: Brill, 2011.

Blackburn, Simon. *Ruling Passions: A Theory of Practical Reasoning*. Oxford: Clarendon Press, 1998.

Braybrooke, David. *Natural Law Modernized*. Toronto Studies in Philosophy. Toronto; Buffalo: University of Toronto Press, 2001.

Calvin, John. *The Institutes of Christian Religion*. Abridged ed. Grand Rapids: Baker Academic, 1987.

Carty, Anthony. *Post-Modern Law: Enlightenment, Revolution, and the Death of Man*, edited by Anthony Carty. Edinburgh: Edinburgh University Press, 1990.

Cherry, Mark J. *Natural Law and the Possibility of a Global Ethics*. Philosophical Studies in Contemporary Culture. Vol. 11. Dordrecht; Boston: Kluwer Academic Publishers, 2004.

Cicero. *On Moral Ends*. Translated by Raphael Woolf, edited by Julia Annas. Cambridge: Cambridge University Press, 2001.

Copleston, Frederick Charles. *A History of Philosophy, Vol. 1: Greece and Rome*. Petaluma: Search Press, 1994a.

A History of Philosophy, Vol. 2: Augustine to Scotus. Petaluma: Search Press, 1994b.

Copp, David. "Belief, Reason, and Motivation: Michael Smith's 'the Moral Problem'." *Ethics* 108, no. 1 (1997): 33.

Darwin, Charles. "The Origin of Species by Means of Natural Selection." In *Darwin*, edited by Robert Maynard Hutchins. Vol. 49. Chicago: Encyclopedia Britannica, 1952.

Derrida, Jacques. *Writing and Difference*. Chicago: University of Chicago Press, 1978.

Descartes, Rene. "Meditations on First Philosophy." In *Descartes: Philosophical Writings*, edited by Norman Kemp Smith. New York: Random House, 1958a.

"Rules for the Guidance of Our Native Powers." In *Descartes: Philosophical Writings*, edited by Norman Kemp Smith. New York: Random House, 1958b.

Dewey, John. *Creative Intelligence: Essays in the Pragmatic Attitude*. New York: Octagon Books, 1970.

The Essential Dewey: Pragmatism, Education, and Democracy. ed. Larry Hickman and Thomas M. Alexander, Bloomington: Indiana University Press, 1998.

Dworkin, Ronald. *Justice for Hedgehogs*. Cambridge, MA: Belknap Press of Harvard University Press, 2011.

Finnis, John. *Natural Law and Natural Rights*. Oxford: Oxford University Press, 1980.

Foucault, Michel. *The Order of Things*. New York: Vintage Books, 1973.

Galileo. "Letter to the Grand Duchess Christina of Tuscany." http://www.fordham.edu/halsall/mod/galileo-tuscany.html (accessed March 12, 2008).

Gangadean, Surrendra. *Philosophical Foundation: A Critical Analysis of Basic Beliefs*. Lanham: University Press of America, 2008.

George, Robert P. *In Defense of Natural Law*. Oxford: Clarendon Press, 1999.

Natural Law, Liberalism, and Morality: Contemporary Essays. Oxford: Clarendon Press, 1996.

Gibbard, Allan. "Wise Choices, Apt Feelings." In *Moral Discourse and Practice*, edited by Stephen Darwall, Allan Gibbard, and Peter Railton. Oxford: Oxford University Press, 1997.

Gillespie, Michael Allen. *The Theological Origins of Modernity*. Chicago: Chicago University Press, 2008.

Grisez, Germain Gabriel and Russell B. Shaw. *Beyond the New Morality: The Responsibilities of Freedom*. 3rd ed. Notre Dame: University of Notre Dame Press, 1988.
Grotius, Hugo. *The Rights of War and Peace*. Ithaca: Cornell University Library, 2009.
Guth, Alan. *The Inflationary Universe: The Quest for a New Theory of Cosmic Origins*. Reading: Helix Books, 1997.
Habermas, Jürgen. *Moral Consciousness and Communicative Action*. Studies in Contemporary German Social Thought. Cambridge, MA: MIT Press, 2001.
Harman, Gilbert. "Ethics and Observation." In *Moral Discourse and Practice*, edited by Stephen Darwall, Allan Gibbard, and Peter Railton. Oxford: Oxford University Press, 1997.
Hart, H. L. A. *The Concept of Law*. 2nd ed. Oxford: Clarendon Press, 1994.
Hawking, Stephen W. *A Brief History of Time*. New York: Bantam Books, 1988.
Hawking, S. W. and Leonard Mlodinow. *The Grand Design*. New York: Bantam Books, 2010.
Hobbes, Thomas. "Leviathan." In *Great Books of the Western World 23*, edited by Robert Maynard Hutchins. Chicago: Encyclopedia Brittanica, 1952.
Holmes, Oliver Wendell. "Natural Law." *Harvard Review* (1918).
Holton, Richard. "Reason, Value and the Muggletonians." *Australasian Journal of Philosophy* 74, no. 3 (1996): 484–487.
Hume, David. *Hume's Enquiries*, edited by L. A. Selby-Bigge. New York: Clarendon Press, 1966.
A Treatise of Human Nature. Mineola: Dover Publications, 2003.
Huxley, Thomas Henry. *Evolution and Ethics and Other Essays*, edited by Thomas H. Huxley. New York: D. Appleton and Co., 1896.
Johnson, Paul. *Modern Times: The World from the Twenties to the Eighties*. New York: Harper & Row, 1983.
Johnston, G. A., ed. *Selections from Scottish Common Sense Philosophy*. London: Open Court, 1915.
Kant, Immanuel. *Critique of Pure Reason*. Translated by Norman Kemp Smith. New York: Palgrave Macmillan, 2003.
Kent, Bonnie. "The Moral Life." In *The Cambridge Companion to Medieval Philosophy*, edited by A. S. McGrade. Cambridge: Cambridge University Press, 2003.
Kierkegaard, Søren. *Concluding Unscientific Postscript*, edited by Alastair Hannay. Cambridge: Cambridge University Press, 2009a.
Repetition and Philosophical Crumbs, Oxford: Oxford University Press, 2009b.
Locke, John and Peter H. Nidditch, eds. *An Essay Concerning Human Understanding*. Oxford: Oxford University Press, 1979.
Lyotard, Jean-Francois. "The Postmodern Condition: A Report on Knowledge." http://www.marxists.org/reference/subject/philosophy/works/fr/lyotard.htm (accessed July 18, 2007).
MacIntyre, Alasdair C. *Whose Justice? Which Rationality?* Notre Dame: University of Notre Dame Press, 1989.

McInerny, Ralph. "Ethics." In *Cambridge Companion to Acquinas*, edited by Norman Kretzmann and Eleonore Stump. Cambridge: Cambridge University Press, 1993.

Montesquieu. *The Spirit of Laws*. Translated by Thomas Nugent, edited by J. V. Prichard. Chicago: Encyclopedia Britannica, 1980.

Moore, G. E. and Thomas Baldwin. *Principia Ethica*. Rev. ed. Cambridge; New York: Cambridge University Press, 1993.

Newton, Isaac. "General Scholium." In *Newton, Huygens*. Vol. 34. Chicago: Encyclopedia Britannica, 1952.

Norris, Christopher. *Derrida*. Cambridge, MA: Harvard University Press, 1987.

Norton, David Fate. "Hume and the Foundations of Morality." In *The Cambridge Companion to Hume*, edited by David Fate Norton. Cambridge: Cambridge University Press, 1993.

Nozick, Robert. *The Nature of Rationality*. Princeton: Princeton University Press, 1993a.

Nussbaum, Martha Craven. *Women and Human Development: The Capabilities Approach*. The John Robert Seeley Lectures. Cambridge; New York: Cambridge University Press, 2000.

Plato. "Gorgias." In *Plato: Complete Works*. Translated by Donald J. Zeyl, edited by John M. Cooper. Cambridge: Hackett Publishing, 1997a.

"Meno." In *Plato: Complete Works*. Translated by Donald J. Zeyl, edited by John M. Cooper. Cambridge: Hackett Publishing, 1997b.

The Republic, translated by Benjamin Jowett. Chicago: Encyclopedia Britannica, 1980, 397.

Popkin, Richard H. *The History of Scepticism: From Savonarola to Bayle*. Rev. ed. Oxford; New York: Oxford University Press, 2003.

Pufendorf, Samuel von. *Of the Law of Nature and Nations*. Eighteenth Century Collections Online ed. Oxford: L. Lichfield, 1703.

Putnam, Hilary. *The Collapse of the Factvalue Dichotomy: And Other Essays*. Cambridge, MA; London: Harvard University Press, 2002.

Ethics without Ontology. Cambridge, MA; London: Harvard University Press, 2004.

Railton, Peter. "Moral Realism." In *Moral Discourse and Practice*, edited by Stephen Darwall, Allan Gibbard, and Peter Railton. Vol. 3. Oxford: Oxford University Press, 1997.

Ratnapala, Suri. *Jurisprudence*. Cambridge: Cambridge University Press, 2009.

Rawls, John. *Political Liberalism*. New York: Columbia University Press, 2005.

Raz, Joseph. "On the Guise of the Good." In *Desire, Practical Reason, and the Good*, edited by Sergio Tenenbaum. Oxford: Oxford University Press, 2010.

Rommen, Heinrich Albert and Thomas R. Hanley. *The Natural Law, a Study in Legal and Social History and Philosophy*. St. Louis: B. Herder Book Co., 1947.

Ross, W. D. *The Right and the Good*. Oxford: Clarendon Press, 1955.

Rousseau, Jean Jacques. *A Discourse on the Origin of Inequality*. Translated by G. D. H. Cole. Chicago: Encyclopedia Britannica, 1980a.

The Social Contract. Translated by G. D. H. Cole. Chicago: Encyclopedia Britannica, 1980b.

Smith, Michael. *The Moral Problem*. Cambridge: Blackwell, 1994.
Spencer, Herbert. *The Principles of Ethics, Vol. 1*. Indianapolis: Liberty Classics, 1978.
St. Augustine. *City of God*. Translated by Henry Bettenson. London: Penguin Books, 2003.
Strass, William and Neil Howe. *Generations: The History of America's Future, 1584–2069*. New York: Morrow, 1991.
Swan, Kyle. "A Metaethical Option for Theists." Journal of Religious Ethics 34, no. 1 (2006): 3.
Thomasius, Christian. *Essays on Church, State, and Politics*, edited by Ian Hunter, Ian Ahnert, and Frank Grunert. Indianapolis: Liberty Fund, 2007.
Tierney, Brian. *Foundations of the Conciliar Theory: The Contributions of the Medieval Canonists from Gratian to the Great Schism*. Oxford: Oxford University Press, 2008.
White, Michael. "The Problem of Aristotle's *Nous Poietikos*." *The Review of Metaphysics* 57.4 (2004), 725–739.
Wolfe, Christopher. *Natural Law Liberalism*. Cambridge; New York: Cambridge University Press, 2006.

Index